C000258504

African History Archive

Over the past forty years, Zed has established a long and proud
tradition of publishing critical work on African issues, offering
unique insights into the continent's politics, development, history
and culture. The African History Archive draws on this rich backlist,
consisting of carefully selected titles that even now have enduring
relevance years after their initial publication. Lovingly repackaged,
with newly commissioned forewords that reflect on the impact the
books have had, these are essential works for anyone interested in
the political history of the continent.

Other titles in the archive:

A History of Africa
Hosea Jaffe

*The Story of an African Working Class: Ghanaian Miners' Struggles
1870–1980*
Jeff Crisp

Yours for the Union: Class and Community Struggles in South Africa
Baruch Hirson

About the author

Basil Davidson ranks as one of the most remarkable Africanist historians of his generation. Born in Bristol in 1914, he worked as a journalist for *The Times*, the *New Statesman* and other publications, as well as serving in the Second World War as an intelligence officer in Nazi-occupied Europe. After the war, he went on to become a leading authority on Portuguese Africa, and was one of the first scholars to emphasize the pre-colonial achievements of African civilizations, as well the damaging effects wreaked on the continent by colonialism. Davidson was also a passionate advocate for contemporary anti-colonial struggles, and witnessed many of these struggles first hand. Among his many notable books are *The African Genius* (1969) and *The Black Man's Burden: Africa and the Curse of the Nation-State* (1992). He died in 2010.

Zachariah Mampilly is the director of Africana studies and an associate professor of political science and international studies at Vassar College. He is the author of *Rebel Rulers: Insurgent Governance and Civilian Life during War* (2011) and (with Adam Branch) *Africa Uprising Popular Protest and Political Change* (Zed 2015).

No Fist Is Big Enough to Hide the Sky

The Liberation of Guinea-Bissau and Cape Verde, 1963–74

Basil Davidson

With Forewords by Zachariah Mampilly and Amilcar Cabral and a Preface by Aristides Pereira

ZED

Zed Books

LONDON

No Fist Is Big Enough to Hide the Sky: The Liberation of Guinea-Bissau and Cape Verde, 1963–74 was first published in 1981 by Zed Books Ltd, The Foundry, 17 Oval Way, London SE11 5RR, UK. A previous version of the book was published in 1969 by Penguin Books under the title *The Liberation of Guinea*.

This edition was published in 2017.

www.zedbooks.net

Cover design by Kika Sroka-Miller.

A catalogue record for this book is available from the British Library.

ISBN 978-1-78699-066-2 hb
ISBN 978-1-78360-564-4 pb
ISBN 978-1-78360-562-0 pdf
ISBN 978-1-78360-999-4 epub
ISBN 978-1-78360-563-7 mobi

To the memory
of those who have died for the revolution of our times

To the fraternity
of those who live for it

To the understanding
of those who will carry it further

Contents

Foreword
by Zachariah Mampilly

My first encounter with Basil Davidson was in an undergraduate seminar with the Pan-Africanist scholar Pearl Robinson. Resolute in my belief that a colonial-era British secret service (MI6) agent could hardly offer a worthwhile account of post-colonial African life, I was quickly disavowed of my assumptions by the empathy and beauty of Davidson's prose. In well-known works like *The Black Man's Burden*, Davidson's lyrical language laid bare the savagery of colonial rule and the challenges confronting Africa's newly independent nation-states.

Over a decades-long career that began with the excitement of anti-colonialism and its inevitable backlash, continuing through the independence era and past the end of the cold war, Davidson's oeuvre covers the range of colonial and post-colonial dilemmas confronting the African continent. He was often a first-person observer of the events and figures he documented. Yet his analysis is always clear-eyed about the challenges confronting ordinary Africans as well as African leaders, many of whom he knew personally. Deploying both first-person narratives that draw on his experiences on literal and figurative front lines as well as an impressive grasp of both historical and social scientific research, Davidson's work is intellectually rigorous and emotionally resonant. Moving between different levels and modes of narration, he maneuvers deftly, at one point narrating a casual encounter with a legendary African leader that dismantles the superhuman aura around them while in the next moment withdrawing to consider the scene from a different, more structural vantage point. It is bravura writing and all the more impressive for his ability to make it appear natural.

No Fist is Big Enough to Hide the Sky: The Liberation of Guinea-Bissau and Cape Verde possesses many of the strengths of Davidson's best work, as well as some of its excesses. If it appears that Davidson juggles between different narrative modes, that is the inevitable outcome of a book written in two distinct time periods with multiple agendas to serve. Conceived as an insider's look at the fledgling Partido Africano da Independência da Guiné e Cabo Verde (PAIGC), the first version of the book served two purposes – to offer a compelling and sympathetic account of the PAIGC's campaign against Portuguese colonialism, especially the thinking of its charismatic leader, Amilcar Cabral; and to provide support for the ongoing liberation struggle by sharing the PAIGC's well-formulated plans and philosophy with the world. It is simultaneously analysis and a call to action.

Based on three separate visits to PAIGC-ruled territory, we see the front lines and liberated zones through Davidson's eyes. However, the early narrative energy Davidson generates with his first-person account of life behind rebel lines is waylaid by the ambitious role he hoped his text could play in supporting the PAIGC, which he clearly admired. This section remains a fascinating trove for scholars interested in the internal structure and behaviour of one of the most novel and inclusive armed groups of all time. It also offers insights into a variety of subjects that have emerged at the forefront of social scientific research on conflict over the past decade, including the microdynamics of political violence, the ways the group sought to mobilize popular support through establishing autonomous and democratic village governing councils (rebel governance), and relations between the PAIGC and foreign countries (rebel diplomacy).

Through extensive quoting of PAIGC party positions and rebel leaders, Davidson takes on a central argument that has long defined the strategic choices of would-be violent insurrectionists. On one side, a Cuban-style insurgency in which violence triggers an outpouring of latent popular support versus the meticulous person-to-person outreach that Cabral, channelling Frantz Fanon, championed. In other words, should revolutionaries focus on capturing the state or capturing society? Davidson's sympathy for the latter is clear. Drawing from his experiences traveling with the rebels, he describes PAIGC cadre engaging civilians with patience and foresight. This was the dynamic that the organization rightly gained global attention for, culminating in the famous speech Cabral delivered to the Tricontinental Conference in Havana in 1966.In front of representatives sent by revolutionary states and armed groups around the world, Cabral insisted on the importance of generating popular support during a conflict in order to avoid the post-colonial malaise many revolutionary regimes experienced soon after the heady days of independence.

If this was all the book accomplished, it would remain an important achievement – a first-hand account of the life and work of Amilcar Cabral, especially during the early years of the war with the Portuguese. But what makes this work stand out is Davidson's decision to return to the manuscript four years later, beginning in 1972, though the newly expanded version would not appear until 1980. Guinea Bissau and Cape Verde are newly independent nations ruled by the PAIGC, a seeming success story that cements the heroic legacy of Cabral.

We encounter two versions of Cabral – the guerrilla and the prophet. In the first section of the book, Davidson journeys with PAIGC cadre through rebel-controlled rural areas meeting local peasants and chatting with thoughtful young rebels. Here is Cabral as brilliant guerrilla strategist, an organic intellectual with deep empathy for the rural peasantry. He hoped to lead them to a better future, one that could reconcile the collapse of the old ethnically defined social order in favour of a modern nation-state defined by its commitment to egalitarian pan-African and socialist ideals. Davidson's faith in the project is irrepressible no matter how much he tries to present the PAIGC in an objective manner. But his belief in Cabral's vision is also a blind spot, as this part of the book devolves into barely edited statements and quotes from PAIGC members. It is propaganda, in both the original and more common usage of term.

But it is the newer material, where Davidson returns to a newly liberated Guinea Bissau, that provides the book with its emotional heft. Rather than presiding over a newly independent state, Cabral is dead, killed by his own cadre in the final days of the independence struggle. Though the PAIGC emerges victorious, Cabral's premonitions and warnings about the perils of national liberation bedevil his successors. Disavowed of the romanticism that tinges his more adulatory account of the independence struggle, Davidson recounts the events that led to his friend's death. But instead of lingering in his sorrow, he instead looks for signs of hope amidst Cabral's successors.

Luis Cabral and Aristides Perreira, Cabral's confidants and successors, struggle to apply theoretical insights developed in the bush to the actual task of ruling two newly independent states. Amidst a weakening Third Worldism in which institutions of global finance are deployed to bend radical regimes that refused to submit to the emerging neoliberal order, they struggle to heed the warnings Cabral put forward. Instead, both emerge as strongmen, ruling their respective countries in ways unrecognizable to their depiction as hopeful revolutionaries in the text. Yet, regardless of the disappointing trajectories both Guinea Bissau and Cape Verde have taken, the PAIGC's struggle for liberation deserves the attention it is only now starting to receive.

Zachariah Mampilly
October 2016

Acknowledgements

I wish to thank the political bureau and general secretariat of the PAIGC for their hospitality on many occasions, during the liberation war and since, as well as for making available to me a rich docu mentation from their archives; Jose Araujo of that secretariat for much help in working through these documents; Gerard Chaliand for allowing me to quote passages from his *Lutte Annee en Afrique* (Maspero, Paris, 1967); Ronald Segal for his constant and constructive interest in the original edition of this book; and many other friends for helpful comment and encouragement at various times.

Note on typography

Due to the technical limitations of the typesetting of the 1981 edition, the correct accent marks are regrettably missing over certain letters in Portuguese words.

Author's Note

A shorter version of this book, called *The Liberation of Guine,* and published in 1969, carried the story of the origins and development of the national liberation struggle of the peoples of Guine and Cape Verde down to 1968.

This new edition, considerably longer, adds four chapters on the periods of 1968-72; 1973, with the loss of Amilcar Cabral; 1974, with the total liberation of the mainland and a long advance to liberation of the archipelago; 1975 and after, with the outset of reconstruction in both countries.

As before, I have drawn on personal experience of those years, and, for help and enlightenment, wish to thank many persons in Guinea-Bissau and Cape Verde, and, above all, leaders and militants of the PAIGC.

Basil Davidson
January 1981

Preface by Aristides Pereira

In his foreword to the first edition of this book, Amilcar Cabral, incontestable leader of the African revolution which led to the liberation of Guinea-Bissau and the Cape Verde Islands, pointed to one of the factors that had decisively influenced its development. This was the 'wall of silence' raised around our peoples by Portuguese colonialism. Yet the toughness of that wall — where clever hands had sometimes added a seemingly original moulding to the crudity of its construction — was unable to withstand the strength and vitality of the peoples it enclosed: armed with the battering ram of their national identity, they reduced it to rubble. Allied to the pride we may without false modesty feel for the greatness of that achievement, there is also gratitude for the support of those who, at the proper moment, waged the same fight along-side us. And among the supporters of victory it is only just, and for us a pleasure always, to single out the friendly and honoured voice of Basil Davidson.

Endowed with uncommon talent as a writer and born in the golden cradle of the overdeveloped world, Basil Davidson could have confined himself to helping rebuild his own country from the ravages of war. But his restless spirit and profound sense of justice could not accept the calm of a quiet life; and this explains why, twenty years after the liberation war in Yugoslavia, it was through the paddy-fields of Guine, burned by napalm, that he made his way, so as to testify with the truth against the imposed silence.

Published in 1969, when six years of armed struggle had led to the liberation of more than two-thirds of Guine, Basil Davidson's book was one of the most valuable and timely contributions to explaining, for those kept in ignorance by the 'wall of silence', the realities of that struggle and, more important, its justification. To the prestige of his name Basil allied 'field-work': not merely reading well-orchestrated propaganda or taking touristic helicopter trips to besieged colonial urban centres. So the world believed in Basil Davidson, and there came a broadening of understanding and support for the battle then approaching its end: the battle which, in Amilcar Cabral's words, could only evolve — come what might — towards the total liberation of our people.

In presenting a new edition, Basil decided to complete it with the story of the years that followed the appearance of the first edition, years rich with events that burned like torches in the life of our people: events such as the proclamation of the independence of Guinea-Bissau in 1973 and of the Cape Verde Islands in 1975, and of the demolition of Portuguese colonialism. Few are as gifted as Basil for telling that story, since he has combined his talent as an historian with a living experience of events, and integrated himself among the subjects of this history. For Basil, as for all of us, the only cause for bitterness is that the murderous fury of the monster, in its last throes, succeeded in wiping out the physical presence of our immortal leader.

With the brilliance of his words and the clarity of his intellect, Amilcar Cabral would have enriched this book with a second foreword, continuing the lucid and finely poetic text which illustrates the earlier edition. These have been years of patriotic inspiration, during which the clear-sighted policy of our party, the PAIGC, led the peoples of Guine and Cape Verde to national independence and through the first steps of national reconstruction.

The period covered by new chapters here saw the consolidation of territory, as a feature of statehood, with the total liberation of the Boe region, and the decision to proclaim an independent state, a decision carried out on 24 September 1973 after the second party congress. It includes that glorious day which our memory of Amilcar Cabral illumined with his undying spirit, of the winning of independence for the young republic of Cape Verde. And it continues from that new landmark in our history to the third party congress, the first to be held under the full sovereignty of our peoples. On all this, the only shadow is the horror of the assassination of Basil's friend, the founder of our nationality, whose blood fertilized the soil of our lands with the supreme sacrifice of life to the eternity of our free and independent countries.

With the crumbling of the 'wall of silence' that Basil's testimony had broken through, his book about our peoples' struggle and liberation gains a new dimension as a text for study and reflection, now that the emotional impact of its first appearance in 1969 has lessened. A critical appreciation – and this is what the author would want from all his readers, because of the problems he debates and the originality and personal stamp of his approach to them – a critical appreciation, I repeat, is not the purpose of these few words. With these words we would simply like to express gratitude to the admirable friend that Basil has always been, our companion in the inspiring years of African revolution and in the liberation of Guine and Cape Verde. They are brief words at the onset of a book which, if it were ignored in the bibliography of our history, would deprive that history of one of the most valuable contributions to understanding it.

But may the judgements made on ending this preface be critical.

Aristides Pereira
Praia, Republic of Cape Verde

Foreword by Amilcar Cabral

Perhaps it is too soon to write the history of the liberation of the Portuguese colonies. But those who will one day write it will have to recall a fact of characteristic influence on the development of these struggles, whether in their internal dynamic or in their relation with the outside world: the *wall of silence* built around our peoples by Portuguese colonialism. And this at a time when the continental 'wind of change' had begun to announce its message of the *African awakening* and the return of Africans to history.

While hastily modifying the Portuguese constitution so as to escape the obligations of the UN Charter, the fascist colonialism of Portugal also took care to suppress all means of non-official information about its 'overseas provinces'. A powerful propaganda machine was put to work at convincing international opinion that our peoples lived in the best of all possible worlds, depicting happy Portuguese 'of colour' whose only pain was the yearning for their white mother-country, so sadly torn from them by the facts of geography. A whole mythology was assembled. And as with other myths, especially those concerning the subjection and exploitation of people, there was no lack of 'men of science', even a renowned sociologist, to provide a theoretical basis – in this case, *luso-tropicalismo.* Perhaps unconsciously confusing realities that are biological or necessary with realities that are socio-economic and historical, Gilberto Freyre transformed all of us who live in the colony-provinces of Portugal into the fortunate inhabitants of a Luso-Tropical paradise.

Not without success, as shown by an incident during the second All-African Peoples' Conference in Tunis during 1960, where we had some difficulty in being heard. One African delegate to whom we tried to explain our situation replied in all sympathy: 'Oh, it's different for you. No problem there – you're doing all right with the Portuguese'. At least it helped us to see that we could count only on ourselves. So we have intensified our effort to expose Portuguese colonialism, to break through this wall of silence and these lies that surround our peoples.

Yet a few years earlier, in 1954, one man had shown the courage not to believe without seeing for himself, and the audacity to make his way round Portuguese vigilance and to get through this wall. This was an Englishman, the writer Basil Davidson, who, exposing forced labour and racial discrimination

1

in Angola with the irrefutable evidence of his *African Awakening,* drew world-wide attention to our colonial tragedy. In that moment, when we were still taking our first steps towards organization, when we still felt very alone and quite without means of making our case known to the outside world, this work of Basil Davidson's had a significant influence on us, stimulating those who had decided to go ahead and appreciably encouraging the hesitant. If this puts us in debt of thanks to the author, his best reward will surely have been the Salazar government's action against him.

When in 1960 we decided to strengthen our case abroad, we found his good support in London where indifference of 'the specialists' towards Portuguese colonies was practically complete. (I well remember one of them, smoking his pipe with a distant and abstracted air.) So we have thought it right and necessary that Davidson should be amongst us at this decisive time when, fighting on three fronts, we are face to face with Portugal's genocidal colonial war against Africa. Pioneer and veteran of Portuguese colonial problems, he could not turn his back on this major reality in our history, the armed confrontation with Portuguese colonialism. As in the past he was well informed, but he wanted to *see for himself* and draw his own conclusions. So he came to visit us, just as we are sure he will visit Mozambique and Angola. And he wrote this book about his visit, asking us to contribute a preface if we wished.

Nobody can accuse this writer of a lack of objectivity: on the contrary. He accepted every risk and fatigue that could bring him into personal touch with the way our people live now. He entered our country three times and stayed as long as he could, talked with anyone he wanted, lived the everyday reality of our life and struggle. Together we used the same boats, the same canoes, the same trails in the bush; we were present at the same meetings; we drank from the same calabash, ate from the same plate, crossed the same countless southern rivers, waded through the same mud, washed in the same water, lay down and rose at the same hour, were escorted by the same fighters. The same ants pestered us, the same bombers bombed us, the very mosquitoes mingled our blood. We admired the same strange landscapes of Boe, looked at the same Portuguese positions, soiled our clothes with the same lateritic earth as red as the blood of our fighters and the soldiers of Portugal.

But Europe, Cartesian and over-developed, demands the most objective objectivity wherever there is war: the wounds and the corpses. Hit or miss the aircraft came, bombing us day by day. And we saw the same ruined villages, the same populations in flight from the bombs, the same dead burned by napalm, that same fighter scorched to the third degree yet still alive, the same bombs made in the USA dropped by aircraft made in Germany helped by radios made in Britain, the same shells from gunboats and frigates made in France. In smoking fields there was the same courage of our fighters, and their stubborn determination.

And on our side we said to ourselves: yes, happily-unhappily there are killed and wounded, ruined villages, fire, a great deal of fire, because, without them, what value could this visit have beyond that of a simple personal experience? How will he possibly convince his fellow countrymen, those phlegmatic British, that distrustful Europe, that so respectable *Times,* that so well-informed opinion, unless there are corpses duly named and noted, bombs with labels of origin, a napalm case with due degree of injury? Thanks, therefore, to those criminal airmen of Portugal who came in the time of your visit.

But other objective realities you did not see. The flowers of Quitafine, for example. Because, you know, there are flowers: we had no time to show them to you. Blue-yellow-lilac flowers, rainbow flowers, flowers red as the setting sun, and white too (but not like the settlers), white and pure as Picasso's dove. And Lebete Na N'Kanha – this time not the Party militant but the woman, the young rebel as fine as a gazelle, the mother of a family, the wife whose husband listens to her, the producer of rice. No time, again: you didn't talk to Lebete the woman. But did you catch the colour of her eyes, the purity of her smile, the grace of her gestures? Can even the most just struggle, one like ours, have any right thus to monopolize time, to silence the voice of Lebete the woman? Dear guest, how many wives have you? Only one? I know, and they say she is beautiful and intelligent. So do not look at my feet, for they are coarsened by the salt water of our swamps; nor at my hands, for they are full of the scars of harvesting riçe. Look at my eyes and you will see the past, present and future of the women of my country.

Children, too. Not just the ones you saw, well clothed, nicely ranged and singing with voices full of hope the anthem of our Party, of our nation in the womb. But children without clothes, children twisted by malnutrition, children who have no toys but huge stomachs inhabited by worms, children who look like balloon-children. You'd no time to talk to them, either. Solemn children, speaking of our Party, our struggle, of the colonialists, of every sort of weapon, asking painful questions: 'We have seen pictures of children in the countries of the whites. They're happy, they don't have big stomachs. Why?' And yet children who remain children, the reason for our struggle, the future of our people.

You have seen our elders, simple militants or Party workers. White beards on the black rock of their faces: did it remind you of the snow on your mountain peaks? Not bad, if so: it's the snow of experience that no sun will ever melt, and we respect it even if the dialectic of logic isn't always on their side. The elders are our museums, our libraries, our history books – the present and the past. They speak well, too: 'The struggle, it's the big lie that becomes the truth.' They have known how to believe in that lie so as to make it come true, in spite of their doubts and for all the ineffaceable marks of colonialism on their minds and on their bodies. They can rejoice only when dreaming of the future, but already they are astonished by the present. How could we unite all these folk, all these ethnic groups, so that they march together as one man? Listen to the elders: 'It can't be the work of men, it is the work of God.' Perhaps they are right, provided that in face of every threat we can keep and strengthen this great weapon of our struggle, the unity of our people, of all the ethnic groups, of all the social strata.

You loved the splendour of our forests which shelter our partisan bases, which protect our populations and protected you as well from those criminal bombings. These forests are now a real strength for our people, for our struggle. Before, they were a weakness, because we were afraid of our forests, sacred bastions of *iraos* and every kind of spirit. Now we are afraid no longer: we have conquered and mobilized the spirits of the forest, turned this weakness into a strength. That is what struggle means: turning weakness into strength.

Then aside from the wounded, the dead, the enemy aircraft, the bombs, the fighting men, the political workers, the militants, the Party, – how many objective realities still to count! Here with us – did you grasp it? – everything is objective reality: women, children, men, trees, spirits, flowers, even the dead. For we are a society of the living and the dead; and that is not a weakness. On the contrary, it's a strength against the sacrifices we must make.

The situation we have succeeded in creating is rested on the actual reality of our country and our society. We do not like war; but this armed struggle has its advantages. Through it we are building a nation that is solid, conscious of itself. We have liberated more than two thirds of our national territory. We shall liberate the rest. We shall liberate the Cape Verde Islands. Step by step we construct our State. Our present position is that of an independent nation with a part of its national territory, notably the urban centres and the islands, still under foreign occupation. Through this struggle we have conquered the right to our own personality in the international field.

Yes, indeed we know: there is a UN Charter, a right of all people to self-determination, an obligation on the part of the 'administrating Power' to grant independence. But with us the administrating power is in the shelter of its fortified camps, administering only its colonial war. This power has become the aggressor, the terrorist, the criminal attempting genocide. That is the situation here, changed not at all by the political death of Salazar, but which, no matter what happens to the politics of Portugal, will develop only towards the complete liberation of our people, with or without the prior consent of the Portuguese government.

No illusions, though. Everyone knows that Portugal does not make any aircraft, not even as toys for children. Our situation – this Portuguese aggression against our people – also involves the allies of Portugal, including Great Britain and the United States. And there too our struggle brings another gain: it teaches us to know the friends and enemies of our people, of Africa.

Basil Davidson came to us as a friend. In spite of the procolonialist position of Mr Wilson's socialist government in its voting at the UN against the interests of our people and in support of Britain's ancient ally, we take encouragement from the belief that Davidson is not our only British friend. We count on the sympathy of the youth of Britain, of all those in Britain who love liberty and progress including, assuredly, members of the British government and parliament. We have the same thoughts about the United States.

The author has sought to interpret the realities of our life and struggle in the light of what he saw and lived through with us, as well as of a deep knowledge of African history and an awareness of what is essential in the history of today. Whatever we may think about the praise or criticism explicit or implicit in this book, we are grateful to him. And this gratitude applies to all the others from afar — British, French, American, Soviet, and others — who have paid us visits and told about our struggle. Even when such reports have only repeated the colonialist slogans of the Portuguese, they have helped to teach us about the nature of men and the obstacles we must cross.

At a moment when young people and intellectuals of Europe or the United States demonstrate in favour of national liberation struggles, and when a growing number of journalists and writers find inspiration and themes for work in the little-known sacrifices of our peoples, it may not be out of place to recall that the heroic people of Vietnam will surely liberate itself, that our people will complete their liberation, that all oppressed peoples will rid themselves of imperialist rule. History itself demands no less. In our own interest it seems opportune for us to make here an appeal to rebellious youth and to intellectuals who take the side of the oppressed, and ask them to prepare for new stages in this common fight for progress and the good of mankind. Even in particularly difficult conditions we are achieving our duty to understand the reality of our own country, and transform it towards progress and justice. May others make ready to do the same.

It is not for us to pass judgement on the author's opinions about various controversial problems, whether in form or content, concerning Africa and the further struggle against imperialism. Basil Davidson has always answered for himself, and this foreword can in no way undermine such an admirable aspect of personal character.

Amilcar Cabral
Boe, October 1968

1. Why?

Les plus grands, ce sont ceux qui ont su donner aux
hommes l'espoir.
JEAN JAURES

The small jet bomber dives from around five thousand feet, its engine drilling like a monstrous fly. Two others follow: Fiats, I think, of the type they make in Western Germany. About five miles away.

We stand near the edge of the clump of trees that conceals our base, a dozen huts, a small dump of 75 mm. shells: watching. It is otherwise a quiet Monday morning. 9 October 1967.

A great wedge of black smoke fans out above the skyline fringe of coconut palms.

'Napalm', says the man from the Vietcong who is standing beside me, a visitor like myself. His tone is of the bitter weariness that a doctor in a plague might use when identifying yet another onset. Tran Hoai-nam, veteran member of the central committee of the Liberation Front of South Vietnam has seen it all before, has seen it many times.

I myself have seen no warfare since 1945; and then at least there was no napalm. Besides, this isn't Vietnam. This is West Africa. Would the Portuguese – even these Portuguese of Dr Salazar's most imperial Portugal – really drop napalm on villages and ricefields in rural Africa? Somehow I still have a hope that it isn't true.

We move that afternoon. *No pintcha*, as Pascoal is always saying: 'Forward, on our way, let's go'. An appeal as well as a command. It takes me back to Yugoslavia in 1943, to the hills of Bosnia and the plains of Srem: *pokret,* a word to galvanize the limbs even of the weariest partisan alive, a flag of victory or a flail of fear, take it as you can.

No pintcha. We get into line and move out across the ricefields, walking easily. This time it is neither victory nor fear, but routine. We are on a tour of inspection, and Cabral is in a hurry. Guerrilla warfare is nothing if not movement, constant movement, merciless movement, movement in the mind even when you are sitting still, sitting still and calculating what has happened, what is going to happen. Here inside this country which is called a Portuguese 'overseas province', a country of strange wilderness and beauty about the size of Switzerland or Holland, we have moved and we shall move for days and nights.

We slop across ricefields yellow with the weak sunlight of the last of the rains. We splash through miles of ankle-deep water, our rubber soles clopping and clucking to each other. Three villages, one after another on our route, are each encircled by a clump of trees in this thin near-coastal forestland. More rice-fields. After that a big waterway, a mile-width of bottle-green sea that penetrates upcountry from the Atlantic and looks like a river but isn't one. A majestic landscape, superb, defiant.

Canoes. We can stop walking. We load into these long dugouts until their freeboard laps an inch or two above the waterline, and crouch with a relief that doesn't last. There is nothing less comfortable than a crowd of men in a canoe, for you can neither sit nor stand. Balante paddlers take us out into the current. Someone's rifle is sticking into my back. Someone's boots are cradled in my stomach. Never mind. *No pintcha.*

I think of the last time I was waterborne on a guerrilla expedition, crossing the moonlit Danube in the summer of 1944. Now it is daylight, sleepy tropical afternoon-time, but otherwise the mood is pretty much the same. It is so uncomfortable, in a sense so unreasonable, that we have to laugh. The laughter echoes back and forth between the walls of mangrove forest. You might think the Portuguese were a hundred miles away. Actually they are eight or nine: but hard watched, well contained. This is a liberated zone, the coastal zone of Quitafine. Here it's how the kids were singing in a guerrilla school the other day:

> The guerrilla walks proudly on the land
> While the little Portuguese commands the clouds . . .

Those Balante paddlers, their rifles slung, swing their blades as though they will go on for ever. There are moments when I think this is what they are going to do. But all things come to an end, even journeys by canoe. We climb up a bank of mud and walk into the forest as twilight falls. Now it is only the ants, the marching ants, that bother us. Linger in one of their trails for an instant and their black little teeth will be stinging into your ankles, your legs, your thighs. Whenever this happens, we break into a trot, slapping at our trousers, stamping our feet. As for snakes, nobody worries any more. Pascoal said the other day, 'We have learned to live with the snakes.'

Late at night we stumble through trees into another base, at this time the main military base for Quitafine, a regular camp well sentried and composed. Here is Mateus, commander in Quitafine along with Pascoal who is regional commissar. A tall grave figure in the night. Mateus is a veteran of three years' fighting just like Pascoal. Limping from an old wound, Mateus makes us welcome, inquires for news, offers his own.

We stand about, relaxed and even happy. Really there is nothing happy about guerrilla warfare. There are only moments of good effort made successfully, of tasks accomplished, that one afterwards remembers with a certain joy. There are others, of a different kind, that one remembers with horror: or tries not to remember. This is one of the good moments.

The guard section who have come with us go off to feed and rest. We sit in a hut and wash our feet, gently comfortable. The paraffin lamp makes a shadow play. We see each other as fleeting shadows, but as solid ones. Cabral who is the founder of this movement, its inspirer, its leader, its relentless critic: a man of unforgettable moral resonance and strength of purpose whom I first met in 1960 when he came to my house in London, then as 'Abel Djassi', and whom I have stayed in touch with ever since. Tran Hoai-nam and Pham Van Tan of the Vietcong who are as tired as I am but, unlike me, would never think of saying so. Another old friend, Mario de Andrade from Angola, a poet with the history of his people in luminous eyes and dancing hands, a fine intelligence who has not allowed his Latin and Greek, seminary-learned, to cloud a shrewd appreciation of the world.

Amilcar looks across at me. 'What would you say to a glass of Scotch?'

'Ah, don't be silly.'

'You never know,' says Mario, whose talent is for not being surprised.

And after all Amilcar has brought a bottle of Scotch. 'First appearance on this scene,' he chuckles: 'just like you. You see, we think of everything.'

We sit with our feet in warm water and pass the bottle round.

* * *

Next morning we learn that yesterday's bombing was lucky for the Portuguese. After weeks of trying they struck an anti-aircraft gun served by two guerrilla soldiers. One of these was burned to death. The other managed to fling himself clear of the gunpit, but with major burns.

Cabral goes off on business of his own, visiting military units and schools and village committees. Pascoal Alves takes us four visitors to see the wounded man.

On the way we pass another anti-aircraft post, consisting of one four-barrelled gun and with two single barrels, all three from Czechoslovakia and served by eight or ten young guerrillas. These guns are well placed in good pits with an open field of fire all round. The gunners explain their weapons. But will they use them when it comes to the point? After all, these gunners are out there in the open and they know about yesterday's bombing. I don't ask this question. But I think it.

A few minutes later, when we're half a mile along the path, today's bombing begins. The Portuguese seem to come every day at about eleven in the morning, and sometimes after lunch — after their lunch, I mean — with two or three planes from the airbase at Bissau, the country's capital. This time they come with two planes: Fiats again. They go back and forth over us at about four thousand feet and drop high-explosive on a fancied target some six miles away. But my question is answered: down the path our gunners open up on them at once, and with calm short bursts which continue till the planes go away again.

The hospital is in a forest clearing. A few beds for casualties and serious civilian cases, but mainly a clinic and dispensary for the neighbouring population. Daily clinics. One doctor, a quietly confident young man who has lately returned from six years of medical training in Moscow; and three nurses (normally, he explains, there should be five) who have each had one year's nursing training in the Soviet Union. I chat with the nurses in the little Russian that I have. It seems odd to find these young women speaking Russian: but why any odder, after all, than if they'd spoken French or English? Like the doctor, they are absolutely indigenous, absolutely *of the country:* young women who have gone from their Balante villages and learned a useful trade and now come home again to exercise it.

In a darkened hut there is Tengbatu, a Balante soldier. A long figure made huge with bandages that cover almost his whole body. About 23. A nurse hovers. The doctor reassures her. He says to us: 'Tertiary burns only on the extremities. We shall save him.' A few days later the army takes out Tengbatu to a base hospital near Boke in the Republic of Guinea. He went on the same boat as myself.

Next morning, back at base camp in Quitafine, I walk across the parade ground and find, in the shadow of a hut, a large fragment of an unexploded napalm canister dropped at the same time as the one that scorched Tengbatu. It is neatly printed with its identity: FCM-1-55 NAPALM 300 KG – 350L M/61. It is part of the military material which the North Atlantic Treaty Organization supplies to Portugal. For the defence of the Free World. A strange region, this Free World.

Napalm, like high-explosive, has been used by the Portuguese in Africa since the early months of the Angolan revolt in 1961. They use napalm a great deal, although they do not make it themselves, any more than they make jet bombers. The little hospitals and clinics of guerrilla-held Guine are filled with its victims, not only men but women and children as well. Some die from it. Others are mutilated by it.

War is a dirty business. This kind of war can sometimes be – and on this occasion, thanks to NATO, is – the dirtiest of all.

* * *

Genuine revolts against an established order begin with necessity. The penalties of guerrilla warfare can be accepted, can be justified, only when they are suffered as part of a *necessary* self-defence. This is a hard lesson that has nothing to do with revolutionary verbalism.

A few leaders may understand, from the start, this necessity to use violence both in self-defence and as the only means of opening the door to a better future. But they remain powerless until and unless large numbers of people also feel and acknowledge it. Only then can the bitterness and hope take fire.

The examples are there in the history of our times. Not to speak of the great antecedents in Russia and China, this was how it was in Yugoslavia during 1941 and 1942, when Nazi and Nazi-prompted massacres drove the peasants to fight back. It was so in Vietnam, during the reign of Diem in 1954-9, when the peasants saw their newly-given lands being taken away from them again. It was so in Cuba after the horrors of Batista. It was so in Kenya during the Emergency of the early1950s. And it has been so in Guine.

'I understand the need for violence,' observed the Archbishop of Recife in Brazil, the courageous Monsignor Helder Camara, not long ago: 'I respect those men who have chosen to accept it.'[1] He was thinking of his own Latin America. He might have been thinking of Guine.

This country of Guine is a small one, having within it fewer than a million Africans and perhaps three or four thousand civilian Portuguese. Much separates it from its neighbours and gives it an interest of its own. But there are also certain ways in which Guine may be more than interesting in itself, may be microcosmic in meaning – a paradigm of the African situation in the late 1960s: a place not only worth observing for itself but also worth learning from.

The history of Guine under the Portuguese is what explains the armed revolt which began in 1963.

But the history of the Portuguese is much older here than the history of colonialism. This, too, has something to do with the case. Long ago, even before the end of the fifteenth century, the pattern here was set. These were the latitudes where the trans-Atlantic slave trade saw its first beginnings. 'The people who live round the Rio Grande' – so named by the Portuguese because it was the largest ocean inlet south of the Gambia river – 'are Gogolis and Beafares [Beafadas]', Duarte Pacheco Pereira was reporting in 1506, 'and are subjects of the king of the Mandinka', of the king of Mali. 'They are very black in colour and many are naked while others go clothed in cottons. Here you can buy slaves at the rate of six or seven for a horse, even a bad horse; you can also buy gold, though not much . . .'[2]

The dusty centuries that followed brought little change. Europeans of various nationalities set up small trading stations where they bought and sold what they could while the coastal peoples of the Rio Grande took what profit they could find, resisting enslavement as best they might. It was always a small trade, never on the large scale achieved at other points along the Guinea Coast.

So it went on until the rise of European imperialist ambitions after the middle of the nineteenth century. Then the pace began to quicken. This vague territory, which the Portuguese had called Os Rios de Cabo Verde, became 'allocated' to Portugal, largely by British support against French advance, and was renamed Portuguese Guinea, or Guine. Its frontiers as they are today were drawn upon a map by a Luso-French convention of 1886. Thereafter the Portuguese had a new colony.

But for a long time they had it only in name. Their frontiers 'enclosed' a country about which the Portuguese knew almost nothing except that its populations were hostile to them, and where they had not a single post beyond sound of the sea. It became necessary, in colonial parlance, to 'show effective occupation' and 'pacify the country'. This proved difficult. There was African resistance. Wars followed.

It may be worth listing the more important of these wars. In 1878-80 the Portuguese sent an expedition against the Felup and Mandjak peoples at the head of the Rio Grande. The results were indecisive, but sufficient to give the Portuguese a foothold. In 1880-82 there were campaigns against the Fula and the Beafada. In 1883-5, the Portuguese tackled the Balante for the first time.

Other campaigns followed against the Pepel (1886-90), against the Fula of Gabu (1893), the Oinka (1897), the Bissagos (1902), the Mandjak of Churo (1904-6), the Mandinka of Geba (1907-8), again against the Oinka (1910-13), again against the Mandinka of Churo (1914), again against the Pepel (1915). In 1915 the Portuguese in the little capital of Bissau were living, in a Brazilian report, 'behind the defence of their town walls, and no one could go safely into the interior. Bissau was really a camp. Its walls formed a triangle based on the sea, and its people lived inside these walls', outside which they feared the vengeance of the 'fearsome Pepels', while 'even those who were able to go on trading missions had to pay for the Pepel Chief's permission'.[3]

Campaigns of 'pacification' continued every few years until as late in the colonial period as 1936. And even then, there remained pockets of country where the Portuguese had only a feeble or spasmodic hold. Only after some fifty years of campaigning could the Portuguese otherwise claim to have established the 'effective occupation' they had asserted during the scramble-for-Africa Congress of Berlin in 1884-5.

This long resistance has influenced the attitudes of rural Africans in Guinea; and rural Africans compose more than nine tenths of the population. For them the Europeans have always marked a peril, often a vicious one, whether from slave trading in the old days or from military invasion in recent times. Yet the Portuguese occupation was undoubtedly real when at last achieved. It might have been peacefully accepted, as colonial occupation often was elsewhere, but for the nature of Portuguese rule.

* * *

The Portuguese claim to a certain liberalism of spirit towards their enter-prises in Africa has not always been an empty one. Nearly forty years of Salazar's rule have offered the world a face of implacable and blind author-itarianism; yet the features of Portuguese policy before Salazar, whether at home or in Africa (or indeed earlier in Brazil), had expressed other and better meanings. An extreme economic discrimination against their peasants at home, their slaves in Brazil and 'their Africans' in Africa, was always present, being a perhaps inevitable attribute of the narrowly-based social oligarchies which ruled Portugal even under the Republic. But the discrimination was tempered from time to time by a certain human tolerance which had its roots, perhaps, in Portugal's own experience of medieval conquest by invaders from North Africa. If the tradition of the conquistadors was a dark and bloody one, it was nonetheless lit now and then by a respect for some of the

11

conquered peoples, including some of the Africans.

This respect flowered under the Portuguese Republic in interesting ways which nowadays seem quite forgotten. There were newspapers — in the colonies as well as in Lisbon — which thundered against the neo-slavery that was known as 'contract labour'. There were settlers in Africa as well as men in Portugal who risked much to tell the truth about official corruption or brutality. There were openings, few but useful, to higher education for Africans. If the Pan-African movement could hold one of the sessions of its fourth congress in Lisbon, during 1923, this was because the Republic allowed intelligent discussion about a future in which black men might be treated as the equals of white. If there were African 'cultural associations' in Angola and Mozambique which could legally discuss African grievances and aspirations, this was because Republican policy had at least some tolerance for the ideas of 'colonial trusteeship'.

Little of this survived the imposition of military rule in 1926 and, soon afterwards, the clamping of Portugal and its empire within the rigid inhumanities of quasi-fascist rule, of Salazar's *Estado Novo*. Even so, at least within the narrow field of elite advancement, it needs to be remembered that the Portuguese record is a better one, for most of the colonial period, than that of Belgium. In 1960 the Belgians agreed to withdraw their direct political control of the Congo at a time when Congolese university graduates numbered no more than seventeen. The comparable number for Angola at that time may have been as large as a hundred, although Angola's population was perhaps only a third that of the Congo. Such points as these deserve to be remembered. But they do not alter the fact that Portuguese colonial policy under Salazar was no longer open to any idea of African political or economic advancement, much less self-rule.

If a tiny minority of Africans could still acquire higher education, this was only on condition of their quitting their African status and becoming *assimilados*, of being assimilated into Portuguese attitudes and civilization. Abstracted from their own milieu, *assimilados* were (and are) required to forget their own languages, their own traditions, their own people — to the extent, indeed, that even the handful of them who have taken the revolutionary road, men such as Cabral, Neto and Mondlane, have also had to take themselves through a systematic process of 'reafricanization' before they could hope to make progress.

After 1932, when Salazar achieved his personal command of the Portuguese scene, all question of colonial reformism was at an end. The 'cultural associations' were disbanded or transformed into administrative puppet shows. The dissident voices were silenced in prison or in exile. The door to 'assimilation', always narrow, was all but closed. Exact figures are hard to find, but it is reasonable to say that by the 1950s the proportion of *assimilados* in the Portuguese African colonies — of men and women who could hope to live in any way as European equals — was little more than one half of one per cent of the total African population. Only in respect of these could the Portuguese claim to operate 'non-racial' policies, and even towards *assimilados* there were, and are, attitudes of social and economic discrimination within Portuguese society.

As for the remainder of the African population, the 99½ per cent, they lived as the objects of colonial exploitation, either as 'free labourers' employed for as little money as could possibly be paid in order to keep them fit for work, or as virtual slaves whose status was thinly masked under the name of 'contract workers' in Angola or *servicais* in Mozambique. Not for nothing did an Inspector-General of Colonies, Henrique Galvao, inform the regime in a report of 1947 — which was carefully suppressed, but which found its way to publication thanks to Portugal's underground opposition — that 'in some ways, the situation [in Angola] is worse than simple slavery. Under slavery, after all, the Native is bought as an animal: his owner prefers him to remain as fit as a horse or an ox. Yet here the Native is not bought — he is hired from the State, although he is called a free man. And his employer cares little if he sickens or dies, once he is working, because when he sickens or dies his employer will simply ask for another'. High death-rates among forced workers, Galvao added, had never in his experience debarred an employer from being supplied with more men.[4]

In Guine the situation was better than this. There were few settlers, and consequently there was little forced labour of a direct kind, except for the seasonal needs of district administrators who required roads to be cleared or gardens to be weeded. Otherwise the general position was much the same as in Angola and Mozambique. Economically, the colony was run as an appendage of Portugal — or rather of the monopolist trading company, the Uniao Fabril — which supplied Portugal with cheap colonial imports in return for Portuguese exports, the terms of trade being fixed in order to turn the balance of payments as favourably to Portugal as was possible.[5]

This structure could obviously allow only the most minimal 'development' in the way that Africans lived, and there was never any question of lowering the profits of the colonial enterprise in order to raise the standards of African life. Worse still, a considerable segment of the rural population — again as in Mozambique and Angola — was forced to cultivate cash crops for export at fixed prices: in the years before the war began here, perhaps as many as 50,000 African families in Guine were producing groundnuts under these conditions. As elsewhere in Africa, this cultivation of cash crops for export cut severely into the domestic food supply, and deepened the poverty and malnutrition of the peasants.

Not surprisingly, the health situation had become a disgrace by the 1950s. Texeira da Mota, writing in 1954,[6] found that the great majority of the population even in Bissau, the capital, suffered from ancylostomiasis,[7] and that infantile mortality stood at around 600 babies in every 1,000. Sleeping sickness remained endemic in about two fifths of all villages, while malaria was practically ubiquitous in one degree of seriousness or another, not to speak of other afflictions such as bilharzia and various forms of dysentery. Elsewhere the last twenty years of the colonial period saw a great deal of effort directed at tropical scourges such as these. But not in Guine: the colony could simply 'not afford it'.

Although Portugal was regularly taking out as much money, or more, than it was putting into the country, the total administrative health services in 1954 — again according to Teixeira da Mota — were composed of eighteen doctors and two pharmacists, four female nurses, twenty-six male nurses, sixty-six assistant nurses, one midwife and thirty-seven assistant midwives. Even so, the Bissau hospital, mainly for the use of Europeans, employed seven of these doctors, all the female nurses and sixteen of the assistant nurses.

This meant that the whole of the rural population had at best only eleven doctors; and three of these were normally on leave in Portugal. So the practical outcome of Portuguese rule, in health services, was the provision of one doctor for every 100,000 Africans, while the supply of nurses and mid-wives was almost as bad. Most of the colony's 300 hospital beds were in Bissau, and outside Bissau there was only one hospital.

The educational structure was no different. One per cent of the population, at most, could claim some elementary literacy; but only 0.3 per cent was of 'assimilated status' and could hope for something better. There was one government secondary school, but about sixty per cent of its pupils were European, and no mission secondary school. There was no higher education of any kind. By 1960 a total of eleven Africans from Guine had acquired graduate status — as 'assimilated Portuguese' in Portugal.

Now these conditions might have been accepted if there had been any prospect of improvement. There was none. The Salazar regime did indeed produce a few reforms of structure in 1961, under international pressure, but they were paper ones. The status of *assimilado,* for example, was formally abolished: practically, opportunities for education remained exactly as before. The laws on forced labour were improved; the actual condition of the labourer experienced no change.

As in Portugal itself, all initiatives which might lead to any form of effective democratization had been repressed since at least 1930. No political demonstrations were allowed: no gatherings, no debates, much less political parties of any kind. No trade union rights were conceded. No structural reorganization was even considered. What was, under this regime, continued as what should be: now and for always.

With every road to reform thus barred and forbidden, only two alternatives remained. One was continued quiescence, continued surrender to a life of helot misery. The other was revolt, necessarily armed revolt.

Once this conclusion was reached even by a few men and women, as it was in 1956, the trail of Portuguese violence had almost come full circle. With this it can be said, in Fanon's words, that

> The violence which has ruled over the ordering of the colonial world, which has ceaselessly drummed the rhythm for the destruction of native social forms and broken up without reserve the systems of reference of the economy, the customs of dress and external life, that same

violence will be claimed and taken over by the native in the moment when, deciding to embody history in his own person, he surges into the forbidden quarters.[8]

In September 1956, meeting discreetly in Bissau, a few Africans decided to embody history in their own persons. They formed the African Independence Party of Guine and the Cape Verde Islands (PAIGC[9]). They numbered exactly six including Amilcar Cabral, who was their guiding spirit; but they knew where they were going. They proceeded to peaceful appeals for political and social change, and were answered by silence and increased repression. Nearly seven years later, in January 1963, they passed to armed revolt.

* * *

Seven years later . . . Why so long, what had they been doing? A decisive part of the story of this guerrilla war of liberation in Guine lies concealed in those seven years.

When at last they emerged from silence in 1963, these rebels were far more in number than in 1956. But they were also different in themselves, and this difference in quality was more important for their cause even than the swelling of their ranks to several thousand. They had ceased to be rebels. They had become revolutionaries.

Their early bid had been for progressive change, for reform, for equality of rights. Now they spoke another language. 'To be masters of our destiny', they now said, 'that's not simply a question of having African ministers. What we need is that our work, our riches, should belong to all of us, to the people who labour to create this wealth . . . . If we make this war only to chase out the Portuguese, then it's not worth the trouble. Yes, we make it to chase out the Portuguese, but also so that nobody shall exploit us, neither white men nor black men.'[10]

Why this development from revolt to revolution?

Let us begin by looking at the factual record.

In this context, it goes back to 1948. Then it was that three of the African students living at Lisbon's Casa dos Estudiantes do Imperio decided to form, if they could, a Centre for African Studies. They were Agostinho Neto, Amilcar Cabral and Mario de Andrade, and they managed, by stressing their interest in African languages, to obtain the necessary permit. In this way they acquired the means both of meeting for discussion, officially and unofficially, and also of 'reafricanizing' themselves by learning the languages of the peoples they had come from. Andrade became a poet in his native tongue, Kimbundu. Cabral continued to qualify himself as an hydraulics engineer, and Neto, another distinguished Kimbundu student, as a medical doctor. Meanwhile their political discussions began to reach forward to the ways and means, vaguely seen as yet, by which they could play a part in liberating their countries. They began to examine colonial structure. Little by little, they came to the conclusion that no real progress could be made within the organizational framework which the Portuguese had raised. Any real advance would have to follow a far-reaching process of democratization, taking this at every decisive aspect of life from primary education to political leadership.

These discussions carried them no further than an elementary conviction that some form of revolt would almost certainly be necessary at some point in the future, hopefully the near future. For the rest, they still knew little of their own countries, while the only language they spoke with fluency was Portuguese.

They separated. Neto went in and out of political imprisonment. Andrade remained for a while in Portugal and then, escaping persecution, migrated to Paris where he scratched a living in one way or another, for a while as an editor of the review *Presence Africaine*. Cabral returned to Guine.

In Guine Cabral took service with the colonial administration as an agricultural engineer. But it turned out that his duties were mainly concerned with the preparation of an agricultural census. It was a lucky chance. For two years, 1952-54, he tramped the length and breadth of his country acquiring detailed local knowledge, growing into an intimacy with village life, and, as he soon realized, making himself ready for what should come later. Already in 1953 his 'talking against Portuguese rule' had begun to cause him trouble with the authorities. Once again he was lucky. The governor at that time chanced to be a man of liberal inclinations. He called in Cabral and said to him, more or less in these words: 'Look, never mind about my opinions. If you start making trouble for me, I shall jail you. Shut up, or leave the country.'

Cabral had no intention of shutting up, but there was then no prospect of surviving clandestinely in Guine, and so, biding his time, he went back to Lisbon. There he was offered several jobs in Angola, and eventually went out to work on a private sugar estate. He was now 30, and everything that had happened to him appears to have strengthened his convictions. In Angola he linked himself with the handful of educated Africans who were then preparing the way for a movement of liberation, and in December 1956, with his old Lisbon colleague Agostinho Neto, he became a founding member of the MPLA (Movimento Popular de Libertacao de Angola), necessarily clandestine.

But he kept in touch with his homeland; and there, during a visit to Bissau in 1956 a few months before the founding of the MPLA, he took the lead in forming the PAIGC, also necessarily clandestine. Almost exactly three years later, on 3 August 1959, Bissau dock workers at Pidgiguiti began a strike for higher wages. They were shot back to work by the police with the loss of some fifty lives. The whole situation suddenly sharpened.

A month after the Pidgiguiti massacre, Cabral arrived back in Bissau from Angola, bade farewell to his mother who was and indeed still is living there, and disappeared from legal sight. That same month of September, on Saturday the 19th, the leaders of the PAIGC met in secret on the outskirts of Bissau, and declared for a struggle against the Portuguese 'by all possible means, including war'. Among those who took part in this meeting were **Rafael Barbosa, Aristides Pereira, Luiz Cabral, and Fernando Fortes,** with Amilcar Cabral in the chair, their acknowledged leader then and since.[11] No minutes survive from that memorable occasion. But a confidential party record written soon afterwards vividly sets its tone and states its conclusions:

> Having reviewed these three past years of clandestine political work [since the foundation of the PAIGC in 1956] and analysed the political situation, the enlarged meeting of 19 September concluded, in the light of the Pidgiguiti experience and the nature of Portuguese colonialism, that the only way to liberate the country is through struggle by all possible means, including war.
>
> To prepare for this new phase, and on the principle of 'expect the better but prepare for the worse', the enlarged meeting adopted the following plan of action:
>
> 1. Without delay mobilize and organize the peasant masses who will be, as experience shows, the main force in the struggle for national liberation.
>
> 2. Strengthen our organization in the towns but keep it clandestine, avoiding all demonstrations.
>
> 3. Develop and reinforce unity around the Party of the Africans of all ethnic groups, origins, and social strata.
>
> 4. Prepare as many cadres as possible, either inside the country or abroad, for political leadership and the successful development of our struggle.
>
> 5. Mobilize emigres in neighbouring territories so as to draw them into the liberation struggle and the future of our people.
>
> 6. Work to acquire the means that will be needed for success.
>
> So as to guarantee the security of a part of the leadership, and to develop the struggle outside, the Party decided to transfer its general secretariat outside the country.

But to declare for 'struggle by all possible means, including war', was one thing: to conduct it successfully, quite another. Latently, there might be a favourable situation in the country. Practically and immediately, there was no such thing. The PAIGC had some half a hundred active members, but nearly all were in Bissau. Few had any close links with the villages. Out in the villages the peasants remembered their wars against the Portuguese, and grumbled against colonial exactions, but they were still a long way from reaching for arms. They might be easy to convince that there was no third way between continued surrender and armed uprising, but to convince them that the second was both possible and wise could not be done easily, and it could not be done soon. Not for nothing had Cabral tramped the length and breadth of Guine on his census work, listening, talking, asking questions, measuring the peasant mind. He knew what had to be done. But he also knew how difficult it would be to do it.

17

There was, at the onset, the problem of finding and preparing a small group of pioneers. This was far from easy. Despair of ever being able to do anything effective against the Portuguese was widespread. Bissau's African population was for the most part a mixed bag of rootless workers, lay-abouts, small traders, with a handful of artisans and skilled mechanics. Demoralization was common amongst them. So was drunkenness.

What the PAIGC leaders did was to call discreetly for volunteers and then examine each of them with painstaking care. They made some mistakes, but not many. By 1960 they were able to begin sending a small stream of young men and women into the shelter of the neighbouring Republic of Guinea, which had meanwhile won its independence of France in September 1958. Here in Conakry, Cabral established himself in a small house on the outskirts, found rooms close by for the volunteers, and set about preparing them.

Most of those who led the PAIGC in later years went through Cabral's teaching: Osvaldo, commander in the north and then in the east; Otto Schacht, a crack wireless-telegraphist in Portuguese service before 1966 and now a central figure in the movement; many others. Barbosa, however, did not.[12]

A few brief biographies will help to show what happened. I draw the first from Gerard Chaliand's book, and the others from my own notes. Antonio Bana, aged 28, a leading PAIGC worker on the North Front until he was killed in action on 31 May 1968:

> At the beginning of my life, at thirteen, I worked in Bissau as a white man's boy. I looked after the white man's son, served at table, did the shopping. They paid me 150 escudos a month [about £2 at contemporary values]. One day I was thinking and thinking about later on. How could I keep a wife on 150 escudos a month? So I thought I would learn to drive. A black chaffeur taught me. But to be a chauffeur you needed to pass a test. Anyone who wanted to be a chauffeur had to know how to read and write. The Portuguese also said you had to have an identity card, but because my parents were not *assimilados* I did not have any card. So I left the idea of being a chauffeur, and I went to work as mechanic for a Portuguese.
>
> This boss had an Austin truck. And as I worked well he said to me: you'll drive my truck. But he didn't pay me like a chauffeur with an identity card. One day he called me and said: you're running the truck. Well I agreed, but I asked him if he would get me an identity card. He said: no, but it's all right, the District Officer is a friend of mine.
>
> I went on journeys into the interior for groundnuts. Whenever I came back to Bissau I had a real chauffeur beside me who showed his card, and they thought I was his helper. But the chauffeurs who had cards learned about that, and because they were short of work they made a complaint against me. The District Officer ordered that no one could drive without a card. So my boss said: you can't drive any more. Then I stayed in the workshop. I worked well. The whites could do what they liked, I couldn't contradict them. In those times it was them

that had the power. Afterwards I worked with a lot of whites, but not one of them ever hit me because I knew the answer to living with them: work well and don't talk back to them.

One day — I was living with a friend, we mucked in together — another friend came to see us and we got talking. He said there was a Party. I didn't know what a party was. So this comrade explained that this Party was for getting independence, for fighting against the Portuguese, for the liberty of the people, for winning a new life. Well, I knew all right that the Portuguese had always kicked our people around. When I was a kid I used to believe that people could become white or black, and that it was a white skin that made you bad.

We asked this comrade questions. We'd felt the same things, but not clearly. Now he explained it was suddenly quite clear. We met again, several times, That's how I became a volunteer in the fight against the Portuguese.

Since then I've done everything I could for the Party. The Party can count on me. I worked for the Party and I listened to Cabral speaking, to Barbosa[12] — that was in 1959 — but I didn't know them myself. My job was to mobilize people. I used to hold little meetings among the folk I knew, first of all with those I could trust, and explain that the time had come to fight for being free, and that the PAIGC was fighting for this . . . Then later on I was sent, I and others, into the countryside to mobilize the peasants . . . .[13]

Pascoal Alves, aged 29, a senior political commissar on the South Front:

I'm from Bissau. My father was a commercial clerk. I'd just finished primary school when there was the massacre in Bissau [of dock workers, in August 1959] and Cabral came back. I had some friends. They knew about the Party. I didn't wait. I joined the Party. We worked hard to mobilize people. We held little meetings, we gave out leaflets. Then the Party began sending some of us to Conakry, and they sent me too. There I went to the Universite Ouvriere in 1961 and 1962. I learned a lot, I grew up. In 1962 I came back again, and at first I was fighting in the zone to the north of the Corubal, up there in that country. Down here on the coast I have been for a year now . . .

Ibrahima Camara, aged 28, PAIGC supply administrator:

I left Bissau and went to Senegal about eight years ago, not long before the massacre. I wasn't satisfied with the life I could have there. Then after the massacre my father and the rest of our family came to Senegal. We lived near the Casamance, maybe fifteen kilometres from our frontier. I went to school at Ziguinchor. I finished primary, and lycee when I was 22.

That was when I joined the Party and the fight, with my friends and

some of my family. The Party sent me to Conakry, and then Cabral
sent me to Czechoslovakia to study how to run co-operatives. I was in
Prague for six months, and at Loviste. That was in 1961. Then later
on, after that training, the Party sent me to Kindia [Republic of Guinea]
for army training.[14] I was there for a bit and then I was sent into our
country in 1964. Mostly I have worked on forming co-operatives, on
teaching how to run them, and on arranging food supplies for our
forces. I was about two years in the country before going back to
Conakry again . . .

Sala N'tonton, about 30, PAIGC soldier:

I was a farmer [Balante: from Quinara in the central area of Guine],
and our village was a poor one. We'd pigs and chickens. The Portuguese
bought these, but they gave us bad prices. We had to pay a lot of taxes
without ever seeing the benefit of them. Where was the school, the
clinic? There weren't any, no matter what taxes we paid. So I joined
the Party [in 1963]. I wanted to have a hand in putting things right . . .
    Yes, before that I'd been in the army, the Portuguese I mean. That
was in 1957, maybe I was 20, in Balamo. Two years and six months I
served them. They didn't treat us well. The whites had all the promotion. We had the dirty jobs. Then I went back to my village and I stayed
there. That was the time that a comrade from the Party came to our
village. He began talking about how things were and what we had to do
to put things right. I listened to him. I knew he wasn't telling lies. I
knew that things were like he said. I'd seen it for myself. I joined the
Party after that . . .

In the Republic of Guinea they found other problems; but that is a story to
be told later.
    By the end of 1962 they were ready for warfare. Yet it was to be warfare
not simply to chase out the Portuguese, but above all to reorganize the country
on new lines. If there had to be warfare, it was to be for revolutionary ends.
    They appear to have reached this conviction by several stages. Those who
had studied in Lisbon had acquired some familiarity with revolutionary
traditions of thought, notably Marxist, but they seem always to have been
well aware that any revolution in Africa would have to be indigenous in form.
What might succeed in Europe or Asia would certainly be fruitless in Africa.
Here there were none of those basic conditions upon which revolution in
Europe and Asia had been founded: no large proletariat, no crystallized
working class, no masses of peasantry deprived of land except in marginal
and special circumstances (such as the imposition of cash crops). At the same
time it was just as clear that mere revolt, no matter how successful, could
never in itself justify the sufferings it would cause, because a mere extension
of Portuguese structures under African elite control could never guarantee

those changes, whether in material living standards or in cultural expansion, that the people of Guiné really needed. Revolt must imply revolution, or it would be better not to start at all.

There were other clinching arguments. The fruitlessness of a nationalist struggle which aimed merely or mainly at putting Africans into controlling jobs held by Europeans was repeatedly brought home to the leaders of the PAIGC during their years of preparation, as well as later. They saw countries acquiring self-rule within the same basic socio-political structures as before, and with the result that most of these fell at once into the paralysing constriction of elite rule. They found themselves invited to presidential or ministerial receptions and conferences where nothing seemed changed except the outward trappings and the colour of official skins. They watched the flow of national liberation vanish in the sands of popular disillusionment. Were they to tackle the Portuguese, with all the death and misery this must cause, simply for that?

Besides, could a movement with any such limited aims possibly get off the ground? If they went to the peasants and said: You must back our struggle, the peasants would answer, Why? If they said, For a better world, or To put us in power, the peasants would simply turn away. Big words would mean nothing to them; nor would the careers of other people, of men from the towns. 'The big words', as a Vietnamese revolutionary has put it, 'are useless . . . The peasants listen to their own immediate interests. . . .'[15] So it all came back to the same conclusion. To make revolt worthwhile, even to make it *possible*, its objectives had to go far beyond a substitution of the persons in control. They had to comprehend a total reform of structure at every level of life. Only then would PAIGC policies be able to answer the interests of the peasants, and the sufferings be accepted as a price that could be paid.

All this became ever clearer as the PAIGC wrestled with its problems, both before and after the struggle turned to war. Here, as elsewhere, the practical shape and meaning of revolution were forged in the doing, in the acting, in the fighting, in the day-to-day search for right solutions. What these solutions were will be seen in due course. Meanwhile it may be said that the experience of the PAIGC confirms a few basic principles.

First among these is that one cannot make the revolt first, and think about the revolution afterwards. All anti-imperialist revolts take a revolutionary direction. That is their nature. But only those come to fruition which realize, in the course of the struggle, a complete integration of military and political effort within a framework of thought and aim that is revolutionary.

Another principle, flowing from the first, is that methods, structures, and objectives must be profoundly and increasingly democratic. Here there can be no question of a group of leaders or fighters, no matter how devoted and sincere, 'making the revolution' on behalf of others. Unless and until the mass of people actively and continually participate in changing their own lives, there will be no change, or none of any value. Not until the farmers in the villages and hamlets embrace the revolution as their own work, as their own thing, does success become possible. And so 'Keep always in mind that the people are not fighting for ideas, for the things in anyone's head. They are fighting to win material benefits, to live better and in peace, to see their lives go forward, to guarantee the future of their children. . . .' And so, again, 'Practise revolutionary democracy. . . . Hold frequent meetings . . . . Hide nothing from the masses of our people. Tell no lies. . . . Claim no easy victories. . . .'[16]

Guerrilla war without such aims and methods, non-revolutionary guerrilla war, is either a romantic fantasy on the road to defeat or a squalid adventure deserving no support.

Anyone who applies these principles to the history of our times will see their value. During the Second World War in Europe, to offer an example within my own experience, the Yugoslav nationalist guerrillas under General Mihajlovic certainly revolted against German and Italian occupation of Yugoslavia. But they had no more programme and objective than to preserve the *status quo ante* and ensure their own command of the state, or the command of men like them, once the war was over. They calculated that if the war was lost, they were probably lost with it, though some began to reinsure themselves against this. On the other hand, if the war was won, it would be, they thought, the West that would win it – and then they would in any case inherit the power or else be awarded it.

So they quickly fell into inactivity, into a mere waiting for the war to be over; and from inactivity they fell still further into collaboration with the enemy; and from collaboration with the enemy they dwindled, most of them, into the squalors of a kind of banditry. I remember that the same phenom-enon occurred, though on a far smaller scale, during the last six months of the war in Italy, when large forces of guerrillas challenged German occupation. Now and then it happened that a bunch of fighters would find it pleasant to retire into a mountain, reach agreements with the Germans which ensured an effective cease-fire between them and the enemy, and live as comfortable but idle heroes until the Allied armies should arrive and give them medals. Some-thing of the same thing, one gathers, occasionally happened in China during the Chinese revolutionary wars: the Chinese Communists neatly called it 'mountain-topism'.

It has also happened in Africa. Kinshasa may not be a mountain-top; but the self-styled Angolan government-in-exile of Mr Roberto Holden is none-theless guilty of 'mountain-topism'. Waiting for the war to end, they organize ministries and share out titles. The liberation of Algeria offers another case in point. The Algerian FLN was certainly not 'mountain-topist'. It made a revolt and promised a revolution. But in making the revolt, however success-fully, it promoted an 'outside army', in Tunisia, which had evidently less interest in making revolution. When the revolt was over, and the French expelled it, it suddenly became clear that the revolution was to be largely one of words, all too liable to be banished from the scene by internecine quarrels and an army *coup*. This is not to say that the liberation of Algeria failed, only that the liberation has not been what was promised.

There is one last preliminary point that needs mentioning here, and especially in respect of Africa. Historically, Africa is in transition from the pre-colonial structures of the past to quite different structures which can absorb and use the knowledge and technology of the modern world. This is bound to be a long and difficult transition, partly because of Africa's technological backwardness and poverty in accumulated capital, but also, and even more, because this transition calls for a profound cultural upheaval. It is necessary not only to draw Africa's rural millions into the orbit of new forms of production, to build roads and railways, industries and schools. It is also necessary to displace traditional attitudes and ways of thought by modern attitudes and ways of thought; to consign to a dignified memory the beliefs of a past where religion, with its ancillaries in witchcraft or magic, explained the workings of the world; and to enter a new world where these old but no longer valid explanations have no decisive place.

Now it took the Europeans, as we know, a long time and many bitter ideological battles to make this great transition for themselves. Up to the close of the Middle Ages, and even later, the Church claimed the ability to explain everything, condemning science as Anti-Christ. The change was made in the end, but the history of its making is littered with casualties, with men like Bruno burned at the stake, with men like Galileo reduced to silence; even today you will find no few outbreaks of 'flat-earthism' in the mental habits of Europe.[17]

This great renewal of attitudes cannot be easy for the Africans, any more than it was easy for the Europeans. But it has to be made. Here lies another large reason why political change in Africa will remain of little long-term value unless it is also cultural change.

Yet cultural change becomes possible only when men and women fight out their mental battles for themselves. Any liberation movement which fails to be a profoundly democratic one — calling not only on the energies and courage of ordinary people, but also on their intelligence, their daily participation, their capacity for confronting new problems in new ways, their ability to think things through for themselves — will remain a movement whose roots lie on the surface, and lack the nourishment to endure.

How deeply have the roots of the PAIGC reached down into their peasant soil?

References

1. *Le Monde*, 26 April 1968.
2. *Esmeraldo de Situ Orbis*, edited and translated by R. Mauny, Bissau, 1956, p.73. Rio Grande is the Geba Channel.
3. M. Archer, *Terras onde se Fala Portugues*, Sao Paulo, 1962 quoted by M. de Andrade, *Revolution Africaine*, 7-13 December 1967.
4. Quoted in B. Davidson, *The African Awakening*, London and New

York, 1955, pp.204-6.

5. By 1968 the Uniao Fabril's comparatively huge stake in the colonial exploitation of Guine had long caused sceptics in Lisbon to call this war 'the Company's war'. Holding a virtual monopoly of export-import trade with Guine, whether on its own or through its associated companies (such as SARL), the Companhia Uniao Fabril (CUF) has several thousand employees, its own shipping, secondary industries, and so on. Through the Mello family, its ownership is linked closely to other monopolist private interests in Portugal, such as the steel industry which, like other major Portuguese interests, is in turn closely linked to foreign capitalist groups in Britain, France, West Germany, etc.

    In 1962, for example, CUF signed a large contract with the Societe Francaise d'Etudes et de Financements Industriels, providing for a considerable investment by the French concern. In 1963 CUF obtained large credits from French and West German sources, and went into partnership for textile production with the US Ludlow Corporation. . . . The case was typical for every major Portuguese enterprise: if the repression in Guine was 'the Company's war', it was no less the war of many non-Portuguese companies as well.

6. Quoted in A. Cabral's *Report* to United Nations, 1961.

7. A chronic debilitating infection with nematodes, commonly known as hook worms. The bloodsucking activity of the worms, plus malnutrition, leads to anaemia. Infected children may be retarded physically and mentally.

8. F. Fanon, *The Wretched of the Earth*, Paris, 1961; Penguin Books, London, 1967, p.31.

9. *Partido Africano da Independencia da Guine e Cabo Verde* — the word 'African' being there to emphasize that there was no question of claiming independence for assimiles or settlers, but for the whole people.

10. In Chaliand, *Lutte Armee en Afrique*, Maspero, Paris, 1967, p.49.

11. If the names of many Africans of Guine are Portuguese, this is usually to be ascribed to the traditional practice, in the past, of giving Africans the European names of their owners or long-term employers. This applies to Africans in towns where there was also, of course, a certain *metissage*.

12. Rafael Barbosa, the nominal president. Public works foreman by trade, Barbosa was born at Safim near Bissau in 1924 of a Cape Verdian father, who was a travelling small trader, and a Guinean mother. Praised by his colleagues for awakening young people in Bissau to nationalist ideas and aims, Barbosa joined the PAIGC in 1958, and was arrested after a clandestine year on 13 March 1962, since when the PIDE (Salazarist political police) have held him in their prisons at Bissau. The first congress of the PAIGC, February 1964, reconfirmed him in the presidency. Barbosa is married with five children. (See Ch.5 note 7 for his arrest. After release in 1968, he changed sides. See p.140.)

13. *Op. Cit.*, pp.92-4.

14. Raised in 1964 by decision of the 1964 congress, the PAIGC army or FARP (Peoples' Revolutionary Armed Forces) was formed inside Guine out of various fighting units that were already in being: these included mobile units on all three fronts — South, North and East — as well as

local guerrilla units. A few picked men were sent for training outside the country, and some of these to Kindia.

15. Nguyen Van Tien, 'Notre strategie de la guerilla', *Partisans*, Paris, January-February 1968.

16. Extracts from general directives of PAIGC leadership. For fuller quotations, see Chapters 4, 5 and 6.

One may compare them with the experience of others:

'During the years of our resistance, the system we called "the three big democracies" took shape and brought us success:

'Political democracy: to hold regular conferences in our basic units, to give gatherings of fighters the chance to state their views on all questions concerned with the struggle, to carry on education, to examine the daily life of these units: for in our army the political workers have the right to criticize the fighters, and also the other way around.

'Military democracy: in matters of fighting as well as education — if conditions allow it — to hold similar conferences so as to explain to everyone the operational plan, to promote individual initiative, to discuss together the means of overcoming difficulties so as to carry out the assigned task.

'Economic democracy: fighters, like political workers, have an equal right to take part in matters of management, in improving material conditions within the system we call "open finance".

'It is thanks to this practice of a broad democracy that we have succeeded in raising the dynamism and creative efforts of the mass of political workers and fighters, in gathering their wisdom, and in thus resolving extremely difficult and complex problems; while at the same time reinforcing the unity of our ranks and increasing the fighting-power of our troops.' (V.N. Giap, *Guerre du Peuple, Armee du Peuple*, Paris, 1967, p.123.)

17. 'Police were called to a chapel yesterday where three pastors were "exorcising evil spirits" from a sick woman.

'Angry housewives dialled 999 to say the woman had been forced, screaming and struggling, inside the chapel in Treharris, Glamorgan.

'Mrs Mary Davies, who called the police, said: "Two vans drew up outside the chapel and the woman was forced out by two men.

' "She was screaming: 'Help me. Call the Police'.

' "When they got to the gate she placed her feet against it to stop them taking her in. But they forced her inside."

'The three were inside the chapel for 10 hours.

'But when the woman came out, said . . . a local housewife, "she seemed transformed. She was calm, and looked smartly dressed."

'Last night . . . one of the Full Gospel Church pastors said: "It might have seemed as though she was taken to the chapel against her will, but she did not have any will. She was possessed of evil spirits."

'The woman's husband said last night: "I knew my wife was possessed of evil spirits and I asked the pastors to help. . . ." '
(*Sun*, London, 22 May 1968.)

2. How? With Whom?

What has to be achieved is that people themselves discover
the need for armed struggle. As for guns, those you can
always find . . . .
NGUYEN VAN TIEN[1]

On a day towards the middle of October, we come back down that long arm
of jungle-green sea towards the coast, towards the frontier. More tightly
packed, if anything, than the last time. Darkness. A moon half splintered in
a slate-grey night. I grumble to Mario. Your boot, I say, is bothering me. He
replies: so is yours. We relapse into a comfortable discomfort and talk about
a lunch we had the other day with some Cubans in Conakry. Do they believe
in the need for political preparation or don't they? They say — they said the
other day in Conakry — that armed revolt is only, but only, 'the highest form
of struggle': that it supposes a process, that this process has to be political.
All right, but then on the other hand they also insist that a resolute handful
of armed insurgents can in fact (and haven't they proved it?) set off a whole
political movement. Certainly: but what if the people they're among don't
know who they are or what they want or why they want it? What about all
those Indians of Latin America: what do you do about them? How does your
handful of armed men get on if they can't even speak to the Indians in the
Indians' own languages?

We agree, say these Cubans, but you exaggerate. In Bolivia, they say, a
number of Indians called up by the military regime to track down Che
Guevara and his group actually passed over to support of the guerrillas,
because they had learned that men of their own people had already done that.[2]
Perhaps: but elsewhere? (And later, this same night after the canoe journey,
we hear Radio Dakar telling us of Che's capture, and stare at each other in
silence.) Elsewhere, it's not so good: that is agreed. In Brazil, for example,
there have been mistakes about the Indians: the Indians have been left out.
In Peru as well, mightn't they also have added? Did any of the group with
Luis de la Puente speak fluent Quechua when they went up into the Andes?
And is a single one of them still alive or at liberty? I recall something that
Cabral was saying the other day. 'When I was in Cuba I met a revolutionary

26

from Central America. I said to him: "What about the Indians in your country — after all they're a big part, aren't they, of your rural population?" And he said to me: "Oh, the Indians, yes, you see, the Indians are a sort of reserves ..." '

I sit or rather I crouch in that canoe in this slate-splintered night on a river that is like a black flood, unknown, unmarked on the maps, and with a name that nobody seems to remember; and I wonder about all those other guerrillas, those who are fighting in southern Africa, in Mozambique, Angola, the grasslands of old Zimbabwe, against the Portuguese and South Africans and the settlers of Mr Ian Smith. What happens to them when their scouts enter a dark village and the dogs begin barking? Do the faces in the doors of huts know who they are, what they want, why they want it? Do those village folk wait for them and welcome them? Do they know the local traitors, and stop them flitting off into the night?

Africa today is full of such questions. And those who could give the answers have, at the moment, more pressing things to do, or are lost to sight beyond the frontiers.[3]

* * *

We arrive towards dawn at a bankside of almost unfathomable mud and somehow we scramble out. Across the rice fields, trees stagger in that brief bad time before the sun breaks through. We pass them in a dream, lifting our boots out of water, miles of water, and putting them down again. Then at last there is C–, a Balante village raised on good dry ground. I am going to sleep for at least three hours. Error. Otto says: 'We are going out by ship tonight, so there is a farewell meeting now and Cabral will speak. . . .'

It takes place in a pleasant clearing shaded by the sun. The army section at this frontier base has even brought chairs for us: four chairs, and the others will sit on the ground. I hear Otto's voice, translating into French. I begin to make notes. I fall asleep.

But not all the time. I do make notes.

Cabral says:

> I am saying good-bye for the time being and I want to thank you, especially you members of the committee of C–, for your help and your support. You have been brave in the face of these bombardments. You have not abandoned your village. On the contrary, you have opened new rice fields, and that is a great encouragement for us. . . . What is important now is that you hold meetings of all branches in this area, all through Quitafine, in all these villages. . . .
>
> We have brought in some anti-aircraft guns, we shall try to bring in more of them. . . . Our army is stronger. It is strong enough to attack their barracks. I know our army is attacking their barracks often, but I want them to attack more often. I want you to say to army commanders: How many barracks have you attacked? Because the army is your army . . . .

Now we are going to hand out rifles to the members of village committees. This is because we are ordering our army to leave its bases and
go over to mobile warfare, to move constantly and attack the enemy at
many different places where the enemy does not expect it. So the army
is leaving C— and we are giving you rifles so that you can have some self-
defence if the enemy tries to send men here to pester you . . . . (At the
time of this speech, the Portuguese still had three embattled garrisons in
the zone of Quitafine, including a large one at Cacine, and were
expected to try occasional sorties into villages normally held by the
PAIGC).

Everyone who can handle a rifle will have a chance of getting one . . . .

So we all have a lot to do this coming year. Already you have given a
fine example with rice. But there still isn't enough cassava and potatoes.
Shortly we shall send you a trained man, an agronomist, who will help
you to grow more, and grow differently, so as to have a better diet, not
only rice. . . .

Cabral talks for three quarters of an hour and as though he had just had a
good night's sleep. In fact I know that he walked twenty-five miles yesterday.
spent the night huddled in a canoe, and is really not much less tired than I am.
After he stops there is a debate. Six or seven men and women speak. A tall
young man in a blue and white striped gown apologizes for some of the
committee members who are absent: they had to come from a distance, they
couldn't arrive in time. . . . He says the anti-aircraft guns have helped, they
can't knock down those planes but they give people courage, that's why more
rice is being grown than last season. . . . But there is one problem: why don't
the People's Shops[4] buy palmoil and palmnuts? They should do this. . . . (A
debate follows. Cabral says that the installing of these shops hasn't been
easy, needs time to iron out shortcomings. But after all the people are paying
no taxes to the PAIGC. They ought to make gifts at least. . . . Pascoal inter-
venes to explain that the principle of buying oil and nuts is in fact agreed and
will now be put into practice. Cabral comments that this is one thing on which
he's obviously out of touch. . . .)

An old man rises with an elder's dignity. He says that he supports the Party.
Living under the Portuguese was like living in a cave. Now, since the Party
came, the Portuguese are afraid, things are different. . . . 'We didn't think it
could be different. Party work and Party talk: it's like a big lie at the
beginning. But in the end it's the real truth'.

He is followed by a youngish woman who begins with slow ceremony,
rewinding her cloth so as to ensure that the baby on her back is safe and
comfortable. She is Na N'kanha, and she is chairman of the village committee
of C—. She speaks in Balante, which someone else translates into Guine Creole,[5]
which Otto translates to me in French, so that I do not get the savour of what
she says. But what she says is evidently liked: there are smiles all round, the
nodding of heads. She compares the Portuguese with the ant. He bites you,
but it isn't he who built the house. 'Here we sit in the shade, and they come

and bite us. But soon we will chase them out into the sun. . . .'

The meeting ends and the rifle distribution begins. Who can handle a rifle? About fifteen peasants stand up. Cabral hands out the rifles one by one, embraces each recipient, says a few words. I note that they are new rifles, well-oiled; and that they come with ammunition.

* * *

'Party work and Party talk: it's like a big lie at the beginning. . . .' That old man had put the problem, *the* problem, in a nutshell. How do you convince the peasants? How do you get them even to listen to you? How do you face their disbelief? How do you reach the point, as here in Quitafine, where they have themselves discovered the need for action, for acceptance of the sufferings involved, for participation in political responsibilities of an entirely new kind? How do you help them to leap that mighty gap between the thinking of the past − of the old resistances, of the old beliefs, of the old magic − and the realities of the modern world?

A long business. The PAIGC needed three years of active political work in the villages before they could reply to the Portuguese with guerrilla warfare, and even then they could not do it everywhere successfully or at once: not for six months after beginning in the south could they develop warfare in the north, and it was to take them another six months to spread their armed actions to other main regions. Even in 1968, nine years after they began, there were still areas where people would not listen or were afraid to listen.

The difficulties were, of course, specific to the country. Not least among these difficulties was ethnic diversity. Guine's African population of some 800,000 is divided into five main groups, each with its own language, cultural traditions, and sense of separate identity, as well as several smaller groups:

Balante	250,000
Mandjak	140,000
Fula	100,000
Mandinka	80,000
Pepil	50,000
Mancagne or Barme	35,000
Felup	15,000
Bissagos	15,000
Others *(Beafada, Bairote, Cassanga, Banhun, Sarakolle, Balanta-Marne, Pajadinca, etc.)*	115,000

Of these, the Fula and Mandinka, together with some smaller groups such as the Beafada and Pajadinca, are Muslim, while the remaining 70 per cent have their own African religions. Christianity is represented only by a very small minority of urbanized or semi-urbanized fragments. The Fula and Mandinka have long had forms of centralized authority exercised by lineage chiefs. But the remaining peoples, except for the Mandjak, are 'segmentary societies', whose principal form of social organization consists of age-grades and village lineage loyalties. In this respect they govern themselves by methods which are much the same, in essence, as those adopted by other segmentary societies in Africa: by such peoples as the Igbo in Nigeria, the Tallensi in Ghana, the Lugbara in Uganda, the Kikuyu in Kenya, the Ndembu in Zambia, and many others. They govern themselves, that is, by councils consisting of family-heads of individual villages or of neighbouring groups of villages.

Nearly all these Guine peoples have always been farmers of one kind or another. Although they have faced Portuguese exactions, they have had no Portuguese landlords. As in other African countries not settled by Europeans, there has been no great problem of land expropriation or rural indebtedness.

About 100,000 Africans live in the towns, but of these no more than a fraction may be said to be fully urbanized: many, on the contrary, have retained links with their villages, return to their villages now and then (or, rather, did so before the PAIGC blockaded the Portuguese-held towns), and take occasional town employment when they can or when they have to pay their taxes. It is a shifting, barely crystallized urban population: with nothing that resembles a working class, but for very small groups such as the dockers of Bissau; and very few individuals who can claim to be middle-class or to live a middle-class kind of life.

In approaching the peoples of Guine with revolution in mind, it was accordingly fruitless to lean for guidance on any of the familiar jargon. Whatever could the pioneers of the PAIGC have done, for example, with advice — proffered in this case by *World Revolution,* a journal published in New York — such as that 'the main forces of the national democratic revolution in Africa are the working class, the peasants, the petty-bourgeoisie and the national bourgeoisie . . . . Marxism-Leninism, Mao Tse-tung's thought teaches us that the worker-peasant alliance is the sure guarantee for the victory of the revolution. . . .' Could Na N'Kanha in Quitafine have made anything of that?

What was clearly necessary, the pioneers of the PAIGC decided, was to know exactly who was who. It would be no good departing for the countryside with general notions of 'the people', 'the peasants', 'the workers': no good talking about liberation in any general terms. Liberation precisely from what, with whom, to which end? And these down-to-earth questions would have to be answered in down-to-earth words for each ethnic group, each region, each set of local circumstances.

They made their own analysis. In 1964, speaking at the Frantz Fanon Centre in Milan, Cabral offered a sketch of it:

> I should like to give you an outline of the situational analysis we have always used as the basis for our liberation struggle. . . .
> In the countryside, first of all. There we have, on the one hand, the Fula group whom we have always considered as being semi-feudal in their social structure, and, on the other hand, the Balante, whom we may call, if you like, 'stateless'. Between these two extremes there are

several intermediary situations. The Mandjak, for example, were already moving at the time of the Portuguese arrival (towards the end of the nineteenth century) into a situation which could be described as feudal. . . .

What is the actual situation among the Fula? First of all there are the chiefs, the nobles and the religious lineages; then the artisans and *dyula* or travelling traders; after that, the peasants themselves. Here I shall not go into the economic situation of each group in any detail. But let me emphasize that the chiefs and their entourages have secured, despite the strength of traditions bearing on the collective ownership of land, very large privileges in terms of land-ownership and the exploitation of labour. Thus the peasants are obliged to work for their chiefs for part of every year.

The artisans play an important role in the socio-economic framework of the Fula, and may be said to constitute the embryo of an industry for processing raw materials: the blacksmiths at the bottom of the social scale, for example; then the leather-workers; and so on. The travelling traders are sometimes said to be higher in the scale than the artisans. This is really not the case, but they do represent the only group with practical possibilities of accumulating money. So it is the peasant group, generally deprived of rights, that is the real exploited element in Fula society.

Aside from property questions, the relative position of women can be a useful means of social comparison. Among the Fula, women have no social rights: they take part in production but possess none of its fruits. Moreover polygamy is a much respected institution, the wife being considered somewhat as the property of her husband.

At the other extreme, among the Balante, we are faced with a society which is completely without stratification, and where the only source of authority is composed of the elders of a village or of a group of villages. Among the Balante the land belongs to the village, but each family has a piece sufficient for its subsistence, while tools and other necessary equipment belong either to a family or to an individual. Though there is a strong trend towards polygamy, most of the Balante are monogamous. Women take part in production, but, unlike Fula women, become owners of what they produce . . . and so Balante women have a certain effective liberty except in relation to their children, which the family head may always claim. No doubt the reasoning behind this is economic: the strength of a family is seen as resting in the number of hands it can mobilize for its own production.

Transitionally, we have a minority group formed by African small landowners (outside the traditional framework) . . . but they have never been very active in the liberation struggle. . . .

In the towns — let me note that we have no Europeans in the countryside — there are the Europeans on one side and the Africans on the other. The Europeans can, of course, be easily sub-divided into the social strata they belonged to in Portugal: senior officials and managers who form a group that is much isolated from the rest of the European population; middle officials, small traders, clerks, professional men; and then skilled workers.

As for urban Africans, their groupings are composed of higher officials, middle officials, some professional men, then minor officials, clerks with contracts (to be distinguished from clerks without contracts, who can be sacked from one day to the next), some small farmers, who can be classed as petty-bourgeois; and then wage-earners. We define as wage-earners all those who work without contracts, for example dock workers, stevedores, and men who transport farming produce; as well as domestic servants who are men for the most part, mechanics in repair shops and the like, and shop workers. All these people we call wage-earners — and please note that we take care not to call them a proletariat or a working class.

Then in the towns there are rootless people who may also be divided, and into two groups. One of these two groups does not really deserve the name of 'rootless', but we have yet to find a better term for them. The other group is easily identified, and might be called our lumpenproletariat, if we had anything in Guine which we could properly call a proletariat: they consist of beggars, lay-abouts, prostitutes etc.

Now it is on the first of these two 'rootless' groups that we have concentrated particular attention, and it is a fact that they have played a very important part in our liberation struggle. They consist of a large number of young folk lately come from the countryside, and retaining links with it, who are at the same time beginning to live a European sort of life. They are usually without any training and live at the expense of their petty-bourgeois or labouring families. But you have to see them differently from spoiled children in Europe: actually, there are certain African traditions and customs which oblige an uncle living in town, for example, to welcome his nephew from the village. And so a social group is created which spends its time in living like townsmen, and which is to play an important role . . . .

Now, given the nature of these social complexities, it was clear that the peasants would be the mainstay in our struggle, but also that their interests in it would not be straightforwardly objective.

Our traditions — or, if you wish, our economic structure — are such that our Fula peasants or our semi-feudalized peasants often have a tendency to follow their chiefs. So their mobilization has required a profound and intensive labour. . . . As for the 'stateless peoples', such as the Balante, these were the groups which offered far greater resistance to the colonial invaders than the others, and it is in their ranks that we have found the greatest readiness to accept the ideas of national-liberation, even though it remains true that for these peasants — and they are all peasants — this is not without anxieties and problems.

Does the peasantry represent the main revolutionary force? This is a basic question. In the case of Guine, I must at once answer that it does not. Will it therefore seem strange that we should have based our whole revolt on the peasantry? The peasantry represents the country as a whole; it controls and produces its wealth; it is materially strong. Yet we well know by experience what trouble we have had in bringing the peasantry into the struggle. Before returning to this point, let me suggest that in China, for example, the situation of the peasantry has been fundamentally different. You need only consider, in order to see this, all the revolts that the Chinese peasantry have set in motion. But in Guine, apart from certain zones and groups where we found a welcome from the start, we have otherwise, and in contrast to the Chinese communists, had to struggle fiercely for peasant support.

To struggle fiercely for peasant support: it seems not to have been an exaggeration. That the peasants could be the great engine of the revolt: so much was obvious. But to get the engine moving, something else was required. This something else was political preparation by the pioneers of the PAIGC, themselves often by origin of that first 'rootless' group which Cabral mentioned, or else 'petty-bourgeois' artisans, mechanics, clerks, the occasional teacher. And this of course is where the jargon can utterly mislead, for the jargon says that the 'petty-bourgeois' is vacillating, subsidiary, of small or no initial account. But circumstances alter cases; and it is circumstances, specific circumstances, that count when it comes to the point.

* * *

This political preparation was extremely difficult. 'But without it', in some words of Cabral's, 'nothing of lasting value can be done. This political preparation is the toughest, most daunting, but also most important aspect of the whole campaign for national liberation'.

If the PAIGC have any ideological ties elsewhere, these have probably been strongest with the Vietnamese. An article written in 1968 by a Vietnamese leader, Nguyen Van Tien, offers an interesting parallel with what was done in Guine.

> Life for our peasants became very hard (he says of South Vietnam in the years immediately before 1959) after Diem had taken back the land they had been given. The political worker's job was to exploit this discontent created by the Diem regime. For example, he would say: What has the Diem regime done for us? It has taken away our lands and raised taxes.
>
> All our political propaganda was based on the daily interests, the personal interests, of the peasants and on the discontent of the poor peasants. To achieve this, you need political workers who know the peasants. With us, some 85 per cent of political workers are of peasant origin. It's not a question of saying that you are fighting for the liberty of the people — that will come afterwards. It's a question of asking:

Why overthrow the regime? And answering, for our own benefit. . . .

What has to be achieved is that people themselves discover the need for armed struggle. As for guns, those you can always find. . . . The whole 'peasant question' hangs by that, and you must never push the pace. If the peasants do not understand, it is dangerous, and often useless to go ahead alone. In 1959 it was the peasants themselves who raised the question of armed struggle.

There is nothing easy about being a revolutionary. Hardest of all is to win the peasants. But once you've done that, you have won the war. Then you cannot be defeated.[6]

Here is one of the PAIGC's political workers, Antonio Bana, one of hundreds, on the same subject in 1966:

We were sent into the countryside (in 1960, in his case) to mobilize the peasants. We used to make contact with the elders, the *homems grandes*. They were the men with influence, and afterwards they talked to the others. Portuguese oppression was bad enough for them to take us seriously, we young men, when we talked to them of independence; and they listened to us. We explained what the Party was. The Balante were the worst oppressed: they were the ones who had to build the roads. They understood us more quickly than the others.

For the mobilization, Cabral used to make us play a scene. In his presence, each of us had to pretend he was going into a village and talking to an elder. While each of us was doing this, the others listened. If we got it wrong, if it didn't work, Cabral made us begin again until we'd found the right arguments to use. Sometimes we had to do this several times over.

Before going into a village to meet the elder, we asked for information about him. You had to be very careful. You found out about his everyday life, his standing in the village, his relations with the Portuguese. At the beginning we didn't go into villages where the elders were hostile . . . .

So you go into a village after finding out about the elder, the *homem grande*, the man who has moral authority in the village (not usually the chief under the Portuguese system: the Portuguese were accustomed to nominating their own chiefs either from 'good villagers' or at need, as with the Balante, from Fula groups); and you're dressed as a peasant. First of all, I ask for the elder. Then I greet him and ask for hospitality. The Balante are very hospitable. The elder answers my greetings and shouts for food to be prepared.

When the food arrives, I look at what they've brought. It's rare they bring rice or chicken. If there's only rice with palmoil sauce, I say to the elder:

'Father, why do you give me only rice? The Balante are a hospitable people.'

'I'm a poor man. No chickens.'

'But how's that, father? You've been working all your life and your haven't even a single cock in your yard?'

'My son, why ask such things. I used to have cows, lambs too, but the whites have taken them for tax.'

'And does it suit you, father, what the whites are doing?'

'It doesn't suit me. But what can I do? They're too strong.'

So far I've been getting an idea about what the old man is like. He's already told me that he doesn't like the colonialists. But I have asked no big questions, I've said nothing important yet. Now I go a bit further.

'Father, if by chance there's something that could give you a better life tomorrow, would you be in favour of it?'

'I would be in favour.'

'Well then, think about it. For now we have a Party that fights the Portuguese so we can be free and so you can keep what you get by your work. If you have a son or daughter, the Party will send him or her to school. But keep the secret of this, for if the Portuguese find out they'll kill you. That doesn't mean you can't talk to other people about it. But only talk to people you can trust. Me, for instance, I've trust in you, father, and that's why I came to talk to you . . . .'

Then I leave after telling him that I want to meet the trustworthy people of the village in a quiet place, and talk with them. . . .

The second time I meet them, the elder has called the trustworthy people . . . and I ask them to question me on what I've told the elder.

Often they'll say:

'We're blacks, we don't even know how to make a safety-match. The whites have guns, aeroplanes. However can we get rid of them? . . .'

And so it went on, by a thousand little meetings such as this, some successful and others not, but always finding arguments, urging confidence, inspiring courage. . . . Gradually they won ground, little by little they found new confidence in themselves.

Antonio Bana, as we have seen, went through Cabral's school at Conakry.

There were seven of us, then: it was 1961. There was Chico, Osvaldo (Osvaldo Vieira, now a member of the central committee and commander in the north-east), Nino (Bernardo Vieira, now commander in the south and a member of the central committee), Domingos Ramos (since killed in action), Constantino Texeira (now a senior military commander in the south). They'd come back from a year's military training (in the Nanking Military Academy: 'They taught us very well,' Osvaldo commented to me afterwards; 'they were serious people'). Cabral gave us a political course, then explained the tasks each of us was to have and how to carry them out. . . .

I came back more solid, more confident. But now we began to be hunted by the Portuguese. Repression started. Some of the people in the villages grew afraid, others grew tougher: 'The Portuguese have killed my father – or my brother – or my son. The Portuguese are our enemies, we must fight them.' We used the repression to explain what the Portuguese really were. Then the more violent their repression, the more obvious was their true face – and they themselves confirmed what we had said about them.

But of course there were difficulties. Some peasants said that all this trouble was our fault: that if we'd stayed quiet they could have lived in peace by paying their taxes. Cabral had told us clearly that we shouldn't think that the peasants would rise with enthusiasm if we talked about independence. There was distrust. To meet the Mandinka you had to dress as a Mandinka: to meet the Balante as a Balante.[7] You had to watch out for Portuguese agents who would at once betray you. You talked in a village and then you went out of that village and slept in the bush.

You had to get yourself known and the Party known. Little by little, the Party sympathizers in the village would come into the bush with food for you. Later you could hold village meetings in the bush: talk to them, explain the struggle, ask for their help. After a while there were those who were with the Party and others who sympathized – then the neutrals and the suspects. Little by little, you had to find a way, thanks to the determined ones, of getting amongst the neutrals and the suspects and seeing that they did us no harm.

This mobilization was far more difficult than the war itself. . . .

In 1968 it often remained difficult. The PAIGC no more consists of saints and sages than any other body of men in their situation, but at least they are usually willing to admit their mistakes. Bana's recital suggests by implication how many minor errors of judgement there must have been, how many overstated arguments, how many tendencies to take for promised what was only half promised or not promised at all.

Besides that, the early village committees tended to be little more than knots of determined adherents, and it could not have been otherwise at the beginning. But with large areas under more or less permanent guerrilla control since 1964, especially in the south and north, steps were taken to democratize these committees in a larger way. The routine by 1967 was to reorganize them after village meetings where there were the time and security needed, and, so far as possible, to promote the election of committees representing and agreeable to all the respective villagers. At the same time it was possible to move towards the erection of regional committees manned by elected local committees, and so, gradually, to lay foundations for a new political structure that could eventually be countrywide.

* * *

One may note in passing that the PAIGC remain careful not to preach to others. What they would probably insist upon, I think, is that there are certain 'ground rules' for success. These are: first, the necessary existence of an ideologically prepared 'party core'; the use of this core to recruit political workers; the commitment of these political workers to slow and detailed work in the villages; the subsequent and planned commitment of these same political workers, or of other political workers according to the situation, to armed actions which begin the war and carry it through its first stage; and thus the close integration of political and military action from the earliest phase.

They would more or less agree with Regis Debray, in his book about guerrilla warfare in Latin America, when he writes that 'the first nucleus of fighters will be divided into small propaganda patrols which will cover the mountain areas, going into villages, holding meetings, speaking here and there, in order to explain the social goals of the Revolution. . . .' But — and it is a big but — they would think that this formulation greatly oversimplified the actual meaning of this work, of the kind of work that Antonio Bana and his fellow political workers have carried out; and they would tend to believe that any such 'patrols', sent out with little or no preliminary political work in the village, must quickly be defeated by lack of contact with the population and the consequent dangers of betrayal.

Furthermore, in their conditions, African conditions, I think that they would vastly dissent from Debray wherever, especially in his later writings,[8] he seems to suggest that 'the guerrilla force should not be subordinated to the party': they would see this, it seems to me, as a recipe for disaster. For without subordination to the party — the political framework of the revolutionary movement — there is no longer any sure means of showing, of remembering, of being utterly convinced, that the war is no more than a means to an end, no more than an extension of politics by other means.

They would argue further, perhaps, that in African conditions the need to convince the people of the rural areas cannot be short-cut by 'starting a military *foco*, a hearth of revolt', to which the country people will somehow rally by a process of spontaneous enthusiasm. It is absolutely necessary, at a given point and time, to start a military *foco*, a hearth of revolt — and this the PAIGC did most deliberately at certain points in 1963 and after: but *only* when the work of political preparation is advanced to a point where a sufficient number of country people will not only take your side, but will actively participate and lead. We shall come back to this point later on. Meanwhile one may also note that other movements of liberation in Africa, and above all the MPLA in Angola and FRELIMO in Mozambique, adopted the same strategy and list of priorities as the PAIGC.

References

1. Nguyen Van Tien, 'Notre strategie de la guerilla', *Partisans,* Paris, January-February 1968.

2. But reading Che's unforgettably painful memoirs a year later *(Bolivian Diary,* Cape/Lorimer, 1968), one saw that the heroism of that enterprise was accompanied by a failure, which of course had complicated origins, to recruit more than a handful of Indian Bolivians. Noting towards the end some improvement in the floundering of the government army (p.153), Che's unfailing honesty adds that 'the peasant mass aids us in nothing and is turning into informers'.

3. When found and in the mood, however, they talk with all the directness that one notes in Guine. Some time after visiting the PAIGC, I went on down to southern Africa and there, in July 1968, was able to be present at the first full-scale congress of the Mozambique Liberation Front (FRELIMO) to be held inside the colony.

   This confident and successful congress assembled in liberated territory about 150 of the Front's political and military leaders, including its president and vice-president, Eduardo Mondlane and Uria Simango; its army commander, Samora Machel, and senior commissar, Casal Ribeiro; and provincial commanders Raimundo of Cabo Delgado, Mabote of Niassa, and Manganja of Tete, together with their political colleagues.

   Elsewhere I was able to interview leaders of the Angolan liberation movement (MPLA), including its president Agostinho Neto; and, elsewhere again, a senior commander of the joint ANC-ZAPU units operating inside Rhodesia.

   All this is part of another story, for telling elsewhere; but here I should record that the answers to the questions posed above appeared, by all that I saw and heard, increasingly favourable to these movements. Since 1966 each had grown steadily in strength and numbers and experience of leadership.

4. Ware-house-stores set up by the PAIGC for the purchase of crops and sale of consumer goods in liberated zones barred to Portuguese trade. See Chapter 6.

5. The Creole spoken in Guine is something like the Portuguese equivalent of the old 'trade English' of the Niger delta: a language having an African base and a large infusion of Portuguese words. It is said to be a good and flexible language. Thanks to the war, it is now coming into general use throughout the country.

6. Nguyen Van Tien, 'Notre Strategie de la guerilla', *Partisans,* Paris, January-February 1968.

7. Cf. Nguyen Van Tien: 'To get a footing amongst our national minorities our political workers have not simply learned their languages, but have pierced their ears when the minority in question pierces its ears, filed their teeth when the minority files theirs. . . . Without patience, you cannot make a revolution.' *(Partisans,* January-February 1968,pp.68-9).

8. Written in 1968; perhaps he has changed his views since.

3. Under What Precise Conditions?

The people are not fighting for ideas, for the things in anyone's head. They are fighting to win material benefits, to live better and in peace, to see their lives go forward . . .
AMILCAR CABRAL[1]

Up here in the north-east it's a different sort of country. Westward the last low foothills of the Futa thrust their small ramparts down towards the Corubal. Grooved with green rivers, these hills have to be crossed in steep climbs and swift descents; but then, after that, it's the rolling grasslands of the east and north, the open grasslands that run from one side of Africa to the other and join the shores of the Atlantic with the stones of Kordofan.

We trot down into these grasslands from the last ramparts of the Futa: Osvaldo, who is commander on this front of Boe, striding, taciturn, preoccupied by many things, not least at the moment by having me on his hands; Armando Ramos, another veteran of the Conakry school and now in charge of trading-and-supply, diminutive beside Osvaldo who is very tall, armed with a sporting rifle as befits his presently semi-combatant role and stopping now and then to pot at birds in looming gum trees; Yamte N'aga, commander of the sector round the Portuguese garrison at Beli where we are now heading; four or five soldiers as an escort who row ahead or astern of me through shoulder-high grass. . . .

The sea of grass spreads wide beneath a sky that is sunlit grey with the last gust of the rains of 1967. It goes on, I know, far beyond the horizon and in every direction except towards the south where, some fifty miles down the map, it will break against the woodland glacis of the great forest. Otherwise this sea of grass spreads onward into Senegal; northward into Mali till it mingles with the Sahara; and eastward, flowing up around the humped summits of the Futa, into splendid prairies which end only with the Nile three thousand miles away.

We walk hard through this sea of grass, rowing with our hands, sweating with the forenoon sun upon our heads.

Sparse villages, miles apart, one or two with the pockmarks of Portuguese bombing in the last two months. Slender populations, a dozen or so Fula men and women met in distant knots, hoeing a field, sitting by their huts. Tall slim folk in grey and white cotton robes, gravely welcoming, saying little. Few guerrillas, too, in this empty land north-east of the Corubal: two or three communication-posts back behind us toward the frontier with the Republic of Guinea, an occasional ammunition dump concealed by thatch. Also few Portuguese: at this time a garrison at Beli and another at Madina, a few hundred troops in each, barricaded and besieged behind their wire and their stockades. An occasional aircraft on supply, bombing, or reconnaissance, buzzing far off.

Solitude, immensity of space, a certain everlasting awareness of one's human feebleness in face of all this land. Eight men heading for Beli, eight pairs of hands rowing through an endless ocean: what can they, what can any like them, possibly achieve? There is a pattern here with two elements, and both are hostile. On one side, the unity of all this immensity, the common lack of frontiers, of framework, of any of that close-knit human network which could impel a tide of liberation, of co-operation, of communication, and move with irresistible force. How shift this giant of emptiness? How achieve momentum? And then, on the other side, the contradiction: that in fact, in painful fact, the giant is a congeries of different limbs, of different types of country, different peoples, different languages, different traditions, and each enclosed within its own difference. How approach each of them? How weld them together? The general always fractures into the particular as soon as you come close; and the particular, the specific, is persistently diverse.

* * *

We have talked a lot, we go on talking: I learn something about this specific in these eastern regions. It is always the specific that they talk about: the problem *here,* the problem *now.*

They had begun here with political work in 1961, though in a very restricted way. Then at the end of 1964 Domingos Ramos[2] established their first military *foco,* their initial hearth of revolt, but the fuel proved hard to set alight. The main difficulties were two: first, the sparsity of the population; second, and more important, the hostility of the Fula chiefs. Like their neighbours across the eastern frontier in the *massif* of the Futa, who had stayed with the French until the last moment in 1958, these chiefs stayed with the Portuguese: predictably, for their interests were more or less the same.

In his Milan lecture, two months before Domingos Ramos led his little band northward into these grasslands, Cabral had had useful things to say on this subject:

> The Fula were themselves conquerors in Guine; and the Portuguese found allies amongst them during their own conquest. So it is that among the people of this group we have found that the leading chiefs and their entourages are tied to colonialism. Their power is closely

integrated with that of the Portuguese administration.

The artisans are in turn dependent on their chiefs, living mostly from the work they do for the ruling groups. Some among these artisans are satisfied with this situation, while others are against it and tend to reject colonial rule. The travelling traders, the *dyula*, are unstable, at any rate in Guine, having no fixed point of loyalty, men whose constant thought is for the defence of their personal interests. All the same we have been able to use their mobility to help our mobilization, to spread the first news of our struggle. To win them at least for this, it was necessary only to offer them rewards, though without these they would not have budged.

How have they handled the problem of hostile chiefs? They faced, to some extent they were still facing in 1968, much the same general difficulty with chiefs as other movements in parts of southern Africa. Partly for Portuguese pay, partly from a justifiable fear that the liberation movement would undermine their privileges, partly from a no less justifiable fear of Portuguese reprisals, and then again from sheer dislike of social change, the Fula chiefs have used their undoubtedly strong influence against the revolt. A few rallied to the PAIGC as it got into its stride in 1965 and 1966; most stayed with the Portuguese.

Now in these circumstances the history of revolt demonstrates two methods of action, not necessarily opposed. One is terror; the other is persuasion. Most successful movements of this kind have used terror: they have singled out the more stubborn or corrupt among the collaborators with their enemy, and have killed them. Some part of terror of this kind is as clearly inseparable from armed revolt as bombing or shelling is from modern warfare. It is necessary to answer the coercion of the enemy with a coercion of one's own. This is another reason, as the records all combine to show, why armed revolt has to be a matter of the most profound conviction.

So far as I know, the PAIGC have been sparing in their use of terror. They have preferred persuasion, and of two kinds. On the one hand, they have argued with the chiefs, or with those they could reach, showing them that history is on the move and that they had better move with it while they can. On the other hand, the PAIGC have multiplied their military attacks on the Portuguese, and therefore, by extension, on all Africans who cluster round the Portuguese for shelter, demonstrating to the chiefs that the Portuguese are weaker, even much weaker, than the chiefs had thought, and thus opening the prospect of a different future.

By 1967 these policies had largely succeeded in the grasslands of Boe which lie east of the upper waters of the Corubal, although westward, towards Bafata and further north, there were still great difficulties.

Armando Ramos:

Here in Boe we now have a liberated zone but for the two garrisons at Madina and Beli. We call a liberated zone an area in which we have everyday control, with only an exceptional need to use our army in the event of a Portuguese sortie from one of their garrisons, and where the population is mobilized for us in the political as well as the military sense of the word.

Such conditions began to emerge in Boe after Domingos Ramos had formed the first fighting units here in December 1964. Osvaldo (who took over command here after Domingos Ramos's death two years later) continued the story for me:

We formed more units in 1965 and after, and made more actions. We attacked their garrisons. Now they have lost the initiative. They have only two garrisons, and they stay inside these except for making sorties now and then. We have these garrisons encircled, we ambush the roads, they can supply themselves only by air, mostly by helicopter.[3]

It is a difficult region for us, for there is little population, as you've seen, and it's only towards the east, towards the frontier with (the Republic of) Guinea, that you find a few villages. But it is also an important area for us, because it leads on to the rest of this Fula country north of the Corubal. Plenty of that is still difficult. Round places like Pitche we still have no regular units, and can carry out only sabotage actions. Further west, towards Bafata, it is even more difficult. Most of the chiefs there are still with the Portuguese, and the Portuguese have more troops.

We think that this situation is beginning to change in our favour, partly because of the Portuguese policy of military violence against the people in the villages — bombing, executions as reprisals, theft, rape and the rest. The people are afraid, but now they are angry too. Then, partly because of our own forward movement. Over there beyond the Corubal we now have small sabotage groups which ambush the roads with automatics and bazookas, especially the Bambadinca-Bafata road which is the most useful one for the Portuguese. I can tell you that our nearest sabotage group to Bafata (the second town in Guine) can now act within ten miles of the town.

To these tactics the Portuguese have replied by reinforcing their units west of the Corubal. I do not have any precise military figures for this, but the total strength of the Portuguese army in Guine was said by the PAIGC to be around 35,000 in 1968, together with about 3,000 African mercenaries (drawn mostly, it would seem, from Fula and Mandinka under chiefly influence). A fairly large proportion of this army is in the grassland area centred around Bafata. This concentration corresponds to what appears to be basic Portuguese strategy: to abandon any hope of regaining the military initiative in zones strongly held by the PAIGC, while so far as possible retaining scattered garrisons there, and meanwhile to concentrate on holding the 'spine' which connects Bissau through Mansoa to Bambadinca, Bafata, and further northward.

Even so, they evidently feel insecure even where they still command. By 1967 they had adopted another policy, that of 'regrouping' the grassland population (and to some extent the populations elsewhere) inside 'strategic hamlets' along the lines of American policy in South Vietnam. The argument here is that it matters little if guerrillas command country that is empty of people: the main object is to 'protect the population against rebel infection'. From the Portuguese point of view, this was undoubtedly a sensible policy.

Armando Ramos:

> Generally, the Portuguese and we are competing for the loyalty of the Fula; and the Portuguese, for their part, try to shift villages so as to gather as many people as they can around their armed camps. And the more people they have under their control, of course, the more difficult it is for us.

To cope with this, as we shall see, the PAIGC began in 1967 to change their own tactics, and go over to a more mobile kind of warfare so as to reduce Portuguese control of these 'strategic hamlets'. Reacting against this, the Portuguese were said at the beginning of 1968 to be bringing in still more troops, even though their army in Guiné was already equivalent, in relative population terms, to an American army in Vietnam of 600,000 men.

Discussing such matters, we tramp and wade towards Beli. At about noon Yamte N'aga leads us towards his temporary base, a dozen large thatched huts in a small wood; a sentry, grinning with surprise, waves us in.

It has at present about thirty men, some of them new recruits, who are all around twenty years old or less and who give us a fair and formal salute at Yamte's command.

How far to the Portuguese? A few miles across two flooded rivers. There's no movement possible here until the rains stop and the water goes down. Yamte says that he has small sections round Beli, and mortared its airstrip the other day, but as for me, I'll have to stay where I am. We stay where we are, glad of a rest. There is chicken and rice. We go on talking.

* * *

Yamte talks: in Balante which comes to me in Osvaldo's French, so I get only the sense of what he says. But the sense is interesting. Yamte is older than most, maybe thirty-five or forty, a former soldier of the Portuguese and a peasant by origin and inclination. How much land does he have? 'A lot', he replies with a grin: no problem of land. Then what problem? Many problems. He launches into a long talk about the Portuguese. Evidently it is full of savour: there are smiles and interjections; All I get is that Yamte knows the Portuguese very well indeed, and does not like what he knows.

This is a general problem. You ask: 'Why are you fighting the Portuguese?' And they reply – it happened to me often – by something such as: 'To liberate our country.' A slogan? Yes: but what would the average volunteer of the Second World War, in the British army or any other on our side, have answered to a similar question? The self-evident needs no explanation.

But Yamte is interesting in other ways. A small dark man, moustached, compact, powerful: a Balante peasant. But also a Balante elder. 'The Balante circumcise late in life, maybe around the age of 25. Before that you're a young man, a warrior, a *blufo:* after that you're a leader, an elder.' Yamte is a leader, one of the few Balante elders who are active in the units of the PAIGC. 'The Balante think that elders should not go to war: that's an affair for the young men.'

Yamte has been with the PAIGC since 1961. Till lately he was commander in the Madina sector, but they demoted him. Says Armando Ramos with a grin: 'He made a mistake'. They don't tell me what it was. Lack of discipline? Peasant obstinacy? Whatever it was, Yamte is now commander of the Beli sector, and is not in the least put down. Beli, after all, is the district capital of Boe. I lie on my back and listen to their voices.

* * *

Africa's dealings with Europeans of the colonial period now cover about a hundred years, and it is beginning to be possible, thanks partly to the opening of official archives, to look back on this long experience with a fairly objective eye.

Throughout this period Africans resisted the incursion of Europe on many occasions and in many different ways. This is so to the point where it can be said that much of their history in this hundred years can best be seen and understood through their resistance. It is possible to divide this experience into different types, according to time and place: to draw up, in short, a typology of African resistance. This typology can help one to see the evolution of African beliefs and attitudes through a broad spectrum of ideologies which run from 'traditional' to 'modern'.

At first the Africans fought back as they had always fought invaders: the societies with kings and chiefs, and also the 'segmentaries' which had neither. At this primary stage of resistance, the first fought more than the second, the 'segmentaries', who often saw in Europeans a possibly useful ally against neighbouring societies with kings who dominated them, or tried to dominate them. There were famous wars: of the Ashanti against the British, of the Fon against the French, of the Xhosa and Zula, of the Hehe and Herero, the Algerians, the Kongo and Mbundu, many others. Hero-kings led their armies in defence of their lands: Ahmadu and Samory, Cetshwayo and Mkwata, Abedkader, Queen Zhinga against the Portuguese long before.

These primary resistances were hard to overcome, but they were overcome. In the fifteenth-sixteenth centuries, the Portuguese had needed nearly a hundred years to overthrow Ndongo and Matamba. Far in the south, during the nineteenth century, there were no fewer than seven 'kaffir wars' against the Xhosa and their allies. Only in 1900 did the British complete their last but seventh campaign against Ashanti.

Then the Europeans claimed 'effective occupation', but they did not really have it. Other resistances followed: delayed-primary in type. Many of these were now fought by the 'segmentaries', who had woken up to find that their European allies meant to be their European masters. Some of them proved hard to beat: the Tiv in Nigeria, for example, the Balante in Guine. Having no chiefs or kings, their system of authority could not be beheaded by the killing or deportation of a leading man or little group of leading men. Quashed in one corner, revolt burst forth in another. Delayed-primary resistance went on for a long time. Not until the 1920s did it flicker into silence.

All these wars had their strong religious motivation. These were peoples who believed that God had given their land to their ancestors, and that their ancestors, guardians of the living and the yet unborn, were dishonoured by European intrusion. Having disturbed the God-given equilibrium of tradition, the Europeans were to be identified with Evil. Calling on their ancestors, the Africans sought for divine aid in order to restore things as they should be.

This religious motivation was important in the primary wars, in the delayed-primary revolts against European authority, and in later forms of resistance which now took shape. In 1896 the Ndebele of the lands between the Zambezi and Limpopo rose in revolt against European soldiers and settlers who had seized most of their cattle and much of their land; months later they were joined by the Shona of the same region. Both peoples fought under the general inspiration and even under the orders of spokesmen of the great spirits of the Earth who had been revered here for centuries: the spokesmen of Mwari, as the Shona called God, and of great ancestor-spirits such as Nehanda. It was much the same with the widespread and stubborn Maji Maji rising against the Germans in Tanganyika ten years later: here too the inspiration and leadership were provided by spokesmen of the spirits of the land. There were many other if lesser cases of the same kind.

Especially in central-southern Africa, this kind of resistance began to move outside the framework of African religion and acquire Christian forms. There came the rise of 'Ethiopianism': of that wide range of Christian-influenced movements which sprang from the prophecy that Ethiopia – meaning Africa, the whole of black Africa – should 'soon stretch out its hands to God': should be redeemed, that is, and restored to dignity and independence. Africans began to form independent Christian churches of their own, vowed to the idea that the Christian God was also *their* God who would give back Africa to the Africans. By 1920 there were hundreds of independent Christian churches under the leadership of African pastors; and nearly all of them, or those with most influence, fed a powerful political content into their beliefs. To this the colonial authorities replied with administrative repression. In 1921, for example, the little community of 'Israelites' who had settled on the Bulhoek commonage, far south in the Cape Province of South Africa, were ordered to move because the land was 'reserved for Europeans': refusing to move, they were attacked by the troops of General Smuts, and 163 of them were killed. Elsewhere there came the rise of famous religious leaders such as Kamwana in Malawi and Zambia, Simon Kimbangu in the southern Congo, Simao Toco in Angola, all of whom, with others of their kind, were duly packed away into colonial jails.

But from 'dissident Christianity' there were Africans who now moved to 'dissident politics'. Harry Thuku of Kenya is a case in point. As early as 1921, this telephone operator in Nairobi declared for political, not religious, action against European domination; and much flowed from his initiative. Similar ideas were strong in West Africa, where educated men were already talking the language of European nationalism, and claiming the right to form parties that should agitate and work for African advancement. Others were doing the same in North Africa, in French-speaking West Africa, in South Africa.

National parties were formed after the Second World War in many British and French territories. They came to fruition, as we know, in the political independence which began with the Anglo-Egyptian Sudan, Morocco and Tunisia in 1956 and with Ghana in 1957.

But these national parties were mass movements rather than structured organizations. With few exceptions they were led by minorities of educated men, mainly in the towns, and they carried the peasants only by a broad and general process of acclamation. They spoke of a new millennium, and the peasants were not against it. But the peasants were seldom more than faceless masses to whom the nationalist leaders promised much but from whom they expected little. After independence, the gap between the leaders and the led, between the towns and the villages, soon became painfully apparent. Dangerously often it became habitual for national leaders to visit their constituencies only when they needed votes.

Out of this there arose growing rural discontent, most evident where central government failed to meet its responsibilities. Revolts broke out in the Congo in 1964, for example, at a time when the central government seemed not only far away, but also powerless to make any useful change in the way men lived. These revolts are worthy of close study because they tell a great deal about the evolution of rural thought. In one respect the revolt of Pierre Mulele, for example, was extremely up-to-date: those among his followers who could read were asked to study texts drawn almost word for word from the writings of Mao Tse-tung. Yet the real power behind the movement was still traditional, was still drawn from the religious motivations of the past. Mulele's Pende followers believed that God had prepared a 'second independence', a real one this time, and that when this came there would really be a change in everything. Following the thought of tradition, accordingly, they fortified themselves with charms and spells which should liquefy the white man's bullets, safeguard their own lives in battle, and magically give them the victory.

Now it may be very useful to believe that God is on your side. Nearly all European armies have been encouraged to think so when fighting anyone else or indeed each other. But it is not useful, in fact it is likely to be fatal, to believe that magic can do the job for you. Mulele's rebels melted away in confusion and defeat. They had failed to make the necessary transition from the thought of tradition, from the world of ancestral wisdom, to that of the new world, the world of political revolution.[5]

In the typology of resistance, then, the next stage to expect is evidently one where this transition – in thought, belief, behaviour, attitude to cause-and-effect – will in fact have taken place, at least in large and decisive degree. Here the crucial point does not lie with the thinking of the leaders: although Pierre Mulele acquired a magical reputation among the Pende, and many others, there is nothing to prove that he himself believed in it, or even sought it. The crucial point lies with the thinking of the rank and file. That *they* believe, sufficiently believe, in the primacy of material cause-and-effect, and not in magical guidance, is the proof of their movement's having entered this next stage: this stage where a socio-economic revolution of structures, and not merely a substitution of authority at the top, becomes actually possible.

Of course there are intermediate stages; great transitions in ideological conception can never be simple or clear-cut, as the history of Europe amply shows, and the new necessarily takes shape from a gradual or erratic trans-formation of the old. The big and certainly decisive Kenya rising of 1952-6, the so-called 'Mau Mau' of the Kikuyu, Embu and Meru, falls clearly into one of these intermediate stages between the old frameworks of conception and the new. This vast eruption was the result of political thought and action within the context of modern nationalism: of clandestine preparation for armed revolt when any further hope of far-reaching reform, even minimal reform, seemed vain. It was militarily organized by men such as Dedan Kimathi who clearly understood the material cause-and-effect of modern warfare, and who showed, when it came to the point, a remarkable ingenuity of method. Though greatly hampered by a lack of experienced political leadership once the fighting had begun – either because the established nationalist leaders could not give their support, being imprisoned, or for other reasons would not give it – the forest groups still managed to build an elementary superstructure on national-political lines. Yet they stood outside the ideology of modern revolution; and when at last, in spite of all their courage and tenacity and skill, the weight of British counter-action proved too great, their political organization fell rapidly apart, void and useless. Then 'the dreams and prophecies of the seers became the sole remaining basis for hope among those of the forest who survived. . . .'[6]

And for the PAIGC in this respect?

I had been reading Benoit Verhaegen's invaluable book on the Congo revolts of 1964.[7] I asked Cabral: 'Do you have a lot of magic too?' He replied with a smile: 'Yes, at the beginning: amulets and charms, much of that. But now they've learned that it's better to take good cover and shoot straight'.

The fighting groups I saw in Guine seemed to bear this out. There were lucky charms, of course: what army ever marched without them? But I never saw or heard tell of any 'doctoring' ceremonies of any sort, nor of any reliance on magical aid in the conduct of operations, nor of any of those drugs which were alleged to be common in the Congo[8]. And I think it would have been difficult to conceal these things if they had been present. The only oath taken by volunteers, moreover, is a simple one of loyalty to the PAIGC and the struggle for independence.

There are other lines of transition. It appears to be true, for example, that the Balante age-grade system has grafted itself neatly into warfare under PAIGC formation. It would be interesting to know more about this.

But any claim that the PAIGC does indeed represent a movement of a new kind, of a revolutionary stage, will clearly have to stand or fall not so much by its military success, though partly by that, as by the political content of its convictions, teaching and organization. And the claim will have to be judged not by what the PAIGC's top leaders think and do, for they have clearly made the great transition, but above all by the framework of thought and action within which the wider leadership – the several hundred men and women who are commanders and political workers at every level of authority – now move and have their being.

* * *

The camp at Beli merges behind us into the slender woodlands of Boe. The last I remember of it are two young soldiers, maybe seventeen or so, who bring me their school books. They are learning to read. They spell out their letters and form words for me with quiet astonishment. A new kind of magic? Maybe. But a far more useful one.

References

1. Cabral, from a policy directive of 1965. See also Ch.6, footnote 3.
2. Killed in action before Madina on 10 November 1966.
3. In the following summer, on 19 June 1968, PAIGC units forced the Portuguese to evacuate one of these two garrisons, Beli, and destroyed the electricity plant in a parallel attack on Madina. District capital of Boe (a region enclosing about one tenth of the country), Beli was abandoned by the Portuguese after twelve days of PAIGC attack, following many previous attacks.

   'During withdrawal under strong air cover,' runs the relevant PAIGC communique, 'the enemy forced a part of the population to go with them. After their departure, the Portuguese air force levelled the installations of camp and town. . . .' This withdrawal from a fortified but long-besieged camp came after vain attempts to relieve its garrison by road and air, and was one of about a dozen such withdrawals during the summer of 1968.
4. Writing in *The Times* (24 May 1968) after a visit to Guine on the Portuguese side, Mr J. Biggs-Davison MP claimed that this 'regroupment has brought collective cultivation and cooperatives. Indeed war has stimulated social advance. . . . As more natives are regrouped out of

reach of the PAIGC, the Portuguese position which I found more favourable than I expected, may be expected further to improve'.

One may note that the United States authorities in South Vietnam made repeatedly the same kind of claim in 1966-7. The policy, indeed, has obvious sense so long as its operators can also retain a military initiative in the field. Unfortunately for the Portuguese, they have lost this initiative and seem unable to regain it. In consequence, they have been forced back on static positions which, in 1968, they were losing one by one. For further PAIGC comment, see p.76.

5. I have discussed these matters at greater length in *The Africans,* London 1969 (US title *The Legacy of Africa,* Boston, 1969).
6. D.L. Barnett and K. Njama, *Mau Mau from Within,* London, 1966, p.490.
7. B. Verhaegen, *Rebellions au Congo,* Brussels, 1966, Vol. I.
8. Subsequent information has confirmed all this although, as we have seen, a very different situation developed in 1963, until eliminated by the results of the first party congress of February 1963.

4. By What Political Principles and Organization?

'Building the Party as You Fight'

For my part, the deeper I enter into the cultures and the political circles of Africa, the surer I become that the great danger which threatens Africa is the absence of ideology.
FRANTZ FANON[1]

We are waiting for the tide. A single floodlight bares a yellow cone beyond the bows, a cone splintered by the barrel of an anti-aircraft automatic on the foredeck and patterned by the shadows of men who stand and chat or move about on small time-eating jobs. Dark water drags at the *Tres de Agosto*, so named after the massacre of dock workers at Pidgiguiti in Bissau in August 1959. Sea birds flicker past us through a starshot sky. The night is full of clicks and murmurs, a tropical night whispering with hidden life.

When the tide fills, slapping high into the mangrove swamps which line these 'rios de Cabo Verde', we move with the chocolate flood, on either beam a man pole-sounding and crying out the *brasses*, the Portuguese fathoms, while gradually we shift against the current. In this respect nothing has changed in centuries: this is how the old caravels were sailed in these latitudes. But otherwise everything has changed. Above me I can see the head and shoulders of the captain of the *Tres de Agosto*, a small steel ship driven by diesels, edged over the coping of the wheelhouse-breast: he is an African of Bissau who came from the Portuguese coastal service in 1961, a firm man of middle age and few words who curiously wears a fur-lined cap with the flaps down, maybe from habit or because it's lucky, or just because he feels the chill night breeze. Beside me on the foredeck behind the ack-ack gun his second-in-command, the engineer, lingers with the air that seamen have, listening, waiting, his arms hanging loose but ready: he, too, is an African of Bissau who came over from the Portuguese service in 1961. He wears a regulation army cap in the Cuban style, dark green canvas with stiffened peak: PAIGC caps and uniforms of this dark green cotton are all made in Cuba, it seems, of materials given originally by China. These men look as though they know their work; and they do know it. They've been ferrying men and

equipment back and forth between the Republic of Guinea and Quitafine for
at least a year now.

Pascoal and Otto, who with Cabral and others are taking us into the liberated areas of the south-west, have thoughtfully provided canvas chairs. We
sit on the foredeck and enjoy the sensation of being passengers in good hands.
For some twelve hours there will be nothing that we have to do. It is a good
time for talking, for considering. . . .

* * *

I will come to the question of foreign aid later on: meanwhile, aid for what?
The leaders of the PAIGC have written little upon basic questions of ideological principle, partly because few of them have any practice in writing, and
partly because those few who have such practice, maybe a dozen, maybe even
fewer, have been totally engaged in the work which has flowed from their
principles. But from many conversations and from several existing texts,
published or not, one can detach a number of guiding convictions.

The PAIGC is a revolutionary movement based upon a Marxist analysis of
social reality. But to say this, after all, is to say very little: what other revolutionary movement of the last fifty years ever declared itself to be any
different? The important point is that the PAIGC is a revolutionary movement
based on an analysis of social reality *in Guine:* revolutionary precisely and
above all because its guiding lines are drawn from totally indigenous circumstances. This does not necessarily make its conclusions correct, but it undoubtedly makes them original. As to the rightness of the conclusions, the
proof of the pudding is and will be in the eating; so far, it may be argued, the
proof stands well in credit.

This attitude of independent analysis, of local and specific analysis, has
become a general characteristic of the revolutionary movements of the
middle and latter part of the twentieth century. Unified though they are in
the basic aims of creating socialist structures of society, they differ in their
actual forms as much as they differ in the basic conditions under which they
have to operate. Sometimes this means that they evolve forms which are
more or less closely comparable, like the PAIGC and the Liberation Front
of South Vietnam. More often it means that the forms, the chosen methods,
the day-to-day practice, stand far apart. Here we are miles away from any
notion of centralized control.

Of the texts to hand, the most instructive is probably a paper delivered
by Cabral to the first Tricontinental Conference at Havana, during 1966,
entitled 'Foundations and Objectives of National Liberation in Relation to
Social Structure':

> Our agenda (at this conference) includes themes whose meaning and
> importance are beyond question, and show a central preoccupation
> with *struggle*. Let me point out, though, that one type of struggle
> which we think basic has received no mention, although I am sure that

it was present in the minds of those who drew up this agenda. I mean *the struggle against our own weaknesses* (emphasis in the original).

Other cases differ from that of Guine. But experience in Guine has shown us (of the PAIGC) that in the general framework of the daily struggle this battle against ourselves — no matter what difficulties the enemy may create — remains the most difficult of all, whether for the present or the future of our peoples. This battle against ourselves is the expression of internal contradictions in the economic, social and cultural reality (and so in the historical reality) of each of our countries. I am convinced that any national or social revolution which is not based on the knowledge of this reality runs great risk of failure, even of defeat.

When Africans say in their proverbial language that 'no matter how hot the water from your well, it will not cook your rice', they express a fundamental principle of physics but also one of political science. We know that the evolution of a phenomenon in movement, no matter what its external appearance may be, depends upon its internal characteristics. And we know that on the political level our own reality — no matter how fine and attractive the reality of others may be — can only be transformed by detailed knowledge of it, by our own efforts, by our own sacrifices. It is useful to recall in this tri-continental gathering, so rich in experience and example, that no matter how close may be the similarity between cases and between the identities of our enemy, national liberation and social revolution are not for export. They are — and every day they become more so — the outcome of a local and national elaboration that is more or less influenced by external factors (favourable or not), but essentially is formed and conditioned by the historical reality of each people, and is carried to success by right solutions to the internal contradictions which arise in this reality. The success of the Cuban revolution, taking place only a few miles from the greatest imperialist and anti-socialist force of all time, makes in its content and in its way of evolution a practical and conclusive illustration of the validity of this principle.

But we need to recognize at the same time that we ourselves and other movements of liberation in general (and I am referring above all to African experience) have not given enough attention to this important aspect of our common struggle.

The ideological deficiency within the national liberation movements, not to say the total lack of ideology — reflecting as this does an ignorance of the historical reality which these movements claim to transform — makes for one of the greatest weaknesses in our struggle against imperialism, if not the greatest weakness of all. Yet it seems that a sufficiently varied experience has accumulated to the point where a general line of thought and action may be defined, such as could eliminate this weakness. . . .

Against this background Cabral called for a discussion on the subject, and explained that his further remarks should be taken as 'a contribution, how-ever modest', to such a debate.

He began by asking for a deeper appreciation of the actual situations in Africa. The familiar revolutionary statement that history's motive force rests in the class war should be refined and redefined in the light of these situations. Was it even true that history began with the appearance of the phenomenon of 'class' and hence warfare between classes? To say so would be to consider 'those peoples of our continent such as the Balante of Guine, the Cuanhama of Angola, the Maconde of Mozambique, as living outside history or as having no history except for slight influences imposed on them by colonial rule'. Such a view must be rejected. Consequently, one had to ask what was the 'motive force' before the appearance of classes and class warfare? 'It is to say that *before* class war – and so necessarily *after it,* for there is no *before* without its *after* – another factor or factors' forms the crucial element in historical change. This is to be found in the level of productive forces at any given place and time: 'the true and lasting motive force of history'.

Cabral went on to consider phases of development in general and particular levels of production, concluding this section of his argument with the affir-mation that 'our peoples (in Africa) do indeed have the possibility of passing from a situation of under-development and exploitation to a new stage in the historical process, a stage which can carry them to a higher form of economic, social and cultural life'. Colonialism had built no new basic structures capable of achieving this: 'imperialist capital is far from having realized in our countries the historical mission, whether economic or socio-cultural, which it has performed in the countries where this capital was formed'. Neo-colonialism, the situation of the 1960s, could only deepen the contradictions existing within African society. On the one hand, it promoted the disunity of the nationalist cause by its material and other effects, including religious or tribal separatism. But on the other hand, neo-colonialism also helped to keep the flame of national liberation alight: 'by the necessarily repressive action of the "neo-colonized" State against the forces of national liberation, by the deepening of class divisions, by the actual presence of agents and other signs of foreign domination (settlers who retain their privileges, armed forces,[2] racial discrimination), by the growing impoverishment of the peasantry, and by other and obvious external factors. . . .'

Hence the central concept of national liberation was to be defined not so much as the right of a people to rule itself, but as the right of a people to regain its own history: 'to liberate, that is, the means and process of develop-ment of its own productive forces'. So 'in our thinking, any movement of national liberation which fails to take account of this basis and objective of national liberation may well be fighting against imperialism, but will not be fighting for national liberation'. And since it must be true that the liberation of a colonized or neo-colonized country's own productive forces, given the historical reality of the colonial (the African) situation, 'calls for a profound mutation in the condition of those productive forces, we see that the phenom-enon of *national liberation* is necessarily one of *revolution . . .*' (emphasis in the original).

He went on to consider the question of violence.

> It is obvious from all the facts that violence is the essential means of imperialist domination. If, then, we accept the principle that *national liberation equals revolution*, and is not simply a matter of raising a flag or singing an anthem, we shall find that there is and there can be no national liberation without the use of liberating violence, on the part of the national forces, in answer to the criminal violence of those who promote imperialism. Nobody can question the fact that imperialist domination, no matter what its local characteristics may be, implies a state of permanent violence against the nationalist forces.

The important thing, he concluded, was therefore to decide precisely which forms of violence should be used by the nationalists, in order both to win and to maintain a true independence.

* * *

This much condensed outline of a lengthy train of argument may serve to illustrate the trend and nature of PAIGC thought without, I hope, deforming it. Even this sketch should clarify PAIGC policies and objectives. It explains, for example, what they really mean by revolution: as being that process of structural change which overcomes not only direct colonial subjection but also, and still more decisively, indirect or 'neo-' colonial subjection as well. It shows that what they see as justifying their struggle to be free — their necessarily painful because necessarily violent struggle — is not 'the raising of a flag, the singing of an anthem', much less the elevation of an African elite to the seats and privileges of the Portuguese. It explains, on the contrary, that they see their justification in the vastly more valuable if vastly more difficult task of working through that *profound mutation in productive forces*, in production relationships, and in all that this must mean for cultural and political change at the level of the masses, which can alone enable the people of Guiné *to regain and continue with their own history*. It describes their contempt for the halfway house of national independence which has often gone by the name of 'national liberation' in the Africa of the 1960s. It illuminates their almost explosive insistence on indigenous development, on original and independent forms of revolution.

Not for nothing, perhaps, was Cabral trained as an engineer. This stubborn emphasis on factually analysing the machinery of society, traditional society, colonial society: on inspecting it piece by piece; on considering how far, and if, these pieces can still be used in the building of an entirely different machine; on deciding just what new pieces will be necessary; on conceptualizing, in short, the actual and detailed *process* of socio-economic change — all this comes repeatedly through their talk and such of their policy documents as I have seen.

The aim, then, is to change society so as to renew society within its own reconquered history. To build a new society – in the circumstances, necessarily by socialist means, 'for there are only two roads open to a nation becoming independent now: to go back to imperialist domination (via neo-colonialism, capitalism, State capitalism) or to move towards socialism'. To form a new society, that is, which can draw ordinary people, the village masses and the townsmen, into a voluntary, planned and unified effort at their own salvation. In no other way can Guine regain and continue with its own history in the modern world. In what other way can *any* African country achieve these ends?

First the analysis and the fixing of the main objectives. Then the question, by what means?

> Every people knows best what to do for itself; but it seems to us [of the PAIGC] that you have to create an advance-guard which is united and conscious of the true meaning and objective of the national liberation struggle which it is going to direct. This need seems all the more urgent in that the solonial situation, if with some exceptions, neither allows nor admits the existence of advance-guard classes (a working class conscious of itself, a rural proletariat). . . . Conversely, the generally embryonic nature of the toiling classes, and the economic, social and cultural situation of the peasants – who are the strongest physical force in the struggle for national liberation – do not allow these two principal forces in the struggle to understand, on their own, the difference between genuine national independence and artificial political independence. Only a revolutionary advance-guard, generally an active minority, can understand this difference from the start and can gradually explain it, during the struggle, to the masses of the people.

This formulation belongs to 1966. It came from ideas long fermenting in the mind of Cabral and a few others, and from years of practical experience. The PAIGC had been formed in 1956, but its experience since then has constantly reforged, as the records suggest, its thinking and its modes of action. Up to 1961 it was literally an advance-guard composed only of a few determined men and women; then broadened by the entry of several hundred young volunteers who gradually acquired experience and leadership in the field; then again broadened by further self-enlargement.

Early in 1964, on 13-17 February, the men in control decided that the time had come to reorganize and democratize. A congress of Party militants was called in the southern forest, and major decisions were taken.

For purposes both of political administration and of military command, the country was divided into regions and zones.

The Party itself was given a new and enlarged controlling structure, and was now to consist of:

1. A political bureau of twenty members – fifteen with full membership,

and five candidates – which elected an executive committee of seven members.[3]

2. A central committee of sixty-five members – twenty of whom being candidates – divided into seven departments:

    a) political action of the armed forces;
    b) external affairs;
    c) political control of armed forces and Party apparatus;
    d) secretariat for the training of political workers; for information and propaganda;
    e) security;
    f) economy and finance;
    g) development and co-ordination of Party organization among the mass of the people; in effect, consistent building of village committees and the integration of these in regional committees;

This reorganization of 1964 has since undergone further changes. In 1967 the departments were reduced to five in number, each consisting of five members of the political bureau under the direction of one of them, and, in practice, supervised by an executive committee. These five departments are:

    a) a control commission appointed to watch the actual working of each part of the Party structure, a development rendered advisable by the sheer multiplication of Party members and activities;
    b) a security commission, concerned mainly with intelligence and discretion;
    c) a commission for external relations, now more complex than before;
    d) a commission for national reconstruction, concerned mainly with non-combatant work and projects in the liberated zones;
    e) a commission for 'organization and orientation', concerned mainly with smoothing out inner-Party relations, and with making sure that the Party, as a whole, continued to learn from its experience.

It was decided at the 1964 congress to pass beyond the purely guerrilla stage of military organization – a multiplicity of small units based on their own localities – and to draw a selected number of the best fighters into new regular military units. Subsequently about 2,000 guerrilla fighters volunteered, and a first batch of 900 men was chosen from them. Expanded in later months, this regular army continued to operate by guerrilla tactics, but became highly mobile, with units assigned to three different 'fronts', now defined as consisting of the south and south-east, the north and north-west, and the north-east and east, respectively named the South, North and East Fronts. As we have seen, the East Front in 1964 had still to be opened, but fighting units were strongly established in the South and parts of the North.[4]

By now, too, the expansion in trained men was enabling a closer integration between military and political commanders. The system of appointing commissars to all fighting units was maintained, although it is perhaps necessary to explain that a commissar's duties were not simply to transmit political instruction, but much more to look after all those aspects of military life, guerrilla life, which fall outside the sphere of military operations: health, discipline, complaints, justice, education both political and otherwise. But the tempered military commanders now emerging – men like Osvaldo in the north and Nino in the south – were at the same time drawn closely into the political command. They joined that small group of political leaders – Cabral himself, Aristides Pereira, Luiz Cabral (Amilcar's brother, and afterwards in charge of the Senegalese end of things), and some others – who had formed the core of the advance-guard.

The situation evolved; and favourably. By 1967 it was possible to make greater efforts to democratize and devolve responsibility to village committees in liberated zones now covering about half the total rural area of Guine, and including most of the rural population. Even in 1966 these village committees were a powerful and even decisive element in the whole structure, forming the strong hinges on which the PAIGC, resting more and more securely on peasant support, could turn and open the door to a different future. Here is Chico, senior political commissar in the North, talking to Gerard Chaliand in 1966:

> In each village in liberated Guine we have arranged for the election of a Party committee. We call this a *'tabanca* committee' [*tabanca* is Guine-Creole for village]. It consists of three men and two women. It is elected by a village assembly: that is to say, by all the villagers.[5] First of all, we explain how they should organize themselves, the tasks they should carry out, and, of course, the objectives of the Party. Often it's young folk who are elected. The older ones weren't always happy to see the young folk take their place in running village affairs. Our fighters are nearly always young. But as everyone is fed up with the Portuguese, the older ones who were reluctant at the start have had to follow the young ones. So you see that the committee is elected by the villagers. We – the Party – we're consulted: when we support a candidate, we judge by the work he or she has done for the Party, on the respect which the other peasants show for him or her. In principle, the choice of the peasants is maintained. If they've chosen badly – in our view – we let the choice stand. We wait for the peasants to find out their mistake for themselves. Of course the Party reserves the right to keep out those who use their authority for their own interests. We don't want to build a new lot of chiefs [*chefferie*]. The committee is renewed at the demand of the peasants – from time to time to make sure it doesn't get stagnant.
>
> Village committees have several jobs. One of the main ones, at the moment, is to step up farming production – so as to have enough rice for the peasants and for the fighters. The fighters also produce rice, millet, etc.; but mainly it's the villages that feed the fighters. We have opened new collective fields so that villagers should produce for the fighters. Village committees look after the control and carrying out of jobs; they [also] look after the militia.
>
> The militia consists of young villagers who are not members of the [regular] army but are partisans, guerrillas, without uniforms and

having only rifles. They form village self-defence units; in some zones they also have an offensive role. They live at home in their villages, while the fighters of FARP [the regular army] leave their villages and go with their units wherever the war may decide. Of course they are volunteers. They join us thanks to the political work of explanation that we've done in each village. We do this work in the local languages. In these parts people speak Balante and Mandinka; some peasants also know Creole. My own native language is Pepel, but I don't know it, I've always lived in Bissau. I learned Balante and Mandinka during the struggle.

Political work? That means getting the Party known, explaining why it exists, what it wants. We explain about colonialism, that Guine isn't Portugal, that we can govern ourselves without giving cattle to the Portuguese, without paying heavy taxes, without being knocked about, without being afraid of the Portuguese. We explain that what we're doing isn't something that falls from heaven: that it's already happened in other countries. You have to show our people that the world doesn't begin and end at the village boundary ... that it's a struggle for the whole of Guine, an international struggle, that they must run their own lives, resolve their own village problems, develop production, send their children to school, and have frequent meetings.

So long as the Party is there, the meetings are regular. Otherwise they get farther apart and fall way. Our people are only beginning to be free, you can't get from one day to the next what the Party wants. But little by little we are going ahead. Usually the village committees meet two or three times a month. . . .[6]

* * *

It is really here, in the day-to-day political work in the villages, that the dynamic centre of this whole movement obscurely lies. Continuation of the earlier political preparation which had made warfare possible after 1962, this tireless work of listening and talking, explaining, watching, correcting, suggesting, guiding, and generally *representing* the Party to the peasant and the peasants to the Party — for nothing could work for long in this difficult affair unless the process of communication shuttled back and forth — was what now made the critical difference between success and failure.

This, too, is part of the general history of successful guerrilla wars.

'In principle, the revolutionary political workers [*cadres*] scarcely ever leave their villages', say Nguyen Van Tien, writing in 1968 of the building of the Vietcong during Diem's terror, but stating a general principle of their practice. 'They know the terrain, the people, their own families. We have political workers who have lived for years like this, hidden underground by day and coming out only at night. Some of them have become blind through never seeing the light. . . .'[7]

It has always seemed to me that these political workers, these representatives 'on the ground', are the true heroes in all the wars of national liberation. They have no political power, no physical security, no reassurance in numbers. Often they are terribly alone; always they can act only by personal courage and persuasion. I think of those I knew myself in the enemy-infested plains of north-eastern Yugoslavia in 1943-4; of Baba in Backa Palanka, tenuous northern terminal of the partisan crossing of the Danube, of Proka and Kara, and others in those lands where the next enemy garrison was never more than a few miles away; where the enemy sought them week by week, sometimes day by day; where they clung to their villages through thick and thin, vanishing by day into holes dug in farmyards, holes which the enemy tried to find by stamping with boots or prodding with poles; and where, whenever they were found, these men and women preferred to kill themselves rather than risk talking under torture, or else were taken and tortured by the enemy, and killed just the same.

I think of crossing the Danube in the night and finding Baba waiting for us on the farther bank, almost within earshot of the nearest enemy strongpoint, and leading us to the farmhouse where we should hide, and returning to her little town to listen for enemy intelligence, to warn us of danger, to 'keep the links' no matter how fragile these might become. I think of entering villages before dawn and finding the *terenac*, the local political workers or 'terrainer' who would give us shelter till the next night, or of attending assemblies where he or she strove with peasant doubts, fears, ignorance of what was happening in the wider world around them. I think of hiding in holes myself, and hearing overhead the thud of Nazi boots. In those open plains, there could have been no partisan war without these *terenci*.

And it's much the same here in Africa.

One day in the grasslands of Boe I was with Osvaldo and Armando Ramos in four Fula villages, close by the frontier, which the Portuguese had peppered with bombs a few weeks earlier: the villages of Vendu-Leidi, Burculem, Tabadare, and Dalaba. They were typical settlements of 'cattle Fula', rural Fula: little thatched hamlets with gardens surrounded by pastures where they had their cattle, and fields where they grew millet and maize. These villages may have had a total population of two or three hundred but they represented, in these empty grasslands, quite a solid knot of people: in this case, a knot of people under PAIGC influence. A message ahead had drawn some thirty men and women from huts and neighbouring fields. One of them, I remember, was a hunter clad in skins, wearing many amulets, and carrying a muzzle-loading 'Dane gun' almost as long as himself and goodness knows how ancient: a local sage by virtue of his skill in hunter's lore, and so by extension a man of magical attainments.

We meet in the shadow of a tall spreading tree, not a baobab but something like it. A man in PAIGC uniform and carrying a rifle, whom I have not seen before, materializes from their midst and begins talking in Fula. A slender man, light on his feet, thin and taut. They tell me his name. Mane Kiba. He speaks to the villagers, and someone translates for me: 'This is the man called

Osvaldo. You have heard of him. . . . And he would have come to talk to you before but there was the work in the fields, you couldn't meet. . . . Now he will come back and talk again . . . . So in seeing him twice you will get used to him. . . .'

There is a meeting. Mane Kiba takes part in it. So does Osvaldo. They discuss the bombing. Nobody was killed but everyone was scared. One of them, a member of the committee of these four little hamlets, says in Fula: 'If we held these villages with one of our hands before the bombing, now we hold them with both of our hands.'

Mane Kiba is the political worker, the 'terrainer', of this district. He is a Balante by origin, and about thirty years old. He tells me his story.

> I was chairman of my village committee in Quinara [the central region enclosing the lower course and estuary of the Geba river], and I was chairman in 1963. We fed our guerrillas in the bush nearby, and I was our youth leader. I was also a chief for the Portuguese [one of the 'warrant chiefs' whom the Portuguese, attempting a form of indirect rule, had appointed among the Balante], and so the Portuguese lodged with me when they came to our village, and I had to feed them. So for a time I was feeding both – the Portuguese and our guerrillas. I could supply our guerrillas with good intelligence. Then I was denounced by some of the people in our village but I managed to escape. After that, two of my uncles were killed by the Portuguese, and my father was put in prison for seven months. One of these uncles was shot. The other died because they made him drink battery acid. That was the repression. They burned men alive in that time.

Now back for a moment to the question of external aid. Building their revolutionary party as they fought – and fought against a toughening Portuguese repression strengthened after 1963 by the arrival of seasoned troops and commanders from Angola, where the guerrilla rising of 1961 had failed to hold its ground – the PAIGC could rely on some support from the neighbouring Republics of Guinea and Senegal. This varied in degree and warmth. That of the Republic of Guinea was of great and perhaps decisive value at the beginning, when it was a case of winkling men out of Guine, training them, and arranging for their future training in Europe or Asia; but it is also true that the Guinea government had its early reservations. It was also, understandably, touchy on the subject of clandestine arms imports, facing as it had several attempts at armed intervention or assassination which President Toure has said were directed, according to the evidence, from Paris and Abidjan (the Ivory Coast capital of President Houphouet-Boigny).[8]

Some time in 1962 the authorities in Conakry, the Guinea capital, discovered that a consignment of canned fruit just landed on the dockside was really a consignment of small-arms ammunition. Those who had arranged for this consignment were in fact Luiz Cabral and others of the PAIGC; but they were all arrested and jailed for a while. After that the air cleared steadily, and

the Guinea government came to accept the PAIGC as the only rightful
inheritor of Portuguese power next door: by 1966 relations were excellent.
Just how good they were one could see for oneself in passing along the lines
of communication between Conakry and the frontier with Guine: repeatedly
I saw PAIGC teams welcomed and helped by officials of the Guinea administration. Sekou Toure and the PDG have proved staunch allies. By the end of
1967 the Portuguese had bombed near-frontier villages in the Republic of
Guinea on seven occasions in attempts at intimidation; but the policy has
utterly failed of its object. On 4 October, when I was there, the Portuguese
bombed Cassebetche, a small village in north-western Guinea, and killed
eleven villagers. Toure's answer was to say that next time he would send his
own airforce, which includes some MIGs, to shoot up Portuguese posts.
Meanwhile Osvaldo at once organized a mortar raid on the Portuguese post
next across the frontier, opposite Cassebetche, and apparently with no
small success.

In Senegal President Senghor proved harder to win. For several years the
Senegalese government appear to have favoured the cause of a small splinter
movement called FLING, with an office in Dakar, the Senegalese capital.
Composed of an isolated handful of emigres, FLING presented itself as the
'moderate alternative' to the PAIGC, and probably enjoyed a certain favour
with the Portuguese as the body they could hope to negotiate with, if it
should ever come to the point of negotiation. But FLING remained little
more than its original handful of 'mountain-topists' – with the additional
comfort that their 'mountain-top' was in Dakar, far away from any danger
– gaining only from time to time a few individuals for whom the way of the
PAIGC represented too hard and perilous a sacrifice. By the end of 1967 the
Senegalese government, and President Senghor in person, had accepted the
PAIGC's supremacy in the nationalist cause of Guine. Cabral was invited to
the annual conference of the ruling party in Senegal, being on that occasion
the only fraternal delegate from a non-independent African country, and it
seems that agreements had in fact been signed early in 1967 which fully
regularized the position of the PAIGC on Senegalese soil, giving the PAIGC
something of the same formal as well as practical position they already
enjoyed in relation to Guinea.

Cabral, like his leading colleagues, puts considerable value on the part
played by Guinea and Senegal in helping the PAIGC to grow. But he points
out that the main effort of preparing the anti-colonial war in Guine was
always carried on *inside* the country. And he insists that while it may be true
that a guerrilla rising may in some circumstances be prepared, or even
launched, from outside the territory in question, it cannot be successfully
carried on without development and control from interior bases.

PAIGC practice therefore demands that the manning of exterior bases –
as in Dakar and Conakry – shall be kept to a minimum of personnel necessary to foreign representation, foreign communications, and a certain
amount of long-term planning at the 'paper level'; and that all such personnel must spend a large part of every year inside Guine itself. Cabral himself is

inside Guine frequently, while his leading colleagues, I am told, are there more or less permanently. In 1968, moreover, the condition and size of the liberated areas was such that leading organs of control and representation were being installed both east and west of the Geba, the main river that divides the country more or less in halves. With hundreds of political workers such as Mane Kiba active 'on the terrain', and with mobile military units ranging through more than half the rural areas, the Conakry and Dakar offices had become distant and very secondary facilities, mainly for contact with the outside world: with the governments of Senegal and Guinea, with the Organization of African Unity, and with Europe, Asia and the Americas.

The same general development applies to the PAIGC's relations with its other allies and friends. Inside Guine you find Soviet artillery, Czechoslovak automatics, Cuban-made uniforms of Chinese cotton. You find nurses trained in Moscow, a variety of personnel chosen to direct co-operatives and other such enterprises who have had their training in Eastern Germany, Yugoslavia, Czechoslovakia, Cuba. You find Osvaldo and five others (they had been seven but Domingos Ramos was killed before Madina in 1966) who spent several months in the Nanking Military Academy back in 1961. (Since then it appears that Peking, disapproving of the aid which the PAIGC continue to receive from Moscow and other centres of 'revisionism', regards the PAIGC with strong disfavour.) But you do not find foreigners engaged in any way in PAIGC work – the single exception, so far as I know, being a Cuban doctor working under Dr Domingos de Silva, a PAIGC doctor, at the PAIGC base hospital in the Republic of Guinea: that is, outside the country.

'We want no volunteers,' Cabral said to me on this point, 'and we shall turn them back if they present themselves. Foreign military advisers or commanders, or any other foreign personnel, are the last thing we shall accept. They would rob my people of their one chance of achieving a historical meaning for themselves: of reasserting their own history, of recapturing their own identity.'

This principle the PAIGC appear to have defended with an almost ferocious determination. Towards the end of 1965, as a case in point, Cabral visited a distant African president to explain the PAIGC's need for military equipment of certain kinds. It seems that the president was enthusiastic. 'Let's form a joint general staff,' he proposed, 'and we will appoint officers to advise and direct your campaign.' Cabral replied with suitably polite words and hurried away. 'I told my comrades, when I got back, that it was all over with help from that quarter'.

They have sought, accordingly, three things from the rest of independent Africa and from any other country that will help them: (a) military equipment, especially in small cannon, automatics, bazookas, and ammunition, or medical and other non-combatant supplies; (b) training facilities for non-military personnel; and (c) political and diplomatic support against the Portuguese.

In October 1967, according to Cabral, the PAIGC had 470 members under training in the Soviet Union and the rest of Eastern Europe: a few in branches of higher education such as medicine, but in their great majority learning to be electricians, motor mechanics, nurses, and so on.

Holding a politically non-aligned posture within the framework of their domestic revolutionary policies, the PAIGC would clearly welcome help from elsewhere if they could get it. As an earnest of this they sent a delegate to Paris and London in 1965, a philosophy graduate named Maria Luz de Andrade. In Paris she received a dusty answer, and in London just the same. Asking the British Red Cross for medical aid, especially in antibiotics, she was referred to the Portuguese Red Cross. Even earlier, under the pseudonym of Abel Djassi, Cabral himself had come to London in 1960, scouting for help from the British Labour Party and any others who might favour the anti-colonial cause, but had found few to listen.[9] Returning under his own name in 1965, he was able to hold a press conference in London, speak to MPs at the House of Commons and address several small gatherings; but again nothing came of these. 'Why should we be surprised?' he said afterwards: 'After all, Portugal is Britain's ally. . . .' But he was certainly disappointed.

Yet the sting of disappointment was no longer, perhaps, very sharp. Inside Guine the cause of the PAIGC was now established on powerful foundations: sufficient aid, if only just sufficient, had come from elsewhere. The people of Guine were realizing the destiny that the PAIGC had proffered it. They were reasserting their own history, recapturing their own identity, forging their own means of development into new forms of society. They were proving the truth that Mario de Andrade was to express at a conference of all the nationalist organizations of 'Portuguese Africa' in Dar es Salaam during 1967:

> Warfare for national liberation gives our people the conviction that they can triumph directly over their enemy. Its dynamic creates the most favourable conditions for the resolving of tribal and social antagonisms. By aiming at the total destruction of colonial structures, it accelerates the forming of nations, and it promotes the emergence of those revolutionary forces which will irreversibly influence the conquests of this nationalist phase.[10]

The revolution in Guine could feel the ground firm beneath its feet: native ground, ground absolutely *of the country*, the ground of the past that would also be the ground of the future.

Such has been the political approach, general policy, and development. What of the military means?

References

1. Fanon, *Towards the African Revolution*, New York and London, 1967, p.186.
2. There were still at this time, for example, large French armed forces in nearly all the states of French-speaking Africa. Many remain today.
3. Amilcar Cabral as secretary-general, Aristides Pereira, Luiz Cabral, Osvaldo Vieira, Bernardo Vieira (Nino), and two others. Their average age at the time, I would partly guess, was 31.
4. First Congress: see also pp.72-3.
5. For the early years after 1961, this would of course have been an exaggeration. Even in 1966, as the labours of 1967 were to show, village assemblies could not always be assemblies of all the villagers concerned. In the Fula and Mandinka area, if not elsewhere, there were still those who were against, either neutral or with the Portuguese. See for 1963 Mane Kiba's story on p.60.
6. G. Chaliand, *Lutte Armee en Afrique*, Masparo, Paris, 1967, pp.63-5.
7. Nguyen Van Tien, 'Notre strategie de la guerilla', *Partisans*, Paris, January-February 1968.
8. A.S. Toure, *Defendre la Revolution*, Conakry, 1967, pp.24-38.
9. He had never been in London before and, travelling ostensibly as a tourist, he looked around with fresh and eager eyes. He spent his first night or two in the old Gower Street headquarters of many African independence movements, a ragged old eighteenth-century house that must still be warm in the memory of quite a few of Africa's ministers today, not least Mr Kanyama Chiume of Malawi and Mr Mainza Chona of Zambia. But Gower Street being packed, and my own house being full of family at the time, good English friends (Martyn and Binnie Collins) who live along the river Thames found room for Abel Djassi in a pleasant house on the tree-lined towpath not far from where the boat race ends. . . . .'*(West Africa*, 18 April 1964).
10. M. de Andrade, *La Lutte de Liberation Nationale dans les Colonies Portugaises*, Algiers, 1967, p.42.

5. By What Military Methods?

'Building the Army as You Fight'

*The people's armed forces must take their rise, become
organized, and forge themselves during the course of the
revolutionary war for the conquest of power, and as a
consequence of such warfare.*
Cuban Theses presented at
1st Tricontinental Conference, Havana, 1966[1]

Four phases mark the military unfolding of this long war.

First, there was an initial guerrilla phase set going by the pioneers under
Cabral's leadership – Domingos Ramos, Osvaldo Vieira, Bernardo Vieira, Rui
Djassi[2] and others – who were mainly men of the towns, men of 'petty-
bourgeois' origin who had managed to win for themselves a base, though at
first a narrow base, in peasant support.

One may note in passing that the PAIGC's slender portfolio of ideological
writings lays considerable stress – no doubt as another way of asserting the
specificity of African conditions and of further discrediting familiar jargon
– on the 'petty-bourgeois' origin of many among those who launched the
revolt. By this term 'petty-bourgeois' they mean all those urbanized persons
who have more or less regular employment but cannot be said to belong to
a working class or a bourgeois class, neither of which has any native existence.
The evidence is undoubtedly striking. Osvaldo's grandfather, for example,
had risen to the ownership of some property and served as a *chefe de posto:*
he was, in short, a 'small intellectual'. His son, Osvaldo's father, had secured
good employment in the Ultramarina at Bissau. The father of Domingos
Ramos, pioneer in the north-east, had been a *chefe de posto:* Bernardo
Vieira's, a clerk employed by a French trading company in Bissau; Francisco
Mendes's, a tailor; Rui Djassi's, a nominated chief *(regulo)* of the Beafada
and an honorary lieutenant of the Portuguese army.

Secondly, and in the wake of severe Portuguese repression, there came a
steady widening of peasant support. This was the time, late in 1962 and 1963,
when the peasants 'discovered for themselves the need to revolt': when they

65

made the revolt their own: when they entered the ranks of the guerrillas in large numbers.

PAIGC leaders place emphasis on this phase. The actual launching of guerrilla operations may be an obviously necessary first step; but this first step becomes useless, they argue from their own experience, unless it leads to the second step of active, ever-growing and voluntary peasant involvement. About this there is little that is spontaneous, nothing that is automatic or mechanical. Yet some writings have seemed to imply, notably in relation to Latin America, that all you have to do is to begin, heroically begin, and the rest will follow almost of itself. The Cubans themselves do not appear to think this, though they are not always very clear on the point; but some of the things they have said, or things said in their name, about their own revolt and the possibilities of revolt on the mainland can certainly suggest a reliance on spontaneity or 'automatic' expansion. Thus an armed minority 'establishes itself at the most vulnerable zone of the national territory, and then slowly spreads like an oil patch, propagating itself in concentric ripples through the peasant masses to the smaller towns, and finally to the capital'.[3] It sounds very neat: it sounds infallible . . . and no doubt there is some truth in this formulation of the process. But the truth is obscured, even fatally distorted, unless one sees as well the deeper process, the decisive process of peasant discussion, acceptance, voluntary participation. A few men who want a revolution may launch one: only many men who want a revolution can make one.

Thirdly, there was in Guiné the transformation in 1964 of the best among 2,000 guerrilla volunteers into the disciplines and structure of a regular army, and thus the beginnings of a shift from localized guerrilla warfare to co-ordinated mobile warfare. This was followed by a further extension of the army in 1965, together with the building of guerrilla militias in the villages; and by greater development of mobile warfare in 1966, with stronger and more frequent attacks on enemy garrisons and, now, on 'strategic hamlets'.

Fourthly, and yet to be engaged as these lines are written, there is the direct assault on enemy-held towns coupled with insurrection in Bissau and elsewhere, together with parallel operations in the Cape Verde and the Bissagos Islands, which culminate in the final eviction of Portuguese power.[4]

* * *

It is worth repeating here, perhaps, that the men and women who founded and have led the PAIGC had no desire for this war. They knew it would be hard and long in human cost, and they were neither fools nor adventurers. If they did not shrink from the cost, it was not because they lacked intelligence, moderation, or a sense of responsibility towards other people, but because they were convinced that any worthwhile future could be achieved only by a revolutionary change of institutions: by that independence and self-determination which the Salazar regime had consistently denied and continued to deny, or even to discuss. They may never, in fact, have believed that appeals to the Salazar regime would do any good. But they accepted war only after making repeated appeals for peaceful change.

One of their early appeals, though by no means the first, was conveyed to the Portuguese on 25 September 1960, years before any fighting had begun. In a four-page memorandum,[5] this asked for 'the solemn and immediate recognition of the rights of the people of Guine and the Cape Verde Islands to decide their own future; immediate withdrawal of the Portuguese armed forces and political police (PIDE) from Guine and the Islands; a total and unconditional amnesty and release of all political prisoners; and the installation of a process of parliamentary advance such as would assure the territories of their own organs of democratic self-rule.'

Perhaps needless to say, this fell on deaf ears. A memorandum to Lisbon of December 1960 next proposed a more detailed programme for decolonization. On 13 October 1961, an 'open letter' to the Portuguese government signed by Amilcar Cabral referred to 'the wish of our peoples for national independence, peace, progress, and peaceful co-operation with all other peoples, including the Portuguese'. It again urged that the Portuguese regime should 'now follow the decolonizing example of other colonial powers in Africa', by:

1. Immediate application of the measures proposed in our memorandum addressed to the Portuguese government in December 1960,

or

2. Immediate acceptance, before world opinion and the UN, of the principle of self-determination of our peoples, and the calling, by the end of this year, of a conference between representatives of the Portuguese government and representatives of 'Portuguese' Guinea and the Cape Verde Islands, with the following agenda:
    (a) self-determination and national independence for the peoples of 'Portuguese' Guinea and the Cape Verde Islands;
    (b) co-operation between the Portuguese people and the peoples of 'Portuguese' Guinea and the Cape Verde Islands.

But by now the PAIGC also felt strong enough to sound a warning:

Clearly, if the Portuguese government persists in refusing to reconsider its position – ignoring as this does the interests of our people and even of the Portuguese people – nothing will stop our Party from accomplishing its historic mission: the mission of developing our struggle for national liberation, of replying by violence to the violence of the Portuguese colonialist forces; of completely eliminating, and by every means, the colonial domination of 'Portuguese' Guinea and the Cape Verde Islands.

To this, as before, the gentlemen in Lisbon made no reply. Britain, France,

Italy, Belgium might all have withdrawn from their colonial positions in Africa; so much the worse for them: imperial Portugal, ever aware of the glory of its past though purblind to the absurdity of its present, would never bend. 'We will not sell: we will not cede: we will not surrender: we will not quit one fragment of our sovereignty ... Our constitutional laws forbid it, and even if they did not, our national conscience would do so.' Thus Salazar upon this subject.[6]

Yet Cabral and his colleagues persevered. While preparing for war, they continued to ask and argue for peace. And even when, during 1962, the PIDE and Portuguese army in Guine began a campaign of systematic repression[7] against a nationalist movement clearly growing strong in the villages as well as the towns, they continued to warn that repression could only bring a violent reply. Thus a press statement issued by Cabral in Dakar on 26 December 1962 declared that 'the Portuguese government is now in course of unleashing in "Portuguese" Guine and the Cape Verde Islands actions which grow bloodier every day, with the aim of breaking our people's will to liberation and independence'. And he added:

> These actions will surely provoke much loss of human life which could have been averted and still can be averted if the Portuguese government will reconsider its position, and will respect both the legitimate rights of our people and international law. But there can be only one outcome: *the total elimination of the colonial yoke in our country.*

The last words were underlined with good reason. Less than a month later the PAIGC was to launch its first actions replying by violence to the violence of the Portuguese, and the war began.

There were also attempts to reach Portuguese civilian opinion in Guine. Though Portuguese settlers were few, the PAIGC appears to have seen some possibility of neutralizing at least some of them, if not of actually winning them over. To them, too, appeals were launched. One of these in the files at Conakry, undated but manifestly before the arrest of Barbosa in March 1962, struck a characteristic note by insisting that the PAIGC, though determined to eliminate Portuguese colonialism,

> makes a distinction between Portuguese colonialism and Portuguese settlers, just as we distinguish between a vehicle and its wheels. A vehicle without wheels will not work. Nor can Portuguese colonialism without settlers .... If you lack the courage to support our struggle, guard your dignity as men by refusing to serve the colonialists: take up a position of neutrality towards our struggle for liberation .... Your situation tomorrow will depend on what you do today .... Long live friendship, equality and peaceful collaboration between all peoples! ...[8]

Such words found little or no response. All the same, the Salazar regime appears to have had some doubt on the loyalty of its citizens. At the beginning of 1963, though fighting was still in its earliest phase, it began evacuating all European civilians from outlying areas in the south. Reacting against this in February of that year, the PAIGC publicly declared once again that these civilians were not in danger:

> Our direct action is aimed only at the forces of repression (army, police and colonial agents) who, always armed better than we are, commit grave crimes against our defenceless populations. Our sabotage actions are aimed only at military objectives and economic targets essential to colonial exploitation. Our fighters have never and will never attack civilians — European or not — unless these oppose our struggle with arms in their hands. The European civilians living amongst us are well aware that they have nothing to fear from our fighters so long as they take no part in massacres or, at least, so long as they remain neutral. . . .

* * *

The early years of the first two phases, broadly between the end of 1962 and the middle of 1964 in the south and centre, but onward to the end of 1964 in the east and parts of the north-west, were extremely hard for fighters and political workers alike, although often, of course, these were the same men. The political agitations of 1961 and occasional sabotage acts of 1962 were met with stiff Portuguese repression; as this repression became increasingly indiscriminate, there were many small betrayals and disasters. Good men were lost. Others were seized and jailed. Many villages paid a bitter price for their involvement with the PAIGC. This was the time when the PAIGC wrestled with their battle to survive and grow, and when tough determination and determined vision alone provided this first victory. Little or nothing was heard of all this in the outside world. Whenever news did slip through, it was met with general disbelief or derision. What could a handful of rebels do against the Portuguese, especially now that the revolt of 1961 in Angola was partially quelled, and large Portuguese reinforcements were being transferred to Guiné?

But the PAIGC more than survived this first and most testing phase. Next year a bigger effort proved possible. It was 1963, Cabral wrote afterwards, 'that will be remembered in our history as the year in which, with the people's backing, we really got going with our armed struggle in the south and centre'. The wild repression of 1962 had brought its fruits. 'Now we saw fighters coming to us from the forests, from the swamp regions of the coast, and they came no longer with empty hands. . . . Bridges were blown up, ferries and Portuguese transport. Portuguese patrols, bigger units, barracks were attacked, inflicting in that year more than a thousand casualties on the Portuguese. . . .'

The fighting spread. Betrayed by earlier over-confidence in their power of repression, the Portuguese began reinforcing their garrisons. But reinforcement was not enough. Already in July 1963, PAIGC units under Osvaldo had opened a new front in the north: in the lands on either side of the Farim river. Of one of the earliest of these actions, carried out on 7 July, Osvaldo told me:

> Oh, it went well. We had three weapons. There were ten of us. We ambushed three of their vehicles and killed seven of them. We took eight weapons, mostly Mauser rifles but two automatics as well, and a lot of ammunition and stores. We lost one man killed. But the comrades took courage from this first action. All of them are still alive, I think, but for the one we lost then and another since.[9]

Faced with this impetuous tide of African retaliation, the Portuguese were now at last obliged to admit that something had gone wrong. To an immediate chorus of protest against such frankness by other leaders of the Salazar regime, the Defence Minister, General Manuel Gomes de Araujo, told a Lisbon evening paper, the *Diario Popular* (reporting on 17 July 1963, ten days after fighting had spread from south to north), that 'numerous and well-armed groups' operating south of the Rio Grande (the main dividing branch of the sea) had 'penetrated a zone equivalent to about fifteen per cent of the province [of Guine]', while others had 'made incursions into the territory for short distances, killing, robbing, and cutting communications'. On the same day it was announced that another 2,000 troops had sailed for the colony.

In fact, of course, the General was misleading the *Diario Popular,* and perhaps himself, on two rather important points: in the first place, areas of fighting well inside the country were no longer limited to a few southern sectors; secondly, the guerrilla units were based not outside the country, as the General implied, but solidly inside it. Those long years of preparatory work in the villages had not gone for nothing.

As men acquired experience of battle conditions and more weapons came to hand, actions became more confident, and also more daring. I take at random the following few examples from many reported in PAIGC communiques of that time:

> 1963: night of 25 January: region of Fulacunda [south-east]: the Portuguese barracks at Brandan, installed in a groundnut warehouse which is the property of the Overseas Trading Company, was taken by assault by fighters of the PAIGC commanded by Diallo. The Portuguese lost twenty killed and an unknown number of wounded.
>
> 1963: 9 February: region of Quinara [centre]: two Portuguese units disembarked from the ships *Formosa* and *Corubal* at the port of Enxude on the Geba river, suffered heavy losses (several dozen killed and wounded). Nationalist groups have pushed eastwards, attacked colonialist forces at Bambadinca, and converged towards Bafata, an

important river port and main centre for the marketing of groundnuts. Many European civilians have begun to abandon this central part of the country, and retreat towards the capital.

1963: 10 March: region of Cubisseco [south-west]: our units killed eight Portuguese soldiers during an engagement, including Captain Antonio Machado do Carmo ('killed in action in our province of Guine', admits, for once in a way, the *Diario da Manha*, Lisbon, for 16 March). From 15 March Portuguese troops throughout the southern zone are regrouped in a number of fortified barracks. Their situation nonetheless continues to worsen.

1963: 22 May: island of Colber: guerrillas shot down two aircraft. One of the pilots escapes death: Sgt Antonio Lobato, married, aged 25, is arrested and jailed by the nationalists.

1963: 1 June: island of Camo: liberated since February, this island has been frequently bombed and was again attacked by the colonial forces. Portuguese troops were routed at the port of Catchil by our nationalists under the command of Agostinho de Sa. The latter was wounded, but the [enemy's] troops were forced to retreat on Bolama.

Actions such as these were reported several times a week throughout the year. By the end of 1963, the basic pattern for much of the rest of the war had begun to take clear shape. More or less large and continuous segments of the rural areas were seized by nationalist guerrillas, held and defended. Portuguese administrators, traders and other civilians retreated to the shelter of the towns, where Portuguese troops were regrouped in a large number of garrisons. Ambush actions were multiplied on the roads connecting these garrisons.

At the end of the year the Portuguese command still believed that it could regain the initiative. To do this, however, it needed to prove that it could clear the guerrillas from their strongest-held areas. For this proof they selected the coastal 'island' of Como, really a projection of the mainland divided from it by an arm of the sea. They failed. This hard-fought failure was to prove a turning point.

In previous communiques [Cabral recalled afterwards when speaking in Conakry], we offered a detailed account of the facts of this battle on Como. Here I shall simply outline the essential aspects of a battle which has historic importance for our people. Being the first part of our national territory to be liberated by our forces, Como's reconquest became for the Portuguese at the beginning of 1964 a matter of basic and even vital necessity to their military and political strategy. This was because Como formed an indispensable strategic platform for the Portuguese if they were to control effectively our liberated zones of the south, and also because of the political consequences which could flow from their recapture of the island. For Como's people are well known in our country for their fierce commitment to our struggle, and for their loyal support of our Party.

Using every means they could bring to bear – airforce, navy, ground troops – with a total force of 3,000 well-equipped men including 2,000 other ranks and selected officers transferred from Angola – the Portuguese launched their offensive on Como in January 1964 with the determination to take it from us. Portuguese staff were moved from Lisbon to Bissau in order to follow the operations more closely.

After a battle which lasted seventy-five days, our forces pushed the enemy towards the sea, inflicting heavy losses on them in what was the worst defeat for the Portuguese in their record of colonialism. We calculate the enemy's losses at about 650 men. Portuguese deserters, including some who took part in the battle, have since told us that at least 900 of their fellow soldiers were killed or died of wounds received on Como.

The battle of Como was a test for the Portuguese, but even more for ourselves. Indeed, it has helped us to make a better judgement of our own forces. We have learned about the capacity of our fighters and our people when confronted with the most difficult situations; about the morale and therefore the weakness of our enemy; about the political consciousness and fierce determination of the civilian population (men, women and children) in the liberated zones – now definitely liberated – not to fall again under Portuguese rule . . . .

Furthermore the victory on Como, being won in the dry season, once more confirmed the principle advanced by our Party that the rainy season is not, because of specific conditions in our country, necessarily the best time for intensifying warfare. During the last rainy season (June-November) a considerable number of our fighters were at work in the fields, helping to increase farming production. Taking advantage of this rainy season to improve our political and military organization, and to reinforce our fighting capacity, we were able to launch at the beginning (November-December) of the dry season a series of attacks which had the effect of disrupting the enemy's plans. . . .

* * *

The second phase began with the holding of the first Party congress in February, at a moment when the battle on Como was still raging, and was confirmed by the outcome of that battle.

This first and in certain ways decisive congress[10] was held – again in Cabral's later description of events –

a few kilometres from the scene of operations, and consisted of a large assembly of cadres and delegates, including some sixty political and military leaders of our organization; . . . For seven days (including our preliminary meetings), and in spite of Portuguese bombing and shelling, almost all the party leaders and delegates coming from every part of the country joined in meetings to discuss basic problems of organization and warfare. . . . The practical application of the resolutions and decisions taken during the congress helped us to achieve outstanding results in 1964. These greatly changed the situation in our country. On the other hand, by submitting Party deficiences and mistakes to severe criticism and sincere self-criticism, our congress found ways of overcoming such defects. . . .

Insertion of 1980: The deficiencies and mistakes, in fact, had been extremely serious, as was made public by PAIGC leaders in September 1976. Successful guerrilla operations had been increasingly undermined, after the middle of 1963, not by Portuguese offensives or even by the onset of Guinea-Bissau's torrential rains, but by a breakdown in discipline. Coupled with a resort to traditional beliefs in divination and witchcraft, this indiscipline had turned a number of local commanders into petty despots, *militarists* in the worst sense, for whom the liberating and modernizing aims of the struggle were more or less completely lost. President Luiz Cabral recalled in 1976 that: 'The people were in fear, and our struggle risked destruction at the very moment when our fighters had taken to arms. We found that abominable crimes were being committed in our name. . .' (*No Pintcha,* Bissau, No.228, Sept. 1976)

There had come a hunt for witches, a retreat into tribalism, an abuse of women, and much else of the same destructive sort. These were the things that were about to ruin the big rebellions against neo-colonial rule in the ex-Belgian Congo (Zaire). But they did not ruin the PAIGC because they were stopped in good time. This was possible thanks to the courage and lucidity of the leadership, the steadfast discipline of the best of the commanders in the field, notably Nino Vieira, Francisco Mendes, Osvaldo Vieira, Constantino Teixeira; and then, last but not least, the party congress of February 1964 and its handling by Cabral and his closest comrades. They denounced all who were guilty of crimes, and the congress disarmed and punished these persons by removing them from positions of command. It was the toughest internal test that the PAIGC had had to face, and marked, in its essence, the turn from mere resistance to a positive programme of revolutionary change. Cabral and the leadership emerged with redoubled prestige and set about reorganizing their movement; it is from this time that the real innovations may be dated.

Religion was not, of course, attacked as such; fighters were allowed to keep their lucky charms, their *gri-gris*. But the danger of being dragged back into the confusions and sterility of mere resistance never reappeared. 'Even to the end of the war', Nino Vieira (then armed forces' commander and later prime minister) told me in 1976,

> our fighters wore *gri-gris* if they wanted. They would even ask for leave to go to their villages and undergo the 'cure of the country': that is, receive the blessing of the ancestors. And we allowed this. They came back to us strengthened in their self-confidence. They fought better.

73

They had more courage.

Held in these dramatic and dangerous circumstances,[11] this congress marked a major step towards the maturing of PAIGC practice and theory into long-term programmes of cultural and structural change. (It may in this respect be compared with the 1968 congress of FRELIMO in Mozambique.) *Insert ends.*

Reviewing these politico-military gains of 1964, Cabral noted that the Party was reorganized at all levels, especially at the top and at the base. Civil administration concerned with justice, education and health began to take shape in the liberated areas through the erection of local executives and the creation of special administrative committees. Political work was intensified: not only in Guine but also in the Cape Verde Islands, where, it was reported, preparations were advanced towards an eventual armed uprising. Counter-action was taken to destroy Portuguese promoted or officially tolerated 'puppet nationalist' movements designed to undermine nationalist unity: the reference here was to FLING in Dakar and its attempts to win a foothold inside Guine.

A comparable reorganization was carried through on the purely military side. Command zones were traced; zonal commands were integrated by the appointment of inter-zonal commanders; a supreme council of war was created. But the major change was the formation of a regular army alongside the local guerrialla detachments and village militias. It was also possible in 1964 to form several special units equipped with cannon and anti-aircraft automatics brought in from Czechoslovakia and the Soviet Union.

All this, to win peasant acceptance, required patient explanation. In one of our conversations on the *Tres de Agosto*, Cabral recalled the difficulties.

> First of all, as you know, we liberated the southern and a little part of the north-central regions. Then in 1964 we began to say to our guerrilla fighters in the south that the time had come for them to go into the eastern part of our country. Otherwise, we said, if the struggle remained only in the south and north, the Portuguese would be able to concentrate on them and eliminate them. But we found that our guerrillas were not at all of this opinion. 'We've liberated our own country,' they said to us: 'now let those others [in the east] liberate theirs.' 'Why should the Balante go and help to liberate the Fula? Let the Fula do their own work. ...'
>
> We didn't force the issue. We waited until the Portuguese did in fact begin to redouble their attacks in the south, just as we'd said they would, and then we argued our case all over again. It worked this time, and we could form a regular army that would move, and not stay like guerrillas in their own home zones. We said, 'Free uniforms, better arms, good equipment and so on for everyone who joins: but everyone who joins will go where he's sent.' Two thousand young men volunteered. For a start, we chose 900.

This second phase, the building of a regular army at the same time as the continued building of political support in the villages and now, increasingly, in the towns as well, proceeded through 1964, 1965 and 1966. The liberated zones were expanded to include about half the country, and could be better defended against Portuguese raids. Actions became more frequent in the unliberated zones; they were better prepared and co-ordinated, and they hit harder. The military initiative continued with the PAIGC.

It would be tedious to cite the innumerable actions that took place. Here are a few from a long PAIGC list for 1964:

1964: 19 March: two of our groups [of the army] attacked the barracks at Cabedu, causing some sixty Portuguese casualties.

1964: 23 March: one Portuguese ship sunk in the river Combidjan near Bedanda. Another sunk on the Rio Grande de Buba.

1964: April [undated]: one of our mobile groups [of the army] blew up an armoured vehicle in the middle of Catio, main town of the south of our country, which still has a Portuguese garrison.

1964: July [month's report]: Portuguese troops convoyed in four motor boats were able to disembark on Quitafine at the mouth of the Cacine river. They killed four civilians at Campane. But there, during the night, our fighters attacked them and killed some forty of them. At dawn the Portuguese re-embarked on their motor boats, pursued by our fighters who sank one of the boats.

PAIGC fighting groups assembled from several bases, under the command of Arafan Mane, launched a night attack on the Portuguese fortified camp at Buba. They destroyed several buildings and some underground shelters, causing numerous casualties. . . .

Guerrillas attacked two Portuguese platoons on the road two kilometres outside Empada . . . causing the Portuguese to return to Empada which they had just left. . . .

We extended our actions in the east into the zone of Gabu, the fief of several traditional chiefs who so far have stood with the Portuguese. . . . Our army attacked the Portuguese camp at Djaura and put twenty-seven Portuguese soldiers and [African] mercenaries out of action . . . . We attacked their camp at Patom and killed nineteen Portuguese soldiers and [African] mercenaries. . . . Four Portuguese aircraft bombed our positions near the village of Pri. We shot down one of these aircraft.

And so it went on, not always with success, sometimes with blunders and miscalculations, but with a general development of military skill and political understanding as men became veterans in fighting and in persuading, and as recruits were drawn from an ever wider spectrum of ethnic groups.

The outside world was slow to believe in these successes. Even the Granada film of early 1968, which showed an attack upon the fortified camp at Buba, was here and there greeted with scepticism because it could film no Portuguese soldiers lingering on the outskirts of the camp buildings.[12] Such scepticism as this was not only European. Even other Africans, the PAIGC found, were sometimes hard to convince. In this the sceptics revealed one of the general consequences for African mentality of the colonial experience: the tendency to scoff at 'other Africans', and to doubt that other Africans 'can really do anything against Europeans'.

But the Portuguese were meanwhile providing proofs of their own that PAIGC reports, even if occasionally inaccurate or overstated, were substantially true. In 1961 the Portuguese garrison in Guine had totalled some 1,000 men. In 1967 it was certainly not fewer than 30,000, five sixths of whom were from Portugal. Between January 1963 and May 1964 the Portuguese command was changed four times as reputations crashed. In May 1964 there arrived a new governor, General Schultz,[13] who gathered all military and civilian powers into his hands. He had come from the war in Angola, and he lasted longer than his predecessors. He disposed of more troops, and more sophisticated weaponry.

It was Schultz who introduced the policy of 'strategic hamlets', another proof, if one was needed, of the effectiveness of the PAIGC in the northern and eastern grasslands. Much has been claimed by the Portuguese for this policy. On their side, the PAIGC reply that such claims are much exaggerated.

> The recourse to 'strategic hamlets' [Cabral was noting in December 1966] has not yielded the gains that they anticipated. Created above all in the zones under influence of traditional chiefs, notably in Gabu [the central Fula grassland country], these hamlets have come under violent attack by our forces, and several have been destroyed. More realistic than their chiefs, the people now flee these hamlets, and prefer either to take refuge from the war in neighbouring countries [eastern Senegal and north-western Guinea] or else in the liberated zones or the towns.
>
> Moreover, our information from colonialist circles speaks of a continual lowering of morale among Portuguese troops. Quarrels grow more frequent in their barracks and fortified camps. In April 1965 there was an attempted armed revolt in the airforce, and more than a hundred soldiers were arrested including a senior officer who was condemned to twenty-eight years' imprisonment. . . . For obvious reasons, desertion remains small here – only three Portuguese soldiers have come over to us in the last six months. But in Portugal itself there is now a widespread refusal to serve in this colonial war. More than 7,000 young men called up to the armed forces and ordered mainly to Guine have been able to desert and hide themselves in the country, or flee abroad, especially to France.

On the Portuguese side, by 1966, the war had become one of 'position'. Apart from occasional armed sorties or the running of ground convoys through roads likely to be ambushed by the PAIGC, the Portuguese were now besieged in some sixty fortified camps and towns, where their troops were harassed continually by mobile units of the PAIGC.

PAIGC action in 1966 was mainly of five types:

> 1. Attacks on barracks and fortified camps, especially those still remaining in our liberated areas. These attacks are carried out by mortars, cannon (e.g. 75mm.) and bazookas. Less powerful camps are assaulted with small arms.
> 2. Actions to deepen the isolation of enemy positions: by the use of heavy arms against river transport, by the installation of anti-aircraft guns, by the destruction of strategic hamlets.
> 3. Ambushes and other such attacks on enemy units moving through the fighting zones or those partially liberated. Domination of the roads in these zones.
> 4. Raids on barracks in zones not yet liberated, with the aim of increasing the insecurity of the enemy and those (Africans) who support the enemy.
> 5. Active defence and reinforced vigilance in our liberated zones.

> The use of mortars, cannon and bazookas in attacks on barracks and fortified camps has marked the opening of a new stage. They provide the means of striking at these camps from a useful distance before attacking them from close at hand. This has completely upset Portuguese plans which counted on the relative immunity of troops installed in these camps, so as to allow for their physical and moral recuperation: which counted, that is, on the degree of invulnerability which such installations could expect in the face of attack by small arms. The resultant state of confusion for the Portuguese Command is shown by the paralysis of the enemy's forces during recent months.

> Having delivered more than one hundred attacks on fortified positions, we have succeeded [by December 1966] in ravaging about fifteen enemy camps, several of which were very important, such as those of Madina, Ollosato, Enxale, Cutia, Medjo and Biambi, as well as seriously damaging about twenty others, such as those of Buba, Empada, Mansoa, Beli, Bula, Buruntuna, Canquelifa, Farim, etc. Hastily reconstructed, some camps have been attacked, destroyed, and damaged several times.

> The enemy's growing use of aircraft and helicopters reflects their growing difficulties in the supply of their troops. . . .[14]

Enemy losses during 1966 were estimated in Cabral's report as lying between 1,500 and 2,000 killed or wounded, with corresponding losses in arms and equipment. The comparable report for 1967 noted an intensification of warfare. It claimed 142 major attacks on Portuguese fortified camps; 22 commando-type operations against airfields, port installations and Portuguese buildings in towns; and 476 ambushes and minor engagements, with, among other things, the destruction of 116 military and civilian vehicles and the capture of useful quantities of arms and ammunition, including 86 G3-Fall sub-machine guns, 397 Mauser rifles, 26 mortars of 60mm., and 16 radio transmitters 'in good condition'. Enemy losses were stated as 1,905 killed and an unknown number of wounded. The Portuguese were recorded as having carried out daily aerial bombardment of liberated zones, several large-scale combined operations designed at regaining territory, and a number of *coups de main*, often using helicoptered troops, aimed at burning harvests, destroying PAIGC base-camps, and intimidating villagers.

Portuguese communiques have naturally told a different story. Generally, through the years, they have unfolded a bland tale of well-organized success against desperate or demoralized handfuls of *bandoleiros*, bandits, whose failure is described as ever more apparent. Such claims, however, have become increasingly hard to square not only with the facts on the ground, as many outside observers have seen them and described them in words and on film, but also with the manifold effects of the war on Portuguese recruiting and military spending. This lack of credibility was greater than ever in 1968. I have made a careful reading, for example, of the fifteen weekly communiques which the Forcas Armadas da Guine issued for the period between 1 January and 14 April of that year. They describe in very general terms a long series of minor and unsuccessful 'terrorist' attacks on 'settlements' at various places which are usually not named, together with a large number of effective and even brilliant operations by the aforesaid Forcas Armadas. They are full of evasions such as: '(April 10) In the course of an attack on a post the terrorists caused some damage. The whereabouts of certain elements of the garrison are not known. ...' Yet the PAIGC communiques are always written in very great detail. What, then, are the Forcas Armadas trying to hide?

Besides this geographical imprecision, these weekly communiques abandoned on 20 November 1967 their previous practice of stating just how many attacks 'the terrorists' had carried out, and thereafter remained content with admitting 'some' or 'several' attacks. This was the more suggestive of Portuguese embarrassment not only because PAIGC communiques for the same period give much evidence, and in great detail, of increased operations by their units, but also because, strangely, the fifteen Portuguese communiques of January-April 1968 claimed 'confirmed dead' as 327 enemy and only 63 Portuguese. Why, then, be so coy about the number of 'terrorist attacks'?

Clearly enough, these Portuguese communiques were simply telling lies. The true military position was much nearer to that sketched by an article in the *Economist* on 27 April, just after the period described so triumphantly in General Schultz's weekly handouts.

> Governor-General Arnaldo Schultz actually controls Bissau and Bolamo islands, the little Bissagos isles, two fading patches on the colony's northern shore and a swathe of Fula territory. ... Dotted across the country are beleaguered 'fortified villages' where young conscripts

depend for reinforcements, ammunition and supplies on helicopters and
light aircraft landing on rough dirt fields. . . .

On their side, the PAIGC are reticent about their own losses. They say that
this is because the totals are so small that people will hesitate to believe them.
The general secretary's report for 1967, however, noted a total PAIGC loss
of 86 soldiers killed and 172 civilians, together with 583 wounded including
villagers who suffered from aerial bombardment. 'These figures', it adds,
'are larger than in previous years and reflect the intensification and spread of
warfare.' One is equally free to disbelieve these low military casualty figures,
as the PAIGC leadership suspects that one will; but then one will gravely risk
misunderstanding the nature of well-conducted guerrilla warfare. PAIGC
warfare is undoubtedly well-conducted: its units could not otherwise have
survived and grown. And, as such, PAIGC tactics are aimed at keeping severe
casualties to an absolute minimum.

They have certainly had many lesser casualties which for the most part
have gone unreported. After an attack on Buba, for example, the three-man
British Granada team present there counted six walking wounded among the
bi-group[15] they were with, one of whom had six flesh wounds. These men
were patched up as they withdrew from the outskirts of Buba, and were
evidently expected to recover as best they could. Medical service was still at
a primitive stage, and medical supplies severely lacking: this particular bi-
group had one orderly with a little elementary skill.[16]

One may also note, on the subject of casualties, that regular army commands seem invariably to have overestimated guerrilla losses: I can well
remember being with Yugoslav guerrila units who were 'totally eliminated'
on several occasions — according to the German command. In my own
judgement, the killed and severely wounded in PAIGC units have, indeed,
been few in number. (See also p.161.)

Efforts were in hand towards the end of 1967 to increase the mobility of
army units, and to extend their range of action. Late in February 1968, for
example, it was reported that a mobile mortar unit had attacked the heavily
defended airport of Bissau itself. With all this, the third phase, that of mobile
warfare backed by a network of fixed local militia units acting as guerrillas,
was now well advanced.

Generally, the army now consisted of a large number of units known as
'groups' consisting ideally of twenty-six men including a commander and a
commissar. These groups were organized in pairs, as bi-groups under a single
command, and armed, as far as possible, with six machine guns, six bazookas,
eighteen sub-machine guns and a varying number of rifles. Such bi-groups
commonly acted together with their neighbours under regional commanders
and commissars, so that it was possible to commit several hundred men in a
co-ordinated action, and with a considerable fire-power.[17] Up to the end of
1967 these formations were based on camps such as the one I visited on the
outskirts of Beli, but the intention was to close these bases and keep
formations steadily on the move, fed and guided and informed by the

political and militia network which continued to expand alongside them.

* * *

Such is the history of this war in general outline up to the autumn of 1968. As things then stood, the Portuguese retained fortified camps in most parts of the country, but these were fewer and more isolated than before, and could increasingly be supplied (except in the central areas) only by aircraft and mainly by helicopter.[18] In June-September, moreover, Brigadier Spinola ordered the evacuation of ten such camps, and was clearly preparing to evacuate others. As we shall see, the initiative stayed firmly with the PAIGC.

This brief survey may perhaps suggest a smooth rise from one success to the next. Any such impression would be misleading. Every PAIGC leader with whom I have discussed the past eight years has spoken of the persistent difficulty experienced at two main points: at the beginning, in persuading the peasants to accept the revolt and make it their own; later on, in transforming the guerrilla 'localness' of 1963-4 into operations increasingly detached from any fixed or familiar base.

The degree of mobility, as of combativeness by individual commanders in the field, seems to have varied. At times it has been by no means as great as the PAIGC leadership desired. As always in such forms of warfare, there has been a tendency for units to content themselves with the supervision of their own immediate areas. This would partly reflect the protracted nature of the war, as well as the fact that the Portuguese had by 1966 so clearly lost the initiative. Besides, a certain danger of military stagnation is usually present in guerrilla warfare, even when units have passed to the mobile and co-ordinated phase. In movements less coherent than the PAIGC, this can degenerate into 'mountain-topism', into tacit agreements with the enemy; while in coherent movements it can also degenerate into 'military commandism', into situations where the military commanders lose sight of political objectives, throw their weight about, and generally invite disaster.

From these weaknesses the PAIGC have clearly suffered in various ways, and their leaders have not failed to say so. Such failings were relentlessly condemned in a long policy directive of 1965.

> We should recognize as a matter of conscience [this stated] that there have been many faults and errors in our action whether political or military: an important number of things we should have done we have not done at the right time, or not done at all.
>
> In various regions — and indeed everywhere in a general sense — political work among the people and among our armed forces has not been done appropriately: responsible workers have not carried or have not been able to carry through the work of mobilization, formation and political organization defined by the party leadership. Here and there, even among responsible workers, there has been a marked

tendency to let things slide ... and even a certain demobilization
which has not been fought and eliminated. ...

On the military plane, many plans and objectives established by the
Party leadership have not been achieved. With the means we have, we
could do much more and better. Some responsible workers have mis-
understood the functions of the army and guerrilla forces, have not
made good co-ordination between these two and, in certain cases, have
allowed themselves to be influenced by preoccupation with the defence
of our positions, ignoring the fact that, for us, attack is the best means
of defence. ...

There had been arguments between commanders in the same area; wastage
of munitions or misuse of certain weapons; lack of drive and courage among
some responsible men.

And with all this, as proof of insufficient political work among our
armed forces, there has appeared a certain attitude [*mania*] of
'militarism' which has caused some fighters and even some leaders to
forget the fact that we are *armed militants* and not *militarists*. This
tendency must be urgently fought and eliminated within the army ....

These dangers have been met by ruthless analysis; by keeping leaders repeatedly and even continuously on tours of inspection; by emphasizing the right
of village committees to criticize the action or inaction of mobile units; and
by reinforcing the degree of free-for-all discussion at all levels. When I was
with Cabral in Quitafine, for example, he spoke to village committees along
these lines. A year earlier Gerard Chaliand, then with Cabral in the north-
western area, had heard another speech of the same kind:

Armed struggle is now developing in every part of our country [Cabral
told a large meeting of military and civilian personnel]. But in the
liberated areas there are some zones which are quiet and others where
there is fighting [against remaining Portuguese strong-points, sorties or
convoys] every day. This is not good enough. If ten men go to a rice-
field and do the day's work of eight, there's no reason to be satisfied.
It's the same in battle. Ten men fight like eight: that's not enough. I've
discussed this with Osvaldo and Chico [then, respectively, senior
commander and commissar of the north-eastern areas]. They say: it's
not enough because we haven't enough arms. But I say that it's the
result that isn't enough. One can always do more. Some people get
used to the war, and once you get used to a thing it's the end: you
put a bullet up the spout of your gun and you walk around. You hear
the motor [of a boat] on the river and you don't use the bazooka that
you have, so the Portuguese boats pass unharmed. Let me repeat: one
can do more. We have to throw the Portuguese out. And I tell you
clearly that if their boats pass it's not to be tolerated. . .[19]

Experience of guerrilla warfare in many countries has shown that there are only two ways of dealing with such dangers of stagnation. The first is to make armed units constantly subject to criticism by the peasants, who have provided the bulk of the fighters, and who know very well that ineffective armed units can only open the gate to more or less fearful enemy reprisals on village communities. The second, integrated with the first, is to keep the leadership constantly and closely involved with action in the field. The PAIGC have practised both these ways. By 1968 they could claim to have practised them with success.

* * *

Certain aspects of this warfare in Guiné are worth looking at within a wider perspective. If detailed policies are always specific, always dependent on local realities, certain underlying principles evidently have a general application.

On the question of transforming local guerrilla units into mobile regular units, for example, all successful wars of this kind appear to point the same way. Thus Mao Tse-tung, on the Chinese position in the 1930s:

> The fifth strategic problem in the anti-Japanese guerrilla war is its development into mobile war, which is necessary and possible because the war is protracted and ruthless. If China could defeat the Japanese invaders and recover her lost territories speedily, if the war were neither protracted nor ruthless, then it would not be necessary for guerrilla war to develop into mobile war. But as the actual situation is the reverse: i.e. the war is a protracted and ruthless one, it is only by developing itself into mobile warfare that guerrilla warfare can adapt itself to such a war. Since the war is protracted and ruthless, it becomes possible for the guerrilla units to go through the necessary process of steeling and to change gradually into regular armies. . . .[20]

Out of this policy came the Red Army that carried the Chinese to independence and then to revolution.

It was the same in Nazi-occupied Yugoslavia during the Second World War. The history of 'our people's Liberation Struggle may be divided into four stages,' Tito has written.

> These are as follows:
> First, the capitulation of Yugoslavia [in 1941] and the launching of the people's uprising which was from its onset featured by the formation of numerous Partisan Detachments [local guerrilla units] to fight the occupiers;
> Second, the growth of the Partisan Detachments into regular military units, battalions, brigades and divisions, and the creation of the People's Liberation Army;
> Third, the growth of the People's Liberation Committees into a real

people's government and the setting up of the Anti-Fascist Council of People's Liberation;

Fourth, the stage we are in now [November 1943], that is, the transformation of the Anti-Fascist Council of People's Liberation from a general political body into the supreme legislative body and the creation of the National Committee of Liberation as a provisional people's government. . . .[21]

Stage Two, the formation of a regular army, had come in the autumn of 1942; and it was this, while maintaining partisan detachments in all especially difficult areas, that made it possible for the Yugoslav partisans to carry their armed resistance into every part of Yugoslavia, repeatedly to seize the military initiative from an extremely strong and aggressive enemy, escape their own annihilation, and share in the final victory over Hitler.

A few years later, the Vietnamese were stating the same conclusion for themselves.

We often say: the guerrilla war must grow and develop. But to survive and develop it must necessarily evolve into a war of movement; and this is a basic principle. Because, in the actual conditions of our resistance, there can be no mobile war without guerrilla war; but also, without the development and transformation of guerrilla war into mobile war, there can be no carrying out of the strategic task of annihilating the enemy's forces, while, at the same time, the guerrilla war cannot otherwise survive and develop.

To say that it is necessary to develop guerrilla warfare into mobile warfare certainly does not mean stopping guerrilla warfare. It means that at the very heart of a well-developed guerrrilla war there must be the progressive expansion of regular units able to act as mobile units, of units around which it remains necessary to maintain guerrilla formations conducting guerrilla warfare. . . .[22]

It was with comparable thoughts in mind that the PAIGC, as already noted, set about persuading local guerrilla groups in 1964 that they must provide men who would leave their villages — their own particular and personal 'liberated areas' — and march to the defence of other villages and people far away.

Another general principle concerns terrain. A great deal of nonsense has been talked about terrain. The history of these wars shows that almost any terrain is suitable for guerrilla warfare: provided always that the warfare is sufficiently rooted in the sympathies and support of the people who inhabit the terrain in question. What at first sight may seem, on the other hand, to be the 'best' particular sort of terrain for operations of this kind can often prove to be the worst. During 1944, as one example, a group of brave but misguided French officers decided to establish a strong resistance base in the mountainous ramparts of the Vercors *massif* of south-eastern France. They assembled men and arms in relatively large quantities, and were helped in this by the parachuting of stores from Allied bases in Italy and elsewhere. The Germans replied by blockading the few passes into and out of that rock-bound plateau, and the consequences were disastrous for the French.

At much the same moment, as it happened, Yugoslav partisan detachments were operating with outstanding success in the wide plains that lie immediately to the west and north-west of the Yugoslav capital of Belgrade, then strongly in German hands. In those plains of Srem — and I myself spent some twelve months of 1943-4 with partisan detachments fighting there — enemy garrisons were so thick on the ground as seldom to be more than a dozen miles apart, and often much less. Roads were good and plentiful. And, to crown it all, down through those plains there ran the main strategic railway connecting Germany with the southern Balkans, a railway with no cover on either side that was patrolled both by night and day. Yet in this apparently impossible guerrilla territory we moved and operated night by night and week by week. That railway was blown up, often with great segments of rail levered and twisted down its embankment, not once but on scores of occasions. We even succeeded in evacuating severely wounded fighters to hospitals in liberated Italy under the very noses of the enemy. All through that June of 1944, with the help of the Royal Air Force flying in DC3s from Bari, we kept open an airstrip, usable at night by the flares of maize-stalks, that was only five miles from the nearest enemy garrison, a fairly large one at Ruma, and fewer than twenty miles from the outskirts of Nazi-occupied Belgrade. Standing there in the darkness before the DC3s came down, we could even see the distant glow of city lights.

How was it done? On nights when we used our airstrip, the roads leading to it were ambushed by partisan fighters. The wounded who were to be sent to Italy were gathered from neighbouring villages where the peasants had hidden them — from Popinci, Karlovci and others, big villages lying four-square on roads patrolled and searched by the enemy in daytime. The planes came down along our flarepath of burning maize heaps, stayed for the hour that was needed to lift our wounded into them, and departed well before dawn. At dawn the enemy arrived. But we had vanished from the scene, hidden in twos and threes by peasants who had dug more or less well-hidden holes in the ground of their farmyards. The secret was a simple one. It lay in staunch peasant support. Where that is present, any kind of terrain is good terrain.

'Training' is another general aspect. To judge by many outside reports of guerrilla warfare, one might conclude that success must always and continuously depend on the existence of foreign bases and foreign training. At the beginning, no doubt, this may often be true. In African conditions, for example, it is obviously so. In preparing for warfare on the Portuguese, the PAIGC depended on facilities provided by the neighbouring Republic of Guinea, just as their companion movement of Angola, the MPLA, have depended on Congo-Brazzaville and Zambia; or FRELIMO of Mozambique, on Tanzania; or the South African and Zimbabwean and South West African movements, on Zambia and Tanzania.[23]

But the measure in which such foreign bases or dependence on foreign training remain important after guerrilla revolts are well launched, and have got into their stride, may be safely taken as a measure of their growing failure or success. The case is very clear, for example, with Robert Holden's UPA movement in relation to Angola. Once safely established on its 'mountain top' in Kinshasa, next-door in the Republic of the Congo, the UPA rapidly degenerated to a stage where the foreign tail wagged the native dog — and wagged it, accordingly, with increasing feebleness or futility. With the PAIGC, at the other extreme, the external offices in Conakry and Dakar had as rapidly become expendable, and were used mainly as an additional convenience and reinforcement of diplomatic and supply facilities. These external facilities have continued to be useful. But they have ceased to be necessary. The PAIGC could certainly survive without them.

Then there is the policy of creating liberated areas: zones, as Armando on the way to Beli defined them, where the population can be mobilized politically, and can thus continue to mobilize itself, in general if not complete security from enemy action on the ground. Their existence after the early phases of insurrection is crucial to the further building of party and army, and so of the revolution itself. This building of liberated zones has to be begun, even in a small and partial way, before the movement is strong enough to ensure major control of large areas. But the movement cannot be successfully developed into further and finally victorious phases without the continued extension of liberated zones in the political, social, and cultural senses as well as in the military one. Liberated zones are a proof of a nationalist fighting movement's efficacy, a demonstration of what is to come after victory, but also a vital means of achieving that victory. In the case of the PAIGC, liberated zones can be seen to have yielded their full meaning after 1963 in the emergence of a modern if still limited socio-economic structure of an entirely new kind.[24]

References

1. In *Partisans*, Paris, July–September 1967, p.56.
2. Killed in action in 1964.
3. 'Latin America: The Long March', *New Left Review*, London, September–October 1965, p.27.
4. As in preceding pages I have preferred to let these lines, written in 1968, stand just as I wrote them. Things worked out rather differently, as we shall find in due course; but this was how we saw it at the time.
5. All quotations from PAIGC documents in this book are from originals in PAIGC archives or from copies in my possession.
6. Anyone who wishes to measure the frenzied quality of official attitudes in Portugal then, or indeed since, should take a look at a journalistic anthology, from which the above words of Salazar are quoted, edited for the

regime by Mota de Vasconcellos with the appropriately helpless title of
No!, Lisbon, 1961.

   Or there was the extraordinary case of the old Portuguese slaving
'fort' of St John the Baptist at Ouidah on the Dahomey coast of West
Africa. When in 1960 the newly-independent government of Dahomey
insisted upon including this acre of 'inalienable Portuguese soil' within
its own sovereignty, the Portuguese officer who 'governed' it burned
down his house, on leaving, by orders from Lisbon. Can one be less
intelligent?

7.   This repression became severe early in 1962. Some of the PAIGC leaders
   were among its victims: 'At dawn on 13 March [1962] the Portuguese
   colonial Gestapo (PIDE), backed by a unit of their armed forces,
   attacked a clandestine party centre near Bissau. The PIDE arrested two
   leaders and a militant of our Party and seized some *materiel*, including
   arms, flags, documents and badges. Other leaders who were in the house
   managed to escape.

   Those arrested were Rafael Barbosa (Zain Lopes), aged 37, public
   works foreman, Chairman of the Central Committee of our Party;
   Mamadou Toure (Momo), aged 23, married, barman, political secretary
   of the Bissau Zone and member of the Central Committee; and Albino
   Sampa, aged 29, bachelor, mason. The two leaders had been living
   underground.

   This communique of 24 March 1962 went on to note that 'the
   situation is more tense than ever in Bissau, and protest and revolt have
   swept into various other regions. Thousands of lives are under threat
   from the modern arms of the troops and police of Salazar, ready to
   drown in blood the liberation of our people. . .', and concluded with
   another appeal to all democratic peoples and governments for their
   support.

8.   Signed by Amilcar Cabral, Seydi Camara, Zain Lopes (Rafael Barbosa),
   Badara Toure, A. Diallo, and W. Barreto.

9.   This laconic account disguises the quality of Osvaldo's courage on that
   occasion. Cabral told me that Osvaldo and his little group found the
   peasants in the north both sceptical and little welcoming: the peasants,
   in other words, thought that either these guerrillas would not do what
   they said — attack the Portuguese — or, if they did attack, would
   miserably fail. 'So Osvaldo laid an ambush to show that they really
   meant business, and weren't just talking. This ambush was a fortunate
   one. It was very successful. It started the peasants on a change of mind.'
   See also the account of Antonio Bana, who was with Osvaldo, in
   Chaliand, 1967, p.102.

10.   See pp.55-6 for its principal decisions.

11.   A fuller account is in B. Davidson, *Africa in Modern History*, Lane/
   Penguin, London, 1975, Ch. 30.

12.   See pp.109-10.

13.   Trained in Nazi Germany, Arnaldo Schultz had been one of Salazar's
   Ministers of the Interior and, later, operational commander in the
   Cabinda enclave of Angola. He arrived in Guine with the reputation of
   being in Portuguese eyes 'the strong man who would put things back in
   order'. He resigned in 1968, having failed to do anything of the kind.

'Sa demission (a la fin de son mandat, ce qui n'enleve pas las significance du fait) est une grande victoire pour nous,' Cabral wrote to me on 22 May of that year, 'car il etait venu pour faire cesser la lutte en six mois. Et la lutte n'a fait que grandir.'

Schultz was followed as governor by Brigadier Antonio Sebastiao Ribeiro Spinola, a former cavalry officer who, like Schultz, had served as an operational commander in Angola since the outbreak of the nationalist uprising there in 1961. Spinola initiated the policy of 'strategic withdrawal' from besieged camps — from those very camps for which Schultz had promised so much.

14. A. Cabral, *Report* for 1966.
15. *Bi-group:* 'The army must be formed of units with their own commands, and at this stage we should not create larger units than the bigrupo. Each bigrupo must have a commander and political commissar, and be formed of two groups . . .' (internal directive of November 1965).
16. I am indebted to Mr John Sheppard for this eye-witness information.
17. For an actual example of operational orders to a pair of bi-groups, see p.105, footnote 1.
18. Portuguese use of helicopters considerably increased in 1967-8. As with the rest of their sophisticated equipment, the helicopters were mainly of NATO provenance.

I have said little here of the assistance which the Salazar regime has received for its colonial wars from its NATO allies. This was and remains considerable, and in certain ways crucial. All such *materiel* as jet bombers, helicopters, napalm, small naval vessels, and certain types of cannon and bazooka were and are provided by one or other of the NATO powers. Of the latter, the most important in a military sense have been Britain, France, the United States and West Germany, though not necessarily in that order.

It appears, in fact, that West Germany has been Salazar's most useful ally in the field of military supply. The aid is not all one way. Official reports quoted from Reuter from Bonn and Lisbon, and published in *Le Monde* of 20 June 1964, tell a great deal about Luso-German co-operation and are worth reprinting both for what they say and for their implications:

'Portugal has begun putting up buildings for West German military units at an airbase near Beja in southern Portugal, the Portuguese Embassy in Bonn announced on Thursday. These installations are for the training and logistic support of the Bundeswehr [West German Army] as envisaged by an agreement reached on 12 June [1964] between General Manuel Gomes de Araujo, the Portuguese Defence Minister, and his German counterpart, Herr Kai Uwe von Hassel.

'Besides this, Portuguese soldiers wounded in Angola and Guine [the Mozambique revolt had yet to begin] are being treated in German hospitals following a bilateral agreement reached last October [1963], it is also announced from Lisbon. The practical application of this agreement was also an object of last Friday's talks in Bonn. . . .'

Those who wonder what effect these colonial wars have had on Portuguese morale at home may well ponder on the reasons why Portugal should prefer to stow away her wounded in West Germany.

19. Chaliand, *Lutte Armee en Afrique,* Maspero, Paris, 1967, pp.50-1.
20. Mao Tse-tung, *Strategic Problems in the Anti-Japanese Guerrilla War,* 1938: 'Development into Mobile Warfare', *Selected Works,* Vol. 2, Lawrence and Wishart, London, 1954, pp.150-1.
21. Josip Broz Tito, *Selected Military Works,* Belgrade, 1966, p.142.
22. V.N. Giap, *Guerre du Peuple, Armee du Peuple,* Paris, 1967, pp.102-3.
23. *Insertion of 1980:* And would be able, after 1975, to count on Mozambique and Angola.
24. A lengthy discussion of the strategy and tactics of 'people's war', above all as practised by African liberation movements in recent years, is in B. Davidson, *The People's Cause,* Longman, London, 1981.

6. Involving What Obligations?

'Building the Revolution as You Fight'

*World history would indeed be very easy to make if the
struggle were taken up only on condition of infallibly
favourable chances.*
KARL MARX[1]

On this particular day they are wondering how far I can walk, and how fast.
I am wondering this myself. A small question, but not so easy to answer.

I ask: 'How many hours distant?'

Yamte N'aga,*via* Armando: 'Well, if we leave in the morning we shall get
there in the afternoon.'

'But about what time in the morning should we have to leave?'

Armando: 'Don't forget he doesn't have a watch.'

In the end, that day, we march all of fifty-three kilometres.

* * *

The undoubtedly remarkable successes of the PAIGC, such as I and others
saw them in 1966-8, rest on a stubborn triumph over technological and
cultural poverty.

An almost completely non-literate people, lacking all the minor aids to
punctuality and orderly procedure, such as watches and clocks, which we
take for granted, has managed to transform itself into an integrated and
efficient military and political organization. This people has contrived to
improve, steadily and surely, its initially far from favourable chances. It has
learned to provide itself with self-regulating discipline, with self-manned
social services, with self-controlled means of economic survival. Somehow or
other, it has overcome its infrastructural weakness: not completely, not
invariably, not in any way abundantly – all this goes without saying – but
in a measure which is sufficient and which has continued to expand.

Even in a short visit, one could see that it is precisely this measure of self-
administrative progress which represents the PAIGC's central achievement.

For it is this progress which reveals the distance travelled between the small group of pioneers, of 'guerrillas of the first hour', and the broad peasant movement of today. Between those two lie the efforts of countless people who have made this revolt and revolution their own, and, in making it their own, have given it a truly liberating character.

The point here is that the revolt was tied from the first into the gradual realization of new socio-economic structures. Without this frank acceptance of the obligation to 'build the revolution as you fight', there could have been no means, except the very limited means of military action, of transforming a movement of pioneers (by itself, inevitably, an elite movement) into a movement of the masses; and so of guaranteeing that revolt stood for something greater and more valuable than a mere substitution of African for Portuguese rulers.

At least up to 1965, this accepted obligation to 'build the revolution as you fight' was persistently hampered by lack of trained personnel. Later, in 1967, this lack was still acutely felt in certain sectors, chiefly those of health, education, and co-operative or other management. Yet there was now at least a general network of personnel with more or less adequate preparation in all these sectors. Many more would be required to run the country. This was one of the reasons, incidentally, why the PAIGC leadership has been content to envisage a prolonged war which will give time for the training of several thousand men and women.[2] But at least the main structures of a new social framework were in place throughout the liberated areas.

This can be seen in several key aspects, including those of economic organization, education and public health.

Economic restructurization has had two aims: to carry on economic warfare, and to build a new marketing system in place of the Portuguese one.

Summing up in December 1966, Cabral noted that:

> For some time now, we have abolished the system of colonial exploitation over most of our national territory. This year we dealt a heavy blow to the remainder of the [Portuguese] trading system, especially in the eastern (Gabu-Bafata) and western (Canchungo-San Domingo) regions. In fact the state of insecurity created by our units in these regions, and our control of certain roads, have made impossible both the growing of groundnuts [the colonial monoculture] and the distribution of warehoused goods in the interior entrepots [of the Portuguese]. Besides this, our ambushes mounted on the Bissau-Manson road have held up the transport of imported goods and local farming products. The greater part of wholesale and retail trade in secondary urban centres has come to a stop, traders and clerks having fled from these centres to the capital.
>
> Some notion of the catastrophic situation of the colonial economy may be had from the fact that the CUF [Uniao Fabril], the chief trading enterprise in Guine, has been in deficit for three years and has had to live off its reserves. Though its continued existence is demanded

by the colonial government, this is limited to the principal urban centres and is no longer in the political picture. Moreover, the colonial authorities have had to import large quantities of rice (10,000 tons from Brazil alone) to feed their troops and the urban populations – and this in a country which normally produces more rice than it needs. Other economic activities are practically paralysed. And except for those of a military character, public works and public construction no longer exist. ...

Having smashed the Portuguese rural market, the PAIGC clearly and urgently needed to provide at least a partial alternative. Given the 'subsistence' nature of peasant life, this alternative required only to be partial. But there had to be at least some market for peasant products outside the Portuguese system, and some means of providing essential goods. So the PAIGC began installing their own system. They began buying rice and other products from village producers at prices fixed slightly above those of the Portuguese – thus eating into the Portuguese system still persisting on the peripheries of urban centres – and selling consumer goods (cottons, hoes, kitchen ware; and so on) at prices fixed slightly below those of the Portuguese. They fixed these exchanges without money, and at values calculated for the needs of barter trade. To this end they began establishing a chain of 'People's Shops'.[3]

In his summing up of December 1966, Cabral could note that:

We have continued to give the closest attention we could to economic development, especially in the promotion of food supplies. New lands were brought under rice and other food crops during the last rainy season (June-November 1966). Harvests promise to be good, and with a net increase of production in certain zones (Saarah, Quinara and Ndjassani) as a result of better political work among the peasants. Large quantities of rice of the last season's harvesting, particularly in the south, have found no consumers because of the difficulty of getting it out caused by lack of transport. All the same, we have been able to move a considerable quantity of rice from the region of Quitafine [south-west]. Small quantities of other products (leather, rubber, crocodile skin and the skins of other animals, palmnuts) have also been taken out and sold abroad.

Efforts were made to help artisans in small local industries. It was hoped to set up a small soap factory on the basis of local palmoil.

To extend the supply of really necessary articles, we have installed two other People's Shops – one in the north and the other in the region of Boe. In this respect, however, we face grave difficulties through lack of goods, in spite of the help we have had from friendly countries.
This supply of essential goods to our liberated areas has proved an important factor in the consolidation of these areas, in encouragement

for the struggle and demoralization of the enemy. The colonialists try to compete with our People's Shops by greatly reducing their prices for imported goods in the areas not yet liberated. We have to be able to outface this competition. Every effort and sacrifice which can be made in that direction will help us to win the war.

Travelling in Boe with Armando Ramos, then in charge of economic organization in these eastern areas, I was able to collect a few details of the position near the end of 1967, about a year after Cabral had made the above review.
Armando:

These Fula grow little or no rice, but concentrate on cattle. Before we began our war, the Portuguese had to provide them with rice from south of the Corubal. But now it is we who control at least two thirds of the rice-growing areas, and this has forced the Portuguese to import rice for their needs. So the shortage of food in the grasslands is even greater than before, and we are consequently obliged to make, from the south, our own rice transfers to these areas [via the peripheral Republics].

Last year [1966-7] we probably exported a total of about one hundred tons of rice for our own needs. But we have thousands of tons that we can't get out of the country, and which are rotting in the villages.

Goods being imported into Boe when I was there included bicycles, large quantities of salt, sandals, soap, writing materials, and cottons. In the convoy brought up from Conakry for Boe, Armando had goods to the value of about 33,660 escudos (or about £420 at the then prevailing rate of exchange with sterling): they were mostly cottons. He showed me his accounts.

Mario: 'All that paper? Too much paper in this war.'

Armando: 'Without paper this war would have no history.'

For the nine months through September 1967, Armando had brought into Boe, a region of sparse population, a total of goods worth 214,200 escudos at prevailing prices or just under £2,675.

Cabral's report for 1967 noted that:

In spite of intensified aerial bombardment and warfare, we have succeeded in considerably enlarging the production of food crops, in diversifying cultivation, and in applying new techniques by means of specialized cadres formed during the struggle. Rice growing, our main food-base, has had good results in the southern regions, the centre-north and the north-west, the biggest productive increase being in Quitafine, the most bombed region. Diversification has taken shape mainly in the growing of more cassava, potato and beans, and in the introduction of certain exotic varieties of beans and other vegetables.

Supply difficulties continued as before, but new Shops had been established. A chief problem lay in shifting goods from the interior, but 'hundreds of tons of palmnut, leather, bees' wax, palmoil and lighter products have been sold on the foreign market, and these sales have made an appreciable contribution to the system. The functioning of our Shops remains dependent, however, on the volume and frequency of gifts made to our Party by organizations in friendly countries': gifts, that is, which enable essential imports to be made in adequate volume.[4]

* * *

We crossed back from Boe into the Republic of Guinea, and found a PAIGC vehicle, a Soviet type of Land Rover, about to leave for Conakry. In this we set out early next morning. After a few miles we dropped a young man who waved farewell and walked off westward into the bush.

Armando: 'That's the teacher for those Fula villages you saw the other day. He's just come from Conakry after ending his training. He's the first teacher they've ever seen. Mane Kiba is up there waiting for him.'

Aside from political organization and warfare, nothing seems to have more exercised the thoughts and labour of the PAIGC leadership than the installing of at least a skeleton network of primary schools. The task was dauntingly difficult because a population that was almost entirely non-literate could offer no reserves of educated manpower. But it was never doubted that this was a task that had to be done. It was done at the beginning by training the pioneers as well as possible, whether in Conakry or elsewhere. Then, little by little, rural schools were opened in liberated zones. Practice and experience brought new confidence. In 1965 a general directive was issued.

> to create schools and spread education in all liberated regions. Select young people between 14 and 20, those who have at least completed their fourth year, for further training. Oppose without violence all prejudicial customs, the negative aspects of the beliefs and traditions of our people. Oblige every responsible and dedicated member of our Party to work daily for the improvement of their cultural formation.[5]

These instructions bore fruit, as the following handful of statistics will show. For the year 1965-6, the PAIGC had 127 primary schools in Guine, with 191 newly-trained teachers and 13,361 pupils. In the following year, 1966-7, they increased these figures to 159 schools, with 220 teachers and 14,386 pupils. (In Conakry they also had a 'pilot-school', with Yugoslav aid, and 87 pupils.) Eighty per cent of these pupils had completed two years' schooling, and the average age was 12. Some fifty young men and women were also sent to Europe in 1967 for technical training in various fields. (*Note of 1980:* The above figures for pupils, as I realized later, included adults in literacy classes. See p.129 below for 1972 totals.)

Health services were likewise expanding in the liberated regions. During 1967 fifty nurses completed courses in Europe, mostly in the Soviet Union, as well as several doctors; there were now about one hundred nurses in all. In their liberated regions, the PAIGC had now installed six field hospitals, 120 clinics, and had twenty-three mobile medical teams at work. A new hospital was being built in the Republic of Guinea for the treatment of severe orthopaedic cases. As with education, health services available to Africans in Guine were already far superior to those of the colonial period.

All this went hand-in-hand with the continued work of politicization, on which its success so largely depended. To this subject the political bureau's confidential directives have given repeated and detailed emphasis.

> In the liberated regions [runs one of these directives in 1965], do everything possible to normalize the political life of the people. Section committees of the Party (*tabanca* committees), zonal committees, regional committees, must be consolidated and function normally. Frequent meetings must be held to explain to the population what is happening with the struggle, what the Party is endeavouring to do at any given moment, and what the criminal intentions of the enemy may be.
>
> In regions still occupied by the enemy, reinforce clandestine work, the mobilization and organization of the populations, and the preparation of militants for action and support of our fighters. . . .
>
> Develop political work in our armed forces, whether regular or guerrilla, wherever they may be. Hold frequent meetings. Demand serious political work from political commissars. Start political committees, formed by the political commissars and commander of each unit, in the regular army.
>
> Oppose tendencies to *militarism* and make each fighter an exemplary militant of our Party.[6]
>
> Educate ourselves, educate other people, the population in general, to fight fear and ignorance, to eliminate little by little the subjection to nature and natural forces which our economy has not yet mastered. Fight without useless violence against all the negative aspects, prejudicial to mankind, which are still part of our beliefs and traditions. Convince little by little, and in particular the militants of the Party, that we shall end by conquering the fear of nature, and that man is the strongest force in nature.
>
> Demand from responsible Party members that they dedicate themselves seriously to study, that they interest themselves in the things and problems of our daily life and struggle in their fundamental and essential aspect, and not simply in their appearance. . . . Learn from life, learn from our people, learn from books, learn from the experience of others. Never stop learning.
>
> Responsible members must . . . take life seriously, conscious of their responsibilities, thoughtful about carrying them out, and with a comradeship based on work and duty done. . . . . Nothing of this is incompatible with the joy of life, or with love for life and its amusements, or with confidence in the future and in our work. . . .

Nor was the enemy forgotten.

> Reinforce political work and propaganda within the enemy's armed
> forces. Write posters, pamphlets, letters. Draw slogans on the roads.
> Establish cautious links with enemy personnel who want to contact us.
> Act audaciously and with great initiative in this way . . . . Do every-
> thing possible to help enemy soldiers to desert. Assure them of security
> so as to encourage their desertion. Carry out political work among
> Africans who are still in enemy service, whether civilian or military.
> Persuade these brothers to change direction so as to serve the Party
> within enemy ranks or desert with arms and ammunition to our units.[7]

The 'big words' also have their place, now and then, in these otherwise most
practical directives. There must be criticism and self-criticism at all levels,
collective control, democratic centralism, revolutionary democracy. But
what do they really mean? What, for example, is revolutionary democracy?
Here is how the relevant directive replies:

> We must practise revolutionary democracy in every aspect of our Party
> life. Every responsible member must have the courage of his responsi-
> bilities, exacting from others a proper respect for his work and prop-
> erly respecting the work of others. Hide nothing from the masses of
> our people. Tell no lies. Expose lies whenever they are told. Mask no
> difficulties, mistakes, failures. Claim no easy victories. . . .

One is repeatedly struck by the bluntness of these directives. What, again, is
collective control? It is control by 'a group of persons constituted as a group,
and not by a single person or some persons of that group. Collectively to
control, in a given group, means to study problems together so as to find the
best solutions; means to take decisions together; means to profit from the
experience and intelligence of each member, and thus of all members, so as
better to direct, to instruct, to command. . .' and on for another hundred
words of down-to-earth definition.

   All these are among the ways in which the PAIGC have taken thought to
'build the revolution as we fight'.

References

1.   Karl Marx, letter to Kugelmann, 17 April 1871.
2.   Cf. *The Economist*, 27 April 1968: the PAIGC 'has now occupied most
     of the territory it wants to take, and will eventually take the rest.'
3.   The general aim was defined in a confidential memorandum written by
     Cabral in 1965 for 'the destruction of the enemy's economy and the
     construction of our own'. In this he ordered 'all necessary measures to

guarantee and develop supplies to the peoples of the liberated zones', specifying salt, sugar, tobacco, cottons, footwear.

Characteristically, he instructed all responsible members to 'Keep always in mind that the people are not fighting for ideas, for the things in anyone's head. They are fighting . . . for material benefits, to live better and in peace, to see their lives go forward, to guarantee the future of their children. National liberation, war on colonialism, building of peace and progress — independence — all that will remain meaningless for the people unless it brings a real improvement in conditions of life. It is pointless to liberate a region if its populations then remain without essential goods.'

As the means of making sure that they did not remain so, People's Shops for trade on a barter basis 'should be established in every liberated region, and brigades for the sale of essential goods to the *tabancas* likewise created. . . Put at the head of all these commercial bodies men who are honest and not corrupted by colonial commerce, and allow these men not the smallest responsibility of a political kind.'

4. By summer 1968 there were, in all, fifteen People's Shops in the liberated regions: five in the north, seven in the south, two in the east, and one other astride the frontier.

    The main goods they were importing were cottons, mosquito netting, matchets, hoe-blades, salt, sugar, tobacco, bicycles, saucepans, sewing machines, fish hooks and lines, matches, torches and torch batteries. The main goods they were exporting were kola, crocodile and other skins (including some leopard), coconuts, rubber, bees' wax, and, of course, in large quantities, rice.

    Of these export products, those most encouraged by the PAIGC were goods requiring labour in their preparation or acquisition, such as woodcarvings and skins, rather than those which simply 'grow on trees'.

5. For anyone aware of African conditions today, this directive would bear quoting in full. Paragraph 5, for example, instructs all responsible members 'to oppose among the young, especially those over 20, the attitude [*mania*] of leaving the country so as to study elsewhere, the blind ambition to acquire a degree, the complex of inferiority and the mistaken idea which leads to the belief that those who study or take courses will thereby become privileged in our country tomorrow. . . .' But 'also oppose . . . any ill will towards those who study or wish to study — the complex . . . that students will be parasites or future saboteurs of the Party. . . .'

6. Cf. similar statements on 'militarism', p.80-1 above.

7. In 1967 the PAIGC acquired an aid to popular education and propaganda in the shape of a short-wave radio transmitter. This is being used for daily programmes of information and instruction, and for special programmes aimed at Portuguese troops.

7. Towards What Future?

There shall be equal rights and duties: a strong union and
brotherly co-operation among citizens, whether from the
standpoint of the individual, of the social system, or of the
ethnic structure, so as to check and defeat all attempts
at dividing people from each other. There shall be
economic, political, social and cultural unity. . . .
Major Programme of PAIGC, January 1962

In its policy utterances, the PAIGC has allowed itself a certain use of the 'big'
words' on liberty, equality and fraternity that follow on the 'small words'
which speak of individual suffering or resentment. Thus its Major Programme, elaborated in 1962, declares for 'a republican, democratic, non-
denominational, anti-colonialist and anti-imperialist government'; for 'a
restoration of fundamental freedoms, respect for all human rights and guar-
antees for the exercise of these freedoms and rights'; for 'general and free
elections to the various institutions of government'; for 'equality of all
citizens before the law without regard to nationality, ethnic group, sex,
social, cultural achievement, professional status, without regard to rich or
poor, religious tendencies or ideological convictions'; and for other such
desirable things.

'Big words' like these tend to evoke scepticism at this point of the
twentieth century. Even the Portuguese legal texts, after all, have in their
bearing on Africa an occasional air of high-minded liberalism, while the consti-
tutions of many newly independent African states declaim commitments to
unity and brotherhood which have little more reflection in reality than
Lisbon's inflated rhetoric. Is it possible, at this stage, to go behind the 'big
words' in the Guiné struggle, and measure their meaning for practical
development?

To some extent an answer is available in documents and conversations.
But the real answer, as the leaders of the PAIGC would surely say at this point,
lies in all that has been done, is being done, to 'build the revolution as we
fight': in those bush schools, village committees, economic initiatives, forest
clinics, and, still more, in the day-to-day process of self-realization

experienced by thousands of young men and women who are active in the struggle through their own will and determination. It is in these things that they would see the true measure of their movement towards new and demo-cratic forms of life, and thus the only sure promise that postwar Guine will not sink into lassitude, inter-ethnic quarrelling, or one or other form of administrative dictatorship. And it is only out of such things, as the leaders of the PAIGC do in fact repeatedly argue, that there can come the effective democratization of the people in terms of 'economic, political, social and cultural unity': in terms, that is, of a people who have recaptured their chance of continuing their own process of development into the modern world.

These people will decide the future in the measure that they *can* decide. For a people conducting a revolution, this measure is not a small one. Big words again: but words in this case with a powerful content, as anyone may see who visits even briefly this revolution. For it happens that guerrilla war-fare cannot, by its nature, be successfully conducted without discussion, endless discussion, among all those who conduct it, whether as commanders or commanded. In this kind of warfare, where superiority over the enemy rests chiefly in superior intelligence, in knowing better than the enemy how to exploit terrain and situation, in retaining always the initiative of attack or withdrawal, everything has to be explained.

But this means that everything has to be explained not by 'staff apprec-iations' or other written briefings, useless among a largely non-literate people but useless anyway as a means of invoking active and intelligent *participation:* it has to be explained by oral statement and debate. For this is a kind of warfare in which individual thought and action count for more than anything else, and count all the time. This is a kind of warfare in which the volunteer – and the notion of a 'conscript guerrilla' is thinkable in terms only of quick disaster – is there not only to fight for himself but also to think for himself. This is a kind of warfare, accordingly, in which orders which seem to make no sense will probably be ignored.

Hence the warfare of the PAIGC involves a great deal of discussion. Accustomed to regular army ways, the two young Englishmen and their Canadian colleague who made the Granada-TV foray into Guine during February 1968 told me afterwards that they were constantly aware of how much talk there was before the two attacks on Portuguese garrisons at which they were present. Written orders might come to attack such-and-such a post, but these orders were then examined by the whole bi-group, or at any rate by most of it, in their actual and intimate details and implications. Action waited until everyone understood not only what he or she had to do, but also what others had to do, and why indeed they had to do it at all.[1]

And it is not only among the fighting units that this need for discussion holds good: even more, it holds good for the parallel civilian structures in villages and hamlets where peasants can be *asked* to grow more rice, stay patient under aerial bombardment, excavate air-raid shelters, suffer the hardships of interrupted trade, shelter or feed fighting units and administer their own affairs in new ways — but where they cannot be *forced* to do any of these things. Guerrillas may find it necessary to counterpose their own terror to the enemy's terror against hostile chiefs and their like: once they begin trying to terrorize the peasantry, they have lost their war. Consequently, there has to be endless discussion with and among village committees: and endless discussion means, in practice, an endless number of individual decisions, while individual decisions mean in their turn the assumption of a new and very personal responsibility by an ever-growing number of individuals. With successful guerrilla warfare, which means revolutionary warfare, it is therefore not a mere use of 'big words' to say that the chance for ordinary people to decide for themselves is not a small one.

I think this process of deciding-for-themselves by large numbers of village Africans, thinking now within a framework of new and hitherto unfamiliar or unthought ideas, forms a central aspect of what has been happening in Guine since 1962. Yet it remains true that the PAIGC has had to act as a 'vanguard', opening and enlarging the war for national liberation in Guine and its offshore islands, including the Cape Verdes; and that, as such, the PAIGC leadership has had to fix its own direction for the long haul as well as for the short. It is reasonable to ask what conclusions they have reached.

In fixing this direction, they appear to have been aware of two poles of repulsion: on the one hand, the sterility of any approach deriving from a mechanical application of revolutionary doctrine evolved in other lands; and, on the other, the helpless *laisser aller* they have seen develop in many of the newly-independent African states. Of these, the second is accepted as the real danger. They have accordingly taken great care to steer away from the 'middle-class solution', from a direction that would take the PAIGC towards those forms of elitist rule which have led, as they would argue, to the neo-colonialist posture and frustration of much of independent Africa during the 1960s.

A passage from Frantz Fanon reflects their attitude. Fanon argues that states which acquire their political independence under the leadership of elites formed by the structures and ideologies of the colonial period — elites which were to provide these countries, as the British and French repeatedly said, with the stable middle classes of the future — are bound to head for trouble.

> National consciousness, instead of being the all-embracing crystallization of the innermost hopes of the whole people, instead of being the immediate and most obvious result of the mobilization of the people, will [then] be . . . only an empty shell, a crude and fragile travesty of what might have been. . . .

And why? Because

> The national middle class which takes over power at the end of the colonial regime is an under-developed middle class. It has practically no

economic power, and in any case it is in no way commensurate with the bourgeoisie of the mother country which it hopes to replace. In its wilful narcissism, the national middle class is easily convinced that it can advantageously replace the middle class of the mother country. But that same independence which literally drives it into a corner will give rise within its ranks to catastrophic reactions, and will oblige it to send out frenzied appeals for help to the former mother country . . . [all the more because] neither financiers nor industrial magnates are to be found within this national middle class. The national bourgeoisie of under-developed countries is not engaged in production, nor in invention, nor building, nor labour; it is completely canalized into activities of the intermediary type. Its innermost vocation seems to be to keep in the running and to be part of the racket. . . .[2]

Written in 1960, these words were to prove all too prophetic. If the PAIGC leadership did not mark the prophecy, they certainly marked the outcome. They travelled through independent Africa on missions of their own, watching and listening, and they drew conclusions which continually strengthened their anti-elitist views.

* * *

They are manifestly proud of what they have been able to achieve in Guine. But they do not make large claims.

What Cabral said in December 1966, summing up on this point, was still the way that he presented the situation two years later:

It would be naive to claim that the progress realized in our liberated areas has radically changed the social situation of their populations. Our people have to face a colonial war whose genocidal intentions everyone can see: they live under difficult conditions. Whole groups have seen their villages destroyed and have had to withdraw into the bush.

Yet nobody goes hungry, nobody is exploited, the standard of living steadily improves. Our populations reveal an enlarged political consciousness day by day; they live and work together in harmony; they face together the miseries of the war that is imposed on us. Except for occasional cases of indiscipline, motivated usually by personal interest or by explicable misunderstanding, our populations are proud to follow the Party's lead.

It is not concealed that difficulties remain: that such cases of indiscipline, for example, are particularly common among the *dyula* or travelling traders, whose intensely personal enterprise sees the revolt either as a threat to their trade or as a means of inflating their profits.

It is not suggested, either, that lack of trained personnel is anything but a serious hindrance to work in the liberated areas. Yet here, too, the position improves.

> Until lately the men whom we had for responsible village work on rais-
> ing levels of productivity were simple folk [Cabral noted in one of our
> talks on the *Tres de Agosto*]. Now we are beginning to be able to
> replace them with men who have some specialized training. Here in the
> south-east [we were off the coast of Quitafine at the time] our health
> service used to be run by a political worker with no specialized know-
> ledge. Now it's run by a fully trained doctor.

Nor is it thought that reconversion to peacetime will be easy. As things had now stood for several years, the peoples of the liberated areas paid no taxes in 1968, neither to the Portuguese nor to the PAIGC.[3] And this had also become true, by 1966, even of the partially liberated areas or the areas still under general Portuguese military control. Even there, Portuguese economic domination embodied mainly in the more or less forced payment of various taxes – in the *cobranca* – had ceased to be possible, because, in Cabral's words,

> the colonial authorities have to tolerate this refusal to pay tax from fear
> that enforcement will cause the populations to flee into our liberated
> areas or into neighbouring countries. Even in the urban centres, inclu-
> ding the principal towns, an effective political control by the Portu-
> guese has become practically impossible by reason of the rising flood of
> refugees from the fighting regions, as well as the pressures exerted on
> these urban centres by our units.

When the war ends, however, the new state will need its own taxes; almost all the fighting units will have to return to their villages and farming life again; the normal requirements of law and order will have to be imposed and met. Only an administration growing from village roots, it was held, would be capable of carrying through this reconversion to peacetime. Only this sort of administration could avoid the perils of becoming a privileged minority, an oligarchical network, a teamwork of corrupted 'beneficiaries': in the last analysis, what Fanon called 'a racket'.

> This means [Cabral continued on the *Tres de Agosto*] that we have to
> build, and start building now, a type of administration which will be
> completely new in personnel and structure when compared with the
> apparatus of colonial times. We may take over some technical personnel
> from the colonial apparatus, though none who have exercised political
> responsibilities. But, so far as we do, these men will be placed inside a
> framework entirely different from the one in which they were formed.
>   The general approach that we have is that all structural decisions are
> to be based on the needs and condition of the peasantry, who are the

vast majority of our people. That being so, this new administration will be strictly without those chains of command familiar in colonial times — governors of provinces and so on. We do not want to copy any structures of that kind.

Above all, we want to decentralize as much as may be possible. That's one reason why we're inclined to think that Bissau will not continue to be our capital in an administrative sense. In fact, we are against the whole idea of a capital. Why shouldn't ministries be dispersed? After all, our country is a small one with passable roads, at least in the central areas. Why should we saddle ourselves with the paraphernalia of a presidential palace, a concentration of ministries, the clear signs of an emergent elite which can soon become a privileged group?[4]

As to economic policy after liberation, the priority will be on raising food production. Agriculture will come first. We haven't illusions: Guine is a small country, and comparatively a poor one. We shall remain small, and for a long time we shall remain poor. But who knows? We shall work together, we shall find new riches under the soil, we shall cultivate better. [He gestured to the silent mangrove thickets lining the bankside a hundred yards away.] Those mangroves. Nobody has yet discovered a way of using them except for timber, and we don't need much timber. But maybe mangroves have another use that hasn't been discovered? Why not? Stranger things have happened. We have countless square kilometres of mangroves. If we could make them yield something, we wouldn't be so poor. That goes for a lot of other things too.

We shall put our whole priority on agriculture. That means more than cultivation. That means realizing what people can do, can actually do. That's a question of village democracy, of village schools, of village clinics, of village co-operation. If after independence we have to stay for a while in a colonial posture from an economic standpoint, exporting raw materials and importing finished goods, it won't worry us — so long as our people can actually live better.

Living better isn't only eating better. It's a question of working conditions too. That is why we turn our face away from any policy of demanding what's called volunteer labour. Because our people don't forget the past, the past they've been living till only yesterday. Then forced labour was part of their daily life, and this volunteer labour could easily seem no different. Oh yes, I know how it goes. At the beginning with drums and enthusiasm. For a little while, all right, this demand for volunteer labour would be possible. But then the peasants would start saying to each other, What's the difference?

We hope to do a lot with producer co-operatives. But there again we haven't any illusions. It's difficult. You can do it at the beginning only with the best men you have, and the best men don't grow on every tree.

Cabral and others talk in much the same direct way about the nature of the state they can build. They see it as emerging from the revolution as embodied in the PAIGC: as being, in other words, a regular articulation of Party organs from base to central committee. In the measure that the PAIGC can achieve its revolution — apart from militarily winning the war — the PAIGC can embody a democratic State, a State which the peasants will feel most intimately as their own and for which, accordingly, they will pay taxes, return to village life, recognize the new legal framework.

'Any other approach seems mere verbalism. In our circumstances the Party equals the State because there is no other means of making the State a truly national, truly liberating organism.' This State is seen as having three elements, and only three. It will have the people who have organized themselves inside the Party or in line with the Party; it will have its armed forces, reduced from wartime size to something very small; and it will have a means of ensuring its security by a police force. This last is necessary, will remain necessary, 'because every organization supposes its opposite, every order its potential of disorder, every State its negation.' Precisely for this reason, they fear the bureaucracy of a privileged elite. Exactly for this reason, they base their hopes on the organized articulation of self-administering village committees. In realistic terms, they argue, there is no other way of preventing the growth of administrative dictatorship, no matter in how veiled a form.

And beyond the independent state, beyond nationalism?

I said: 'Pre-colonial Africa had many hundreds of independent states. Colonialism shuffled these together into some fifty colonies. These are now engaged in trying to transform themselves into as many nations. Can it possibly work?' The radio news, as I was saying this, had just given us the latest bulletin on the breakdown in Nigeria, on the secession of Biafra, on the lamentable war that was developing there. 'These nations', I continued, 'have many internal ethnic divisions. Besides, many of them are far too small to be viable as separate nations in the modern world. Their domestic markets are too narrow, their chances of accumulating capital too limited, their means of economic self-defence too feeble. How do you resolve these contradictions between ethnic separatism and nationalism, between nationalism and inter-African solidarity?'

Cabral:

> My own view is that there are no real conflicts between the peoples of Africa. There are only conflicts between their elites. When the peoples take power into their own hands, as they will do with the march of events in this continent, there will remain no great obstacles to effective African solidarity. Already we see in our own case how the various peoples in Guine are finding co-operation more and more possible and useful as they free themselves from attitudes of tribal strife — attitudes that were encouraged, directly or indirectly, by colonial rule and its consequences. My own view is that this process of integration had in fact begun before the Portuguese conquest, and that imposition of the colonial system stopped it.

* * *

Other conversations illustrate the PAIGC's conviction of how futile would be any policy of merely trying to 'melt' this small country into one or other of its neighbours. Even if this were otherwise possible, it would be seen as denying the whole purpose of the revolution here. This purpose, repeatedly insisted on, is to enable the peoples of Guine to 'realize themselves in the modern world', to lay hold of their identity as peoples belonging to a given place and unity. They are territorially divided from their neighbours by a hundred years of colonialism. They have traditions and often languages which are different from those of their neighbours. They are conducting a revolt in circumstances specific to themselves. In the process they are building a solidarity of purpose and of culture which are equally specific to themselves, even to the extension of Guine-Creole as a language national to themselves.

These peoples can therefore realize their own future, make it their own, only if they themselves command it. Commanding that future, they can then reshape and change it. They will then, the argument continues, be able to co-operate with their neighbours in organic ways, functional ways, such as can set the pattern for a wider unity. But the condition for this, too, is that there shall emerge no privileged elite, no *Interessengemeinschaft* of bureaucratic beneficiaries, no clique of WaBenzi with their bureaucratic hands in business tills, who capture this state, this emergent nation, and degrade it to an instrument serving sectional ends. For once that happens, the chances of effective inter-African unity vanish as rapidly as the chances of internal democracy. Then the hopes of radical improvement disappear into the pockets of a new 'class' of exploiters, and the vision of a new future dissolves in the fog of broken promises.

Meanwhile the PAIGC cultivate their own garden. It is clear they firmly believe that Africa can rescue itself from neo-colonialist control, can realize the hopes of political independence, only with radical changes of internal structure: in the end, no doubt, only with revolution. But 'national liberation is not for export': each people, each group of peoples, will have to make its own revolution.

Of the real position today they have judged by the amount of aid they receive from their African brethren:

> The OAU has recognized our Party as representing the unity and struggle of the people of Guine and the Cape Verdes, and has given us material and financial aid which we consider very useful.
>
> But it has to be recognized that Africa's aid is far from having a regularity, size or efficacy that would correspond to the responsibilities of the peoples of Africa, and even more of the states of Africa, towards our struggle.
>
> While it is true that many African states face economic and financial problems which must notably diminish the degree of solidarity they can show us, it is also true that other negative factors explain the growing

withdrawal of Africa from the sacrifices which our people, and indeed all anti-colonialist forces, have the right and duty to devote to the ending of Portuguese colonialism.

We remain convinced that Africa can and should do more for our struggle. Aside from our neighbours [the Republics of Guinea and Senegal], we can count on the fingers of one hand those who, in one way or other, have given or give us aid within the framework of bilateral agreements. Does this mean that for the overwhelming majority of independent African states our struggle deserves no more than verbal solidarity, or an actual indifference which in fact helps the Portuguese?[5]

While awaiting something better, the PAIGC have got on with their work.

Having proved that it can serve our people as well as serving Africa, our organization remains loyal to its wider principles: total devotion to the cause of national liberation and African unity; a rejection of political labels and sterile ideological debates; non-intervention in the affairs of others and the quarrels between others [in other words, thought and action free from any tutelage but such as can take account of the inter-dependence of interests common to all Africans]. We want to develop fraternal relations of collaboration, mutual respect and co-operation with all African countries irrespective of their politico-economic choices. And our confidence in and hopes for efficacious help from Africa are all the more reasonable in that our enemy have on their side, and with no limits, an efficacious aid from *their* allies.[6]

These words were spoken at the end of 1966. They remained just as true of African aid two years later, with the partial exception that the Liberation Committee of the Organization of African Unity, meeting at Conakry in February 1968, had moved closer to at least a recognition of the need for more effective support. It was, one might think, not before time.

References

1. Here is an actual example from PAIGC archives. It consists of orders issued by the army command for 'Operation Fanta', and signed by Amilcar Cabral, to bi-groups 3 and 4 (between 150 and 200 men in all) on the East Front during 1965 (the orders were, of course, accompanied by relevant maps):

   Phase I: Destruction of Bridge M
   Closing of roads:
      1. Road 10 (near bridge B) — comrade Sory Djalo's group will mine this road.
      2. Road 11-A (near bridge B) — comrade N'Bare Tchuda's group

will mine this road.

3. Road 11-B (near G) — comrade Kemessene Camara's group will mine this road: near T, comrade Temna Kebeque's group will mine this road.

Destruction of bridge:

Comrade Malam Sanha, with four others, one from each group.

Security on roads — Road 10: comrade Malam Numo.

Road 11-A: comrade Hilario Rodrigues.

Road 11-B: comrade Luiz Correia.

After destruction of bridge:

The bi-group Numo-Hilario will safeguard roads 10 and 11 (ambushes). The bi-group Sanha-Luiz will withdraw towards the sector of T, rest, and prepare to attack P. This attack will be carried out on the evening of the next day.

Phase 2: Attack on P

Closing of roads:

1. Road 10 — Group Sory Djalo, with Malam Numo.
2. Road 11-A — Group N'Bare Tchuda, with Hilario.
3. Road 11-B (near G) — 4 men of the group Temna Kebeque (1 light machine gun and 2 sub-machine guns).

Attack on fortified camp of P:

Groups of comrades Kemessene Camara and Temna Kebeque.

NB — The trenched camp at C will be attacked the same night (mortars commanded by comrade Cirilo).

In attacking P follow FANTA operational plan, having regard to changes imposed by the reinforcement of fighters and supplies.

After attack on P:

The bi-group Numo-Hilario will safeguard the roads leading to P.

Attack on the Trenched Camp at B.

Closing of roads:

1. Road 10 (crossroads at D) — Group of Sory Djalo, with Malam Numo.
2. Road 11-A (crossroads at C) — Group of N'Bare Tchuda, with Hilario.
3. Road 12 — five men of Group of Kemessene Camara (1 light machine gun, 2 sub-machine guns, 1 basooka).

NB — After this attack the roads will be mined.

After the attack the bi-group Numo-Hilario will continue to safeguard the roads: patrols and ambushes.

Phase 3: Liberation of OM and other *tabancas* (hamlets) of the Zone: Reinforcement of the Isolating of C.

Attack on trenched camp of OM:

Closing of roads:

1. Road 10 — Group Sory Djalo, with Malam Numo.
2. Road 11-A — Group N'Bare Tchuda, with Hilario.
3. Road 12 — Group Samba Seydi of the first Sub-section, with Pedro Ramos.

Attack on trenched camp of OM:
Group of Temna Kebeque, with Malam Sanha. Group of Kemessene Camara, with Luiz Correia.
Liberation of other tabancas:
Follow plan for safeguard of roads to P and B — bi-group Numo.

Phase 4: Co-ordinate with other forces to attack C.

Phase 5: Co-ordinate with other forces to liberate all *tabancas* of zone and totally isolate BT.

Phase 6: Co-ordinate with other forces to attack BT.

NB — Co-ordination of forces in phases 4, 5 and 6 will be directed by comrade Domingos Ramos.

2.   F. Fanon, *The Wretched of the Earth*, Penguin, London, 1967, pp.119, 120.

3.   The PAIGC are careful to explain to people in the liberated zones the reasons why they are asked to pay no taxes during the war. They would also, I think, point out that, in fact, the people do contribute, and voluntarily, in giving food supplies, the porterage of war material, the building of military installations, schools, clinics, and so on.

4.   *Insertion of 1980:* But these ideas were not to be followed after 1975. There was then much concentration on and in Bissau, the capital; and at the 1977 party congress there was also much well-based rural criticism of this concentration, criticism which, it seems, had no real effect.

5.   A. Cabral, *Report* for 1966.

6.   *Ibid.*

8. With What Wider Meaning?

*During my lifetime I have dedicated myself to this struggle
of the African people. I have fought against White domination, and I have fought against Black domination. I have
cherished the ideal of a democratic and free society in which
all persons live together in harmony and with equal opportunities. It is an ideal which I hope to live for and to
achieve. But if needs be, it is an ideal for which I am
prepared to die.*
NELSON MANDELA[1]

Portugal has refused to decolonize Guine 'because it might set a precedent for
Angola and Mozambique', noted an article in the *Economist* during April
1968. Now the precedent looked like being not withdrawal but defeat:

> Recently, President Americo Thomaz was produced in Bissau city and
> flown to three safe military outposts in Fula country. Communiques
> said the visit showed the PAIGC had no power at all. In answer, the
> nationalists breached the bristling fortress of Bissau island and
> bazookaed Bissau airport. . . .

The PAIGC offered some details in a communique of 5 March 1968:

> Carrying out a decision of our Council of War in line with our actions
> against the bases and fortified camps of the colonialists, on 28 February
> at 23.30 hours a commando of our army mortared the Portuguese
> airforce base at the airport of Bissau, ten kilometres from the colonial
> capital.
>   Also using bazookas, our fighters destroyed the control tower, three
> hangars and two aircraft, damaging as well several other aircraft. Our
> men withdrew without loss. The action was well prepared, and is of
> especial political and military value to our struggle.

Reproduced in the outside world, this communique gave rise to controversy.

After all, if these nationalists could with impunity attack the very centre of Portuguese control in Guine, and at a time when the Portuguese had a relatively enormous army in the colony, Lisbon's continued claims to have the situation 'under control' became most patently ridiculous.

I reported it, for example, in an article in the weekly journal *West Africa.* This drew a reply from Mr J. Biggs-Davison, a Conservative Member of Parliament who had just returned from his third visit to the Portuguese in Guine since the war began there. This little controversy retains its interest. Mr Biggs-Davison questioned the veracity of the communique. 'True, more than two months have passed since February,' he wrote, 'and the Portuguese could have made good the damage. Nevertheless, there were no signs of any new repairs to the control tower, and I was able to inspect them more closely than guerrillas operating long range mortars.'[2]

In a later letter, however, Mr Biggs-Davison had a little more to say on the subject, and the little more, in the circumstances, was not without interest. 'I never said', he wrote, 'that it [the communique] was false. I do say that it was grossly exaggerated. The damage done was minimal.'[3] Yet it is not so difficult to believe that major damage to absolutely vital military installations, such as the PAIGC reported, can be converted into 'minimal' damage by two months' intensive work. The Second World War and later wars have offered countless examples of such 'miraculous repair'.

At the same time Mr Biggs-Davison performed another service. Some viewers in Britain who had watched a Granada TV film,[4] shown on 2 April 1968, were inclined to question the credentials of the attack on the fortified camp at Buba, south of the middle Corubal river, launched in the presence of the Granada team. These doubts arose largely, it appeared, from the circumstance that no Portuguese had been good enough to show himself in front of the camp buildings before, during or after the attack. This absence was scarcely surprising, since Buba had been attacked with mortars and small arms on two recent occasions as well as often in the more remote history of the war. The front of those buildings was not a place that any sensible Portuguese would visit if he could help it. So the buildings looked empty, and it was gratuitously if rather absurdly argued that the whole engagement had been 'mocked up' for the benefit of a TV team without scruples.

As it happened, this particular team had every scruple, and would certainly not have lent themselves to a dishonest film. Nor would the PAIGC have, in any case, connived at dishonesty. They take their war too seriously to play about with fakes. Still, it was hard to prove that the attacked buildings actually contained Portuguese. Mr Biggs-Davison came to the rescue. During his visit, he was taken by the Portuguese to Buba and was able to inspect the results of the attack. On this he wrote in his first letter to *West Africa:*

> It may also interest Mr Davidson to know that the attack on Buba, filmed by Granada Television for which I believe he acted as programme adviser, resulted in civilian casualties and one African woman was killed. I saw for myself the damage that was done to civilian homes. Did

> Mr Davidson realise that Buba houses a civilian population as well as a garrison? Or are civilians expendable in the ideological war against Portugal?

To which I replied:

> I can well believe there were civilian casualties, and we all regret it. But civilian casualties are unfortunately inseparable from war. I think the PAIGC tries hard to keep them to a minimum – unlike the Portuguese who bomb with napalm and high explosive villages and peasants working in their fields.

I also suggested, so far without reply, that Mr Biggs-Davison tell us the count of Portuguese casualties lifted out by the helicopters which the Granada team saw arriving and departing after the attack. On their side, I added, the PAIGC unit accompanied by the Granada team had six walking wounded.[5]

Attacks such as these on fortified posts multiplied after the end of the rains in December 1967. Ten months later, as the (original version of this) book went to press, the military position was much as described in the map on p.vii. About two thirds of the country was now under PAIGC control. The summer had brought many successes, including the forced evacuation by the Portuguese of ten fortified camps. Scarcely a day now went by without effective operations against the Portuguese, whether on land or water, in the small area not yet taken from the enemy. Thus the communique for the period only between 15 July and 3 August gave details of no fewer than eighteen large attacks on fortified garrisons. Furthermore, in a broadcast of 3 August, on Radio Libertacao, good progress was also claimed by Cabral in the Cape Verde Islands. There 'we have made a great advance in the political field, and are getting ready to pass into a new phase of struggle. Throughout the islands the interest in and support for the cause of liberation of our people daily grows larger. . . .'[6]

In this period, too, the PAIGC began taking more Portuguese prisoners than in 1966-7.

> On 10 April [ran one of their communiques of this time] at 23.30 hours a unit of our regular army attacked the colonialist barracks of Santa Cunda in the sector of Candjambari Northern Front, and forced the surrender of the Portuguese garrison. Four enemy soldiers were killed in action and eleven others taken prisoner; the remainder fled. Apart from this, our units captured one 60 mm. mortar, one 3.5 mm. bazooka, fifteen machine guns of the G3 type, fifteen Mauser rifles, one radio transmitter and a big stock of grenades and various ammunition.
>> Here are the identities of the captured Portuguese soldiers:
>> Sgt No. D8865/64 Jose Neto Vaz
>> Cpl No. 23785/66 Jose Manuel Moreira Duarte

Cpl No. 15339/66 Jose da Silva Morais
Pte No. 22697/66 Antonio Angelo Duarte
Pte No. 35357/67 David Gouveia Pedras
Pte No. 15228/66 Luiz Salvador Antunes de Almeida Vieira
Pte No. 24814/66 Domingos Noversa da Costa
Pte No. 31599/66 Luiz dos Santos Marques
Pte No. 51525/66 Joao da Costa Sousa
Pte No. 04927/64 Francisco Gomes da Silva
Pte No. 22535/66 Jose dos Santos Teixeira

All the above were members of Company 1690 of the Colonial Army.

In line with our Party principles, these new prisoners will be treated according to international convention.

A few weeks earlier, three other Portuguese prisoners had been set free in Senegal. Speaking on that occasion in the presence of the chairman of the Senegalese Red Cross, during a brief ceremony, Cabral took the opportunity to offer some remarks on PAIGC policy in this respect.

This gesture of freeing three captured Portuguese soldiers, he said, was

a corollary of a fundamental principle of our Party and our struggle. We are not fighting against the Portuguese people, against individual Portuguese or against Portuguese families. We have taken up arms to free the soil of our country from a shameful colonial rule, without ever confusing the Portuguese people with Portuguese colonialism.

Taking account of the situation as it now is, as well as of the fact that this is the first time we make this liberating gesture with the aid of the Senegalese Red Cross and the International Red Cross, we should like to add the following declaration:

At this very moment the Portuguese colonialists will continue their barbarous crimes against our people in defiance of the most elementary principles of morality and international law.

The Chairman of our Party, Rafael Barbosa, is still in solitary confinement at Bissau after six years of imprisonment without legal charge or judgement. Hundreds of Guinean and Cape Verdian patriots continue to suffer inhuman conditions in the colonial political prisons and concentration camps of the Island of Galinhas (Guine) and of Tarrafal (Cape Verde). These patriots have been tortured by the PIDE (Salazar's political police), and others have been murdered.

Soldiers of our armed forces when captured by colonialist troops are usually executed at once. Others are tortured and forced to say things which the colonial authorities can use in their propaganda. In their vain but no less criminal attempt at genocide, the colonialist Portuguese carry out daily acts of terror against the peaceful populations of our liberated areas, especially against women, children and old people. They bombard and machine-gun our people. They reduce villages to ashes. They burn harvests with bombs of different kinds, especially fragmentation, napalm and phosphorus bombs.

We for our part are freeing prisoners who, like their fellow prisoners whom we still hold, have enjoyed the conditions laid down by international law. In doing this, we wish to call world attention to the crimes that are perpetrated against our country by the colonialist Portuguese — crimes which they could not commit without the political and material aid of their allies.

Cabral concluded by observing that this liberating of three prisoners could be interpreted as a sign of good will.

But it will not be the same towards the government of Portugal, which continues to arrogate to itself 'the right and the duty', together with the racist regimes of southern Africa and by means of terror, napalm, and the most revolting crimes against Africans, of defending Western and Christian civilization on our continent.

As reported by the official Senegalese News Agency, the chairman of the Senegalese Red Cross, M. Rito Alcantara, then expressed his satisfaction at being able to help in the release of three young soldiers, each twenty-three years old, whose families in Lisbon, he added, were already informed. The same source noted that the three men in question were Pte No. 202/65 Jose Veira Lauro, of Company 1423, captured on 6 October 1965 in the sector of Fulacunda (South Front); Pte No. 192/65 Eduardo Dias Veira, captured on 22 December 1965, in the Sector of Gabu (East Front); and Pte No. 669/67 Manuel Fragata Francisco of Company 1690, captured in the Bafata Sector (North Front). Having decided to make their gesture and demonstrate their humane treatment of Portuguese prisoners, it was very like the PAIGC to release one prisoner from *each* of their main fighting fronts. It rubbed in once again the truth of their military claims.

* * *

What was the further outlook towards the end of 1968?

Objectives of the PAIGC — and for obvious reasons no details were offered — continued along previous lines. They were, on the military side, to step up attacks on all fixed Portuguese positions; to move road ambushes closer to the bigger urban centres, including the capital itself; and, generally, to maintain their pressure while seldom embarking on hand-to-hand assaults which could mean heavy casualties in their own ranks. To those who remarked that this strategy must prolong the war, they were inclined to ask what advantage would accrue to them from a different strategy? Given the need for time to train craftsmen and technicians at many levels, what could be worth the casualties that their troops would suffer by full-scale assault tactics? Or again, given their gradual gaining of the upper hand, what arguments could convince peasant soldiers that a strategy of total assault would be preferable to one of steady and successful pressure?

In gauging the answer to such questions, one has to remember once again the almost total lack of 'development' in Guine in terms of modern education, familiarity with sophisticated weapons, or elementary technical training. It is here that parallels with Vietnam and Cuba clearly break down. The PAIGC greatly admired the Vietnamese and Cubans, and valued their fraternal solidarity; but the PAIGC were confronted with a very different situation. Compared with Guine, Vietnam and Cuba were industrially and technically advanced societies. Moreover, the population of Cuba was ten times, and that of Vietnam twenty times, the size of the population of Guine; and while the Portuguese army in Guine may not be as well armed as that of the United States in South Vietnam, the fact remained that in proportionate terms it was numerically as large or even larger. In 1968 the army of the PAIGC could not possibly emulate the Vietcong in their Tet offensive against 100 cities of South Vietnam, in their firepower, or in their capacity to take casualties. For all its mobility, the war of the PAIGC had to remain true to its guerrilla nature.

The great achievements of the PAIGC have lain precisely in their ability to demonstrate that a technologically very backward African people can in fact challenge, and successfully challenge, a colonial power far superior in the number of its troops and the weight of their equipment; and that this can be done by revolutionary warfare in which political objectives, social objectives, remain always in command of strategy.

Cabral had reviewed all this in his long report of December 1966:

> Our central aim is to develop and intensify the war in its three fundamental aspects: political action, armed action, and national reconstruction.
>
> To do this, mainly we must:
>
> (a) Continually improve and extend our political work among the mass of people and in the fighting units, and at all costs preserve our national unity.
>
> (b) Continue to strengthen the organization, discipline and democracy of our Party, adapt it continually to the evolution of the war, make good its mistakes, and ensure strict application by our militants, whether or not in positions of command, of the principles which direct our struggle.
>
> (c) Improve the organization of our armed forces, intensify our action on each of the fighting fronts, and extend the co-ordination of our military operations.
>
> (d) Increase the isolation of the enemy's troops, hit them decisively, and destroy the moments of calm which they still enjoy in certain urban centres.
>
> (e) Defend our liberated regions from terrorizing attacks by the enemy, and guarantee our liberated populations the calm they need for productive work.

(f) Find better solutions for the economic, administrative, social and cultural problems of the liberated areas, increase farming production, develop craft-industry, lay foundations for at least rudimentary industrial production, and continue to improve our health and education services.

(g) Accelerate the training of *cadres*.

(h) Oppose and remove tendencies to opportunism, parasitism, careerism and any deviation from the general line drawn by our Party in the service of our people.

(i) Strengthen and extend our relations with African peoples, states and organizations, tighten the fraternal ties which link us to our neighbours and to the peoples of the other Portuguese colonies.

(j) Strengthen relations of straight-forward collaboration with anti-colonialists and anti-imperialists so as to achieve a useful co-operation in this common struggle against imperialism, colonialism, and racism.

In a struggle for national liberation, no organization would be so rash as to fix, in advance, a date for independence. But we think that we have already travelled the greater part of the long road to liberation, and have passed the most painful stages of it. . . .

For the immediate future, the fate of the Salazar regime was obviously of critical importance.[7]

On our side [Cabral said on board the *Tres de Agosto*], we are perfectly ready to negotiate a peaceful withdrawal of the Portuguese from Guine. But the Salazar regime are now in a painful dilemma. They cannot recover control of Guine. And yet they dare not cut their losses here, as some of them would like to, and sue for the best terms they can get, because in doing so they would undermine their positions in Angola and Mozambique.

The dilemma remained difficult. Towards the end of 1967, it seemed clear that influential voices were being raised in Lisbon favouring a withdrawal from Guine. Such voices were evidently in a minority. Yet they were evidently, too, powerful enough to induce the regime to send out its President, Americo Thomaz, on a state visit in February 1968 as a demonstration of 'no surrender' and a blow at the 'party of withdrawal'. One may note, however, that the relevant arguments for abandonment of colonial positions in Guine were much stronger than any for withdrawal from Mozambique and Angola, not only because of the relative size of these countries and their comparatively far greater value to the Portuguese balance of payments and company profits, but also because Portugal had no settlers in Guine.

This Salazarist dilemma underlined the close political and military links which tied the war in Guine to Portugal's other colonial wars in Mozambique and Angola, and indeed to the whole balance of power in southern Africa.

No one can doubt [Cabral observed in December 1966], neither among our own people nor among any other African people, that this war of national liberation in which we are engaged is a war which belongs to the whole of Africa.

Though engaged in a war of national liberation, essentially a war of revolutionary nationalism, Cabral and his leading comrades never in fact forgot this wider dimension. They were internationalists, and resolutely so. Just how strongly they linked the liberation of their own countries — Guinea-Bissau and Cape Verde — with the liberation of Portugal's other colonies was to be shown very strikingly in 1974.[8] There could be no question, they had long decided, of allowing the Portuguese to cut their losses in Guinea-Bissau so as better to concentrate their forces in Angola and Mozambique. And just how clearly the leaders of the PAIGC connected their own struggles with the wider and different struggles of the non-colonial world could be seen again, and in example after example, by their bid for solidarity with progressive groups and organizations even in the countries governed by the allies of their colonial enemy. This was a wise tactic; it was also a statement of principle.

Yet the organic connexion between the struggle of the PAIGC and the further outlook in Africa could also be seen, even as early as 1968, from other angles as well.

Cabral as well as several others had been able to travel quite widely, by 1968, in search of material aid in Africa and Europe. Mostly, they travelled on diplomatic passports supplied by the government of Guinea (that is, ex-French Guinea) and Algeria, though one or two other African governments also helped them in this way. In travelling, they listened and learned, emerging from the intellectual isolation which the Portuguese system had imposed on them. Returning, they pooled their impressions and reached judgements which became a regular form of internal guidance. Talking to Cabral and others, one could well see that they had a shrewd idea of what was going forward, whether among their friends or among their enemies, and whether in Africa or anywhere else. On all this they were generally willing to say little, and even that in confidence. But it could be noticed that many of their private judgments caused them to strengthen their policy of non-alignment.

Tactically, again, this was wise. But in its essential principle it was also a statement of their conviction that no people can be liberated except by their own efforts, means and understanding. Guinea-Bissau and Cape Verde had to make their own social revolutions; no-one else could prescribe for them. It was another aspect of Cabral's strength as a marxist thinker and activist that he never supposed that any established doctrine, methodology, or set of rules drawn up by other peoples in other circumstances, making other revolutions, could be valid for general application. Talking over the sub-title of this book with him I suggested *Aspects of an African Revolution:* would that be appropriate? 'Yes,' he said, 'of *an* African revolution, that's all right.'

Yet this insistence on the specificity of each people's reality and chance of revolution proved no obstacle to reaching a number of general conclusions.

Some of these concerned the condition already widely known as 'neo-colonial'. Part of the outlook in 1968 was the widespread incidence of that condition. Colonies had become nominally independent. They had raised their own flags and composed their own anthems. They had established their own governments, administrations, diplomatic services. But very obviously they had still far to go before their independence could become real. Their old masters, chiefly Britain or France (and France, it must be said, much more insistently than Britain), remained in power behind the scenes, dominated their economies and influenced their foreign policies, together with the new but relentless drive of the USA.

Cabral was never led by all this into thinking that the 'first independences' had not been worth fighting for and winning. On the contrary, he held to the view that those 'first independences', no matter what their outcome, were necessary and therefore positive prelude to any further liberation of the continent from its colonial condition. Kwame Nkrumah was living in Conakry during these years. Cabral knew him well and admired him. At Nkrumah's death, some years later, he was to praise him as *the* great figure in the fight against 'classical colonialism'; and, for Cabral, there was nothing in the least 'tactical' about that.

Still it was abundantly clear to these men and women of the PAIGC that the general condition of much of independent Africa, in 1968 (if not earlier), reinforced their belief in the need to carry on their own struggle in such a way, and until, they were sure of being able to take over their two countries without, at the same time, having to take over any kind of neo-colonial system. Though careful not to claim an exemplary role which others should then copy or follow, they saw that their success in being able to achieve a complete and untrammelled sovereignty, even in countries as small and relatively poor and backward as Guinea-Bissau and Cape Verde, must be a powerful aid to all those, elsewhere, who were caught in the neo-colonial trap and were trying, however vainly so far, to find a way out of it. They believed that their struggle for a revolutionary outcome – revolutionary, that is, against the whole colonial condition – possessed an international value.

They were sure of this, by 1968, in another African dimension: in the wider struggle against racist regimes in the southern regions of the continent. Here lay a part of their reasons for unswerving solidarity with FRELIMO in Mozambique and MPLA in Angola, although other ties of common suffering and experience also reinforced that solidarity. If the peoples of the Portuguese colonies could win their liberation without compromise, then the outlook in Southern Africa would become very different. So they paid a close attention, as far as they had the time and opportunity, to what was going on in Rhodesia (now Zimbabwe), Namibia and South Africa. And they laboured, in such ways as they could find, to help the liberation movements that were taking shape in those countries.

It was not an immediate prospect that looked very promising. If FRELIMO and MPLA had already organized and fought their way to strong positions in Mozambique and Angola, the same was by no means true of Zimbabwe, where an armed struggle had begun in 1966, two years earlier, with no good results. The cause of liberation was at that time correspondingly weak in Namibia, while as to what was happening inside South Africa there was little that could be surely known. Yet even within that perspective the history of the PAIGC could have its useful lessons. In 1959, when Cabral and his comrades had decided to prepare for armed action, their effective cadres had numbered only a few dozen men and women. Even in 1963, when they embarked on their first actions on any scale (small acts of sabotage had been carried out in 1962), PAIGC units could by no means count upon a welcome everywhere. But what they had been able to do, gradually, was to build a sufficient political base in peasant support, convert that support into participation, and on that basis, extend and grow. On this analogy, the situation south of the Zambezi, and even the much more difficult situation south of the Limpopo, could begin to wear a very different look from the blandly confident assessments of the racist rulers.

It was a point of view, moreover, that began to be heard more widely in this period. What a spokesman of the African National Congress of South Africa had to say in this connexion, in 1968, may be well worth quoting here. He pointed out that:

> The 1950s and 1960s witnessed four impressive nation-wide general strikes all called by the ANC and its allies. The significance of these strikes should not be underestimated. On each occasion, hundreds of thousands of urban workers risked their jobs and their consequent right to remain in an urban area, in quest not of reforms, not for better working conditions, but in response to a purely political call to demonstrate a demand for votes, opposition to racial laws, and so on. In the face of repression, Trade Union organization was minimal — and the above responses were important pointers to the high level of political consciousness which a half-century of urbanization combined with vigorous political leadership had inculcated into the townspeople.
>
> There are many more examples to be found in the '50s and '60s which illustrate the capacity of those in the urban areas to react impressively to calls for action involving both tenacity and sacrifice: the Defiance Campaign of 1952-53, the bus boycotts of the late '50s, women's resistance against extension of pass laws to women, the pre-Sharpeville anti-pass campaigns.
>
> And what of the people in the countryside, which is the focal point of guerrilla activity in the initial stages? Here, too, there is convincing evidence of a peasantry which, despite centuries of intensive repression, lacks submissiveness. In the very recent past and in many important areas, it has demonstrated a capacity for action to the point of armed resistance. In Sekhukhuniland (Transvaal) in the late '50s the peasantry, partly armed, doggedly resisted the attempts by the authorities to replace the traditional leaders of the people with government-appointed servants, so-called Bantu Authorities. In Zululand similar resistance was

encountered. The most intense point of peasant resistance and upsurge was amongst the Pondo in the Transkei. By March 1960 a vast popular movement had arisen, unofficial administrative units were set up including people's courts. From the chosen spots in the mountains, where thousands of peasants assembled illegally, came the name of the movement — 'Intaba', The Mountain. Although this revolt had its origin in local grievances, the aim of the resistance soon became the attainment of basic political ends, and it came to adopt the full programme of the ANC.

What is also significant about many of these actions in the countryside is that despite the traditionally strict legal sanction against the possession by non-whites of any arms or ammunition, they always manage on appropriate occasions to emerge with an assortment of prohibited weapons in their hands.

These, then, are pointers to the validity of the claim by the ANC that the African majority of the country can be expected to respond in growing numbers to a lead which holds out real prospects of destroying white supremacy, albeit in a long and protracted war. The conviction held by all African political groupings (except those sponsored by the government) that the white state can be shifted by nothing short of violence, reflects what is today both an incontrovertible objective fact and a belief held by a majority of ordinary people both in town and countryside.[9]

These clearly careful words might prove right or wrong. What could not be reasonably contested, now on the eve of the 1970s, was the double-pronged thesis on which they were based: first, that nothing but a violent form of self-defence could advance or even save the cause of African equality in Southern and perhaps Central Africa as well; secondly, that this reactive violence, begun after long years of passive or constitutional pressures which had proved fruitless, need not face a hopeless future.

Such was the perspective in which the various angles of internationalism came together. One should perhaps emphasise the influence of the 'neo-colonial spectacle' on the thinking of the PAIGC. Internally, they even had a term of contempt, 'to Malawi-ise' (having in mind Malawi's subjection), for anyone who was ready to sell the hopes of a genuine independence in exchange for minor gains. It was clear to them in 1968, one should perhaps insist, that the reformist regimes of the 'decolonization' period had largely failed to solve the basic problems of development: the problems, that is, of uniting and enthusing the efforts of Africa's rural millions so as to realize those human and productive potentials whose deployment can alone make good the hopes of independence. As things stood, much of independent Africa was in deepening confusion. Only new approaches, new policies, new leaderships could with some exceptions now expect to find the mass response that was required.

In this unpromising situation, it may be one of history's greater ironies that help should come from where least expected: that it should be the peoples of the Portuguese colonies – longest colonized, most harried, least 'developed' – who are among those most effectively pointing the way ahead. No doubt it is true that we are only at the beginning of a long development. Yet it will be hard to think that political approaches, methods and solutions such as those adopted by the PAIGC and their companions of the MPLA and FRELIMO may not prove decisive in tackling the rugged problems of achieving self-sacrifice and unity during the years ahead. The men and women of the PAIGC and their companions showed no sign of wishing to extol their virtues to the rest of Africa. But they drew attention to what they were able to do and how they were able to do it.

What the leaders of the PAIGC have said, in effect, is that they took the road of radical structural change, of revolutionary politics within the context of their own country, because no other road lay open to them except continued surrender; that having taken this road they laboured for years among the rural people of Guine until these hard-bitten farmers had made the PAIGC their own movement, their own vehicle to the future, that with this achievement the PAIGC have been able to evoke and canalize mass unity and individual sacrifice – not only and not even mainly towards fighting the Portuguese, but above all towards opening the way for basic and far-reaching mental and political adjustment to the needs and opportunities of the modern world.

In some words of the Cuban Theses presented at Havana in 1966, this scope and depth of radical change, of necessary change, 'calls for great practical experience in warfare, and for great political talent in conducting that warfare.' The Cubans were thinking of Latin America. Thinking of Africa, one may perhaps conclude that the men and women of the PAIGC are to be counted among those, up and down the wide world of these embattled years, who have most clearly shown what this kind of experience and talent can really do – no matter how great the odds against them – to give harried and despairing peoples a new and vital source of life and hope.

Insertion of 1980: And there, with the gains secured early in 1968, I had to end the first version of this book. Save for a little updating here and there, I have left that first version just as it was written. Yet the liberation process was far from complete in 1968; and its further course and outcome were going to prove still more dramatic and extraordinary, still more successful, even than its origins and early development.

Many observers visited the PAIGC in the next few years. I myself returned briefly in 1968 so as to help John Sheppard make his memorable Granada *World in Action* documentary, 'A Group of Terrorists Attacked. . .' (a satirical title which Cabral, incidentally, particularly enjoyed). Later in 1968 I attended the second congress of FRELIMO, held in Northern Mozambique that July, and in 1970 travelled in some of the fighting zones of the MPLA in the eastern Angolan province of Moxico. In 1972 it was time to return to the PAIGC; the opportunity came towards the end of that year.

References

1. Concluding words of Mandela's final speech of defence at his trial in June 1964: quoted here from . . . *I Am Prepared to Die*, Christian Action pamphlet, London, n.d.
2. *West Africa*, 1 June 1968.
3. Ibid., 29 June 1968.
4. This was John Sheppard's brilliantly achieved 'A Group of Terrorists Attacked . . .'
5. *Insertion of 1980:* Buba, as it happens, had a strong garrison because of its tactical position in relation to forest trails, and was repeatedly attacked for the same reasons. I went there after the war. Two regimental monuments of the Portuguese armed forces were still in place within the garrison buildings, listing the names of personnel killed here. On the first of these monuments, for 1966-68, I counted fifty-one names of the dead; on the second, for the years 1969-71, I counted forty-nine. A hundred men lost, not counting the wounded, in six years. . . and there were several dozen garrisons of an importance comparable with Buba, and as often attacked by the PAIGC.
6. Six months earlier, reporting on 1967, Cabral had noted that the Portuguese in the Cape Verde Islands, 'alarmed by the progress of our Party in 1967, have strengthened their repressive apparatus and unleashed a large operation against the nationalists. Hundreds of patriots have been persecuted or arrested, others deported to Portugal, Angola or Mozambique.
   'These repressive measures have only concentrated the attention of the island populations on the fact of struggle, unmasked the true face of Portuguese colonialism, and nourished the hatred and political consciousness of patriots . . . united round our Party. We have developed clandestine organization in the main islands and prepared the way for struggle at a higher level, so as to enable our people to reply to the violence of the colonialists. . . .
   'This is all the more necessary since the liberation of Guine will not be real so long as the Cape Verde Islands remain a Portuguese base. Given their strategic importance, the liberation of the Islands can even be said to be indispensable to the struggle of the peoples of Angola, Mozambique and South Africa (the aerodrome on Sal Island being a South African base), and to the consolidation of the security of the independent states of West Africa. . . .'
7. Salazar himself was taken critically ill in October 1968 and was succeeded as head of government by Professor Caetano, whose initial programme was to carry on exactly as before. He did so until overthrown in April 1974.
8. See Ch. 12, p.149.
9. J. Slovo, in *Sechaba*, London, May 1968.

9. Carrying Through: 1968–72

'Mon pa mas que grandi e ka na tapa ceu'
'No fist is big enough to hide the sky'

Peasant saying (in Guine Creole)

It is a saying that Cabral particularly liked. He used to apply it to setbacks of
muddle or misunderstanding with all the glee of a man for whom the dry wit
of village humour was a source of strength. He also used to apply it, without
laughter, in its other sense: in its sense of absolute defiance of whatever new
outrage the fury of colonial repression might devise. The fist might be huge
and ruthless; the sky was broader still.

I am remembering it now, on this evening of November 1972. I am tired
this evening – with some reason, after all, for it's my fifty-eighth birthday.
But even the others, who are young, are tired. Yet age and being tired don't
really signify, can't signify. The war is nine years old and the war is being
won; but the war continues. Tired or not, the PAIGC is carrying through.

'Sharp and fine evening light. Good going since 2 p.m. High tide, so not
much mud . . .' You make laconic notes along the way because you're tired,
or there's no long halt, or there's no light to see by, or because you simply
can't be bothered: but the main thing, in any case, is to get down the key
words that can serve as memory's marker-buoys. Then, afterwards, you can
come back and haul on them and find the cable you have made draws up the
past.

The key word in that cable, just now, is not in doubt. *Mud.*

To move about the seaboard zones of these great forests, forked by ocean
creeks or farmed in sodden plains of rice that push away one woodland
border from another with miles of dyke and paddy, you must endure a wilderness of mud. Usually you must walk along the slithering ridge of little dykes,
very hard to see at night; and often you must wade. At low tide along the
creeks, canoes can be reached or left only through swamps of seemingly
bottomless mud.

The peasants do not mind any of this. Whether they carry burdens on their
heads or weapons on their shoulders, they float across these shores of mud
with a barefoot elegance of levitation. The booted visitor plods and then,

121

knee-deep, is stuck. Made presently aware, the peasants come floating back again and help him out.

Today we have taken canoes wherever necessary and walked and talked, and before sundown we have come out of the trees to the ocean creek which divides the liberated island of Como from the mainland in the southern liberated zone of Cubucare. For days we have been meeting the peasants of Como —Vasco Cabral, a PAIGC veteran leader, and myself with him — and now we are on the long journey back again. All this big southern area — Como, Cubucare, Tombali, Balana, Quitafine — forms the oldest liberated zone. Here the revolution in people's lives has been taking shape since 1964. No enemy soldier has set foot on Como since memorable battles in that already distant year. There has been much for me to learn.

Reaching the edge of the water, there's now a little time to rest before the canoes can be assembled. A long sleeve of darkness divides us from the distant shadow of the mainland and the rest of the trail to be marched before dawn. The sky is clear above this ocean creek, for the rains of 1972 are almost over; and beyond the creek, where they glow like luminous mushrooms in the night, we can see the lights of Spinola's garrisons at Catio and Bedanda on one side, and at Cabedu and Cacine on the other: they are like small white circles on the skyline.

We sit around the verandah of a large village house, a group of a dozen or so PAIGC fighters, two or three local political workers, Vasco and myself. Somewhere behind us the sun falls into the western ocean, very quickly as it happens in the tropics; and then, almost from one moment to the next, the air is cool and even cold with the breath of a long night ahead. We lean against one another, and are grateful when daughters of the house offer bowls of rice and roasted chicken legs. There is warm companionship, war's only immediate compensation.

Not far away, perhaps fifteen kilometres as the local pelicans go (more or less straight, zooming along like small white fly-bombs), an artillery battle is in progress. The conscientious Arafane Mane, who is in charge of our party, explains it to me. It is like this. The Portuguese commander and colonial governor, General Antonio Spinola, has his chief strongpoint in these parts at the little town of Catio, just below one of the white 'mushrooms' we can see. Mostly, Spinola can supply this garrison at Catio only by sea, for the forest roads are all cut by the PAIGC; but at Cufar, some eight kms from Catio, Spinola also has an airstrip big enough to take supply planes based on his big military airport of Bissalanca in the capital of Bissau. Only there's a problem for him: the link between Catio and Cufar is a narrow dirt road, and the PAIGC regularly landmine it, so the link is weak and unreliable.

Just now Spinola is preparing a big offensive against this liberated zone — it is going to be his last, though he doesn't yet know this — and he wants more than ever to use his airstrip at Cufar to send in fresh troops and supplies. To this end his men are trying to tar the Catio-Cufar road. If they can do that, they can much reduce the danger of landmining, and they can move fast along the road. Well aware of all these things, the troops of the PAIGC have set themselves to prevent the road from being tarred.

This particular contest will continue for the rest of my time in the zone. It is just one of those countless 'incidents' that lie along the route of a protracted war. It matters enormously at this moment, yet afterwards nobody will much remember it, not even those who took part in it. Day after day, now, it follows a familiar course.

Late in the afternoon, two or three jet-bombers of the Fiat-91 type (manufactured initially for the North Atlantic Treaty powers, and then sold to the Portuguese dictatorship by the West German Government) appear from Bissalanca, on the barbed-wire outskirts of Bissau. These drop their bombs into the forest around the Catio-Cufar road, and then again swoop back and forth while firing off their cannon in the same blind way. I have watched them doing it. Their pilots are reduced to hitting at random because they do not know the location of the PAIGC units in the bush. They hit blindly and go away. Then, at sundown, the PAIGC units move in and set up their mortars and bombard those garrisons at Catio and Cufar, as well as anything worth hitting on the road between. For this they use bazookas as well as mortars and, when they have it, the fearsome *grad* (as the PAIGC call their Soviet-made 122 mm. rocket). This *grad* can be distinguished from far away by the sharp roar of its explosion. They have it this evening, and we can hear it.

'That's Tchu-Tchu,' says Arafane, 'giving them something to think about.' He means Commandant Constantino Teixeira, who commands in these parts.

But now it is time for us to cross. Our peasant host is also in charge of all boat movements on this side of the ocean creek; that is his especial duty as a member of the Como defence militia. He is a local rice farmer with a lively grin, and now he comes to say that the canoes are ready. 'Years ago,' says Arafane, 'when the Portuguese tried to push us out of Como, back in 1964, this was the man who always managed to paddle across to the mainland, and back again, with ammunition.' I haven't time to get his story; it's another among the many that I fail to get for lack of time. Guerrilla warfare repeatedly gives with one hand only to take back with the other: marvellous opportunities for information, but deprived of any time to use them.

The canoes are at the brink of a merciful tide that covers swathes and swamps of mud. Silently we embark and paddle upon mirrors of grey water that are lit now by a failing moon and the distant glow of enemy garrisons, a routine journey without incident and also quite without the 'romance' which somehow, by a vast misunderstanding, seems to have got itself attached to the idea of guerrilla warfare. In a little while we shall disembark on the other side and plunge again into the cold reality of mud and weariness. There is a lot of mud on the other side, high tide or no. There is no romance.

The boats go swiftly with the paddling of tried arms and hands, but the tide is against us and running hard. For me, at least, it seems to be a kind of pause for reflection. Sixteen years after the six men began the journey of the PAIGC, where has the movement got to on this eve of 1973?

* * *

On the military side the PAIGC continued after 1964 to apply the strategy
laid down by Cabral, although with better military means after 1966:

> In order to dominate a given zone, the enemy is obliged to disperse his
> forces. In dispersing his forces, he weakens himself and we can defeat
> him. Then in order to defend himself against us, he has to concentrate
> his forces. When he does that, we can occupy the zones that he leaves
> free, and work in them politically so as to hinder his return there.[1]

But 1968 proved that military as well as political progress could be made from
this 'back and forth' motion, both in reducing the enemy's command of
terrain, and in further undermining his morale. With this progress, the political
and so once again the military capacity of the PAIGC and its whole supporting
and participatory movement could be repeatedly advanced. Looking back,
even from as close as 1972, it was already possible to see that 1968 marked
the point at which the colonial power lost its war in Guinea-Bissau, even if
its power and will to inflict damage and destruction remained as great as ever.
  Ever prudent in prophecy, Cabral felt able in January 1972 to write a
communique surveying the recent past, which remarked that

> the activity of the Portuguese colonialists continues to be dominated
> by this truth, so often recognized by their own leaders: the truth that
> they cannot win this war against our African people. This impossibility
> results not only from the growing combativity of our armed forces, and
> from our successes on the field of battle: it results above all from the
> continuing rising level of our people's political understanding. Knowing
> this, the colonialists have begun to perpetrate by all the means they can
> use the most barbarous crimes against our populations, slaying cattle,
> burning harvests: developing a criminal and terrorist activity which is
> the sharpest possible denial of their claims to be promoting the economic
> and social welfare of our people.

The last point, concerning Spinola's 'claims', was a reference to the Portuguese
commander's belated attempts to develop a form of political welfare. He
initiated a 'programme' called *Guine melhor* ('better Guinea-Bissau') and tried
to set about outbidding the PAIGC by promises of reformist change. Years
earlier, this might have worked to some extent; as it was, neither the Portuguese
fascist mentality nor the means adopted ever brought this 'programme'
within the realms of political reality. Spinola himself came to understand this
very well by 1970;[2] hence his frantic efforts in November of that year to kill
the leaders of the PAIGC by a seaborne commando assault on Conakry, their
external base.
  But what were the military considerations which brought him to this understanding, and were to drive him back, in the end, on a last-ditch hope of
winning some kind of neo-colonial compromise? Though always a commander
who thought extremely well of himself, and regularly boasted of his brilliance

in action, in fact Spinola merely extended the strategy of his defeated prede-
cessor, Schultz. He demanded more troops from home, and received them. He
enlarged the conscription of African levies, and formed an elite force of local
African mercenaries, called 'commandos', who were to number about 700 by
1973. All these he poured into more fixed garrisons and sector offensives,
combined with an increased use of helicopters and aerial bombing.

None of this did him much good, as the military record of events daily
revealed. The army of the PAIGC, with a somewhat better armament in
mortars and machine-guns, but with notably improved training and command
at the unit level, became a steadily stronger weapon of attack. Its precise
numbers, apart from local defence militias which began to receive rifles in
1967-68, were never made public; but one probably won't be far out in
putting the total full-time armed force at about 4,000 fighters in 1968, rising
to an eventual total of about 6,000. In 1968 this force went over to better
co-ordinated operations against selected strong points with the aim not only
of harassing them as before, but also, now, of eliminating them. Such strong
points fell one by one: Beli, Ga Carnes, and nine others by the end of 1968;
and the same work continued after the opening of the 1969 dry season
offensive in January of the new year. More strong-points fell: three more in
February alone. By the end of March 1969 the army of the PAIGC had
eliminated no fewer than eighteen strong-points, as well as launching major
assaults on many more. None was retaken or re-established by the enemy.
So the liberated zones grew wider; their security from enemy attack improved;
and travel through much of the country became relatively safe for couriers
and civilian personnel. With all this, more and better structures of self-rule
could be promoted.

Of the strong-points destroyed in this period, perhaps the most significant
was Madina da Boe in the eastern region of the country. Cabral's communique
of 9 February 1969 announced that:

> After powerful attacks by infantry combined with artillery, our forces
> took the fortified camps of Balana and Gandambel on 28 January, and
> then, on 5 February, that of Madina. The enemy suffered heavy losses.
> Pursued by our fighters, the colonialist troops retreating from Madina
> headed north for the town of Gabu, but were intercepted at the XeXe
> ferry when about to cross the Corubal river [Guinea-Bissau's largest
> waterway]. Attacked by bazookas and automatics, the enemy lost
> about fifty men. Our capture of the fortified camp of Madina com-
> pletes the liquidation of all colonial military presence in the Boe
> region, about 3,500 square kms.

It was during preparations for these operations in Boe, the previous October,
that Cabral wrote the preface to this book. Afterwards, Madina became a
training centre of importance to various arms of the PAIGC.

With their 'saturation' strategy in ruins, the colonial commanders fell back
on different tactics. From now onwards, they relied increasingly on aerial

bombardment in support of brief commando raids by helicopter. These raids were damaging at the point of contact; but the point of contact, more often than not, was with unarmed peasants or local militias. None of this, however painful, could do anything to restore the strategic initiative to Spinola's forces, or prevent the continued enlargement of the liberated zones and the improvement of their civilian structures. Spinola was now fighting a defensive war; and he was losing even this.

Such was not, perhaps naturally, the conclusion reached by a number of supposedly expert observers invited by Spinola and his authorities. Whoever was willing and likely to be 'suitable' was brought out from Britain or elsewhere and given a guided tour, chiefly by air. Some of these observers felt able to reassure their public that all was yet well. In December 1970, even in the wake of all these PAIGC successes of 1968-69, the military correspondent of the *Daily Telegraph,* Brigadier W.F.K. Thompson, could still tell his readers that 'the activity of the PAIGC offers at present no serious challenge. Militarily, the rebel movement is of no consequence. . . .'[3] Another British military commentator, Brigadier Michael Calvert, proved no more adept. As late as January 1972, at a time when Spinola had completely failed in all his efforts to recover from the losses of the last few years, and when the PAIGC had an even stronger hold on the strategic initiative, Brigadier Calvert was still assuring the readers of *The Times* that 'General Spinola is slowly and inexorably reclaiming the whole territory. . . .'[4]

While foreign visitors with a tenderness for Portuguese fascism and its colonial empire were busy reassuring their readers, the position on the ground continued to deteriorate for Spinola and his forces. Summing up in September 1971, Cabral wrote that:

> The first half of 1971 will be particularly remembered in the history of our struggle as the period when, for the first time, we were able to attack all the urban centres still occupied by the enemy, including Bissau [the capital] and Bafata [the second largest town] . . . [a situation which] marks a new stage in the political and military development of our struggle.

Altogether, he went on, the eight-month period of January-August 1971 'Is the best in our eight and a half years of struggle, and represents a decisive contribution to victory'. During that period the forces of the PAIGC

> carried out 508 major actions, including 369 attacks on garrisons in urban centres; 102 ambushes and other operations on roads; 15 major mining actions; 14 actions against river transport; and 8 commando operations in town centres. Our forces put out of action 735 enemy soldiers and agents, including 408 dead. . . . As far as equipment is concerned, we have destroyed or damaged [in this period] 90 military vehicles, sunk 28 boats, and shot down two aeroplanes and three helicopters.

Whatever they might now say for foreign consumption, the fascist commanders knew all this perfectly well, and by this time they were singing a
different tune among themselves. Yet they had begun with all the arrogance
of racist superiority. In 1967 one of the most prominent of Salazar's
generals, that same Kaulza de Arriaga who afterwards was to suffer a
swingeing defeat at the hands of FRELIMO in Mozambique, had given a
series of 'Lessons of Strategy' to a senior staff course in Portugal. 'Subversion',
this general had then taught, 'is a war above all of intelligence. One needs to
have superior intelligence to carry on subversion; not everyone can do it. The
Blacks are not highly intelligent; on the contrary, of all the peoples in the
world they are the least intelligent.' From which it followed, for General de
Arriaga, that African liberation movements must be easy to defeat. He was
going to learn the hard way just how wrong he was; but meanwhile, by 1970,
some of his politically less primitive colleagues had begun to see matters
differently. Early in 1971, a confidential report of the Portuguese General
Staff, entitled 'Report of Psychological Section No. 15', fell into the hands of
the PAIGC, who published extracts. It painted a dark picture of falling
morale at home in Portugal and the rising strength of liberation movements
in the colonies, where, it said, 'the enemy has perfected and increased his
efforts on all fronts, internally as well as externally. ... The psychological
situation is precarious, in the metropole [Portugal] as well as overseas.'

These conclusions were borne out by what one saw on the ground in 1972.
It became obvious in that year that the whole process of popular involvement
in the struggle for liberation was far advanced on the situation of a few years
earlier. Participation had developed from mere sympathy or support to the
point where it was now the core and substance of a new and post-colonial
state. Living in those areas, one could perceive this in many aspects of daily
life. This participatory process, now, already had a history of its own.

* * *

When they began in the 1950s, as earlier pages have shown, the pioneers of
the PAIGC were obliged, like other such pioneers, to present themselves as
'the will of the nation'. As Cabral used to say, they were at that time
'nationalists without a nation', for the ideas of nationalism, of a national
independence, had yet to crystallize in many minds. Making this act of
'substitution', however, the PAIGC did not forget their own weakness. When
the Algerian representative, Frantz Fanon, urged them in 1960-61 'simply
to begin', they dug in their political heels and refused, even at the cost of
losing useful support. Others might imagine that the peasants of Guinea-
Bissau would 'rally to the sound of the guerrilla rifle'; Cabral and his comrades,
one recalls, had no such confidence. They knew that political preparation was
first required, as we have seen; and that they could responsibly launch an
insurrection only when a sufficient peasant support *and* participation were
assured. Otherwise their action of revolutionary 'substitution', no matter
how well intended, could only be an irresponsible adventure.

Their task, as we have also seen, was to ensure that a process of winning mass participation should gain steadily over their initial 'act of substitution'. It was as difficult as the record has shown, but it was possible; and gradually the task was done. Liberated areas were established. The 'militarism' and witch-hunting of 1963 were disciplined and eliminated; and they did not return. Participation gradually won new ground, partly through the install-ation of social services, but, most of all, through the launching and develop-ment of grass-roots structures of self-rule: of *participacao popular* – of people's participation or, as in the related cases of Mozambique and Angola, *poder popular*, people's power – and all that this meant.

By 1972 the process was mature, and had indeed become the most inter-esting of all this movement's work. Studying it, I lived for weeks in liberated zones; I could have lived there for months if I had wished. All that a visitor required for that, once accepted by the PAIGC and therefore by the people, was a stout heart, a sound ability to walk, and of course a capacity to learn. Crucial to the process were the political structures 'at the base': a dense network of village committees which, as they became increasingly elective in nature, repeatedly took over fresh responsibilities. Here one found a new society taking shape in such a way that practically no aspect of *community* life lay outside its influence and action. On Como island, for example, there were at this stage – that is, in 1972 – a total of fifteen such committees; and at various meetings I was able to identify members of thirteen of them. In another sector, that of Cubucare on the nearby mainland, I met representatives of seventeen of its local committees.

New activities were repeatedly added to their tasks. The latest, in 1972, was the promotion of a network of village courts. Each of these tribunals consisted of a local judge (a lay magistrate, as we might say in England) and two assessors (or assistants) appointed by their respective committees. For the time being they were applying customary law (chiefly, here, that of the Nalu and Balante) on lines known to all adult men and women. (Other zones had often to apply other customary laws, according to their ethnic composition; and a national code would have to be a project for the future.) Minor offences, such as trading with the enemy at Catio or Cabedu, were punished by fines in kind (usually rice) or assignment to porterage services. More serious offences could be punished by local imprisonment. The most serious cases were forwarded to a PAIGC military court.

Promoted by the political workers, themselves under the direct super-vision of senior militants who lived in these zones on a permanent basis (veterans, for example, such as Carmen Pereira and Jose Araujo), this unfold-ing process of mass participation became many-sided. It was what guaranteed that the new social services could function: that teachers would be housed and fed; that parents would send their children to school rather than to cultivate the rice fields or scare off marauding birds; that clinics would be supplied with the necessary 'infrastructure' in housing and food; that local defence militias would be vigilant and active; and that, gradually, from these and comparable activities, the new society of the PAIGC would crystallize and develop.

But the key principle always held firm: 'People must do it for themselves'. If peasant committees were ready for the necessary supporting effort, they could have schools and clinics and other forms of developmental aid — not otherwise. As the men and women of the PAIGC saw it, their duty was to *lead*, never to act as 'fairy godmothers' who waved a wand and life changed. The true liberation had to come from inside the culture of these peoples, gradually, deliberately, by an often difficult 'working through' to new perceptions and understandings.

It was a practice that proved fertile. By 1972 the PAIGC had in this way promoted the foundation of no fewer than 156 primary schools inside liberated zones where no such schools had ever existed before and where, moreover, the people were completely non-literate; these schools were staffed by some 250 teachers trained by the movement. Besides these, there was now one secondary school and one nursery school (the latter largely for the children of militants on external service) in neighbouring Guinea. For October 1972, when I was there, the breakdown of attendances showed these results:

First year	6,988 pupils
Second year	849
Third year	506
Fourth year	172
Fifth year	31 (secondary)
Nursery year	28 (in Guinea)

Of this total of 8,574 pupils, 2,155 were girls; and this was another huge break with the culture of tradition. About 7,000 adults were attending part-time literacy and other classes.

Here again Cabral had set the keynote in his 40-page *Palavras de Ordem Gerais* of 1965 in words that are worth repeating: 'Demand from responsible Party workers that they dedicate themselves seriously to study . . . . Learn from life, learn from people, learn from books, learn from the experience of others, never stop learning.' There were many who found it hard to meet such demands, and not a few, no doubt, who failed altogether. But the demands were still made.

Public health was another field for widening participation. In the Como villages, for example, there had been no health-care facilities of any kind during the colonial period, save those provided by local herbalists and diviners: no physicians or surgeons, no trained nurses, no modern medicines. This situation also changed. In 1972 I found a central clinic on Como and several mobile ones. The central clinic had four beds for in-patients and thirteen nurses, eight of whom were women, and all of whom had received at least one year's specialized training in European or African countries. Out-patients were their chief concern. I picked up the register when I was there, and counted the names of 672 out-patients (as well as a handful of in-patients) for the month of October and four-fifths of November. For a local population of some 3,000 persons, the figure was impressive. About one-fifth of the whole island population, in less than two months, had received some form of medical care or advice.

In October 1972 the PAIGC had 125 small clinics of this kind and nine small hospitals where some surgery was possible whenever 'doctors on circuit' were available; as well as these, there were three larger hospitals staffed by fully trained doctors. At least two of the latter were stout-hearted Cuban volunteers, one of whom (I met him in Cubucare) had served with Fidel Castro in the Sierra Maestra. These were the Cubans who were really there, doing their surgery under the most adverse and often dangerous conditions, as distinct from the mythical Cuban soldiers who were alleged to be there by hostile propaganda. All these clinics and hospitals were inside the liberated zones; outside, in neighbouring Guinea, there was another permanent hospital staffed by Yugoslav medical volunteers. Altogether, the medical services of the PAIGC thus provided 488 beds, of which just under 300 were inside the country. Given the needs, it was little enough; but in the circumstances it signalled a tremendous political and material effort.

I think that one should emphasise, once again, the political effort. The Portuguese had ruled by a rigid and sometimes ruthless autocracy, taking all decisions at the top, at no point referring to the people for whom these decisions were taken. But the liberated zones displayed another situation. They showed the beginnings of a grass roots democracy and way of life which was also, in its conception and its structures, the foundation for a modern way of life. This was giving power back to the people, but in forms entirely different from those of pre-colonial times. Here was no sentimental 'searching for roots', no attempt to return to the pre-colonial past: here, on the contrary, the roots of peasant life were in leaf and bud with new ideas and attitudes such as could take these people into the modern world on their own terms, on their own feet.

This insistence on the need and possibility for a modern culture to grow out of traditional culture was characteristic of the whole project and programme. It was emphasised and unfolded at every level of political life. In 1969, for example, Cabral held days of seminar discussion with some 200 young militants then coming up through the ranks to positions of responsibility. Since published in English,[5] these seminar talks by Cabral reveal him, I think, at his most penetrating and effective. He drew out into the light every kind of cultural and political problem of individual or collective development, and examined these problems, often very personal and delicate ones, from the standpoint of PAIGC practice and theory. He discussed the superstitions of traditional culture. He spoke against polygamy, the subjection of women, the distrust of literacy, the contempt for intellectuals (and of intellectual contempt for non-intellectuals), and all those other spectres which haunt people from an old world who have called themselves to enter upon a new one. He talked especially of 'cultural resistance' to colonialism, and of what this must mean: 'A lot of people think that to defend Africa's culture, to resist culturally in Africa, we have to defend the negative things in our culture. But this is not what we think.' A system to replace the colonial system, a new and post-colonial society, could never be a reversion to 'whatever existed before', even if that were possible. Far from it:

> Our cultural resistance consists in the following: while we scrap colonial culture and the negative aspects of our own culture, whether in our character or in our environment, we have to create a new culture, also based on our own traditions but respecting everything that the world today has conquered for the service of mankind.

In 1972 it was time to take a further forward step. Mass participation had matured in the liberated zones. The 'building from the base' had ramified and fructified in many aspects of daily life. All this meant that the new state taking shape here was a plant in no way nourished by the sectional aspirations of a structural or otherwise privileged elite. On the contrary, its leaders answered the prescription of an old Twi saying current in Ghana when it was the pre-colonial state of Asante: *Wobeforo dua a, wofi n'ase na womfi soro* — 'If you want to climb a tree, you must start at the bottom.' Those who ran this new state had indeed done that. They had not been lifted to the top by privilege, corruption, bullying or foreign influence. They had climbed to leadership by the arduous route of service to the community, self-sacrifice, stubborn daring in the face of huge discouragements. Now the state which they led was ready for constitutional definition. The liberation war still raged, but independence stood clear upon the skyline.

* * *

At the outset of 1972 the central committee under Cabral decided to organize a general election throughout the liberated zones. These now covered some two-thirds of the country, with the rest under no more than partial colonial control except in the capital and chief provincial towns. All persons over 18 would be asked to vote by secret ballot for or against lists of PAIGC candidates nominated locally. Those thus elected to regional councils in the liberated zones would then choose from their ranks the men and women who were to form the People's National Assembly (PNA); and this PNA would be the supreme and constitutional organ of the new state. Among other things, it would have the right and duty of proclaiming national independence, and it would expect other states to recognize this, as, in fact, they did when the moment came.

I saw the final phases of this long electoral process of 1972, and attended some of its meetings. It had several objectives. One, as mentioned, was to provide a constitutional basis for independence. Another was to establish an elective means whereby a supreme legislative body — the PNA — would nonetheless ensure the continued leadership of the PAIGC. Given that the future would clearly require a separation of powers and functions between state and party, the problem thus posed was not an easy one, whether in theory or practice. While the PNA was to be sovereign and the ultimate source of all power, the PAIGC was most clearly the only conceivable executive and would remain so. At the time, of course, this kind of problem had little or no meaning. Even the minorities who voted against PAIGC lists did so, for the most part, only because they disliked the candidates in question.

The major objective, in any case, was a different one. This was to carry through another and very wide exercise in the meaning and advancement of *participacao popular*. The people of the liberated zones (and to some extent of the contested zones as well) had been led to participate in their own local self-government: now they were to be led to participate in their own national government. But how, and even why, should this be done? What, in any case, was this new and unknown thing, a National Assembly? Much had to be explained and discussed; and much was, and for many months.

'In the past,' I heard a peasant say at an electoral meeting in the region of Balana-Quitafine, 'the Portuguese plastered our eyes with mud. We couldn't see. We didn't even know what a political meeting was. . . .' And he went on to recall the phases of their evolving participation: of their early committees ('which at first nobody understood'), of their continuing journey into understanding what was what. The senior speaker present, Vasco Cabral on this occasion, replied now as at other meetings where I was present, saying that the object of the exercise was to demonstrate, once again, that *povo na manda na su cabeca*, that 'people have to do it for themselves', colloquially, or 'people rule themselves'.

> We form the People's National Assembly precisely so that the people shall be able to participate more fully in governing themselves and in promoting their interests. . . . So far it is the Party (PAIGC) which has made the laws: now it will be the duty of the Assembly to examine the value of these laws and to make new ones.

By November 1972 the elections to regional councils were all completed, with heavy majorities for the PAIGC lists and small minorities (ranging from 7.5 per cent of the votes in the East to 5.65 in the North and 3.01 in the South) against those lists.[6] These regional councils then elected their deputies to the National Assembly, which was to meet in 1973, and with consequences the next chapter records.

This process of consolidating gains and laying the basis for new advances was continued at the same time in another field — in that of political work on the international scene.

* * *

True to its internationalism, the PAIGC had always seen its work for liberation as part of a wider process. Cabral insisted upon this from the start. His earliest piece of writing addressed to an external audience was a pamphlet entitled 'The Facts about Portugal's African Colonies', published in London in July 1960 and sold in many thousands of copies through British trade unions and other democratic organizations.[7] Its basic theme was the need for alliance and common effort between all those, everywhere, who sought to move the old world forward. This was a theme, by 1968, which had begun to make its mark in many countries. Big successes were scored with the emergence of support committees, as well as a widening understanding of the work and importance of the PAIGC and its companion movements in Angola and Mozambique.

In November 1968, signalling the impact of these successes on the international scene, the General Assembly of the United Nations voted, by 85 to 3 (South Africa, Portugal, Brazil) with 15 abstentions, a strong resolution of support for the national liberation movements in the Portuguese colonies and of condemnation for the Lisbon dictatorship. Here was another 'writing on the wall'. Previously, the Western Powers had opposed all such resolutions; now they contented themselves with abstention.

International support in the capitalist world grew in material ways as well, especially after the Swedish social democratic government had given the green light, in 1968, for its para-statal organization, SIDA, to provide a generous quantity of material aid. Support committees in several countries began to become more effective. If the amount of material aid they could produce was always small, and often only nominal, their educational, moral and political impact was far from negligible. And this was seen on a growing scale until the end of the liberation war. In 1971-72, for example, Cabral scored major political successes while visiting a number of Western countries as well as countries in the Soviet bloc; and in 1973, even in Britain, the British support committee proved able to bring 10,000 people on to the London streets in protest against the state visit to 'Portugal's oldest ally' of the Portuguese dictator, Marcello Caetano (who had recently succeeded Salazar).

Meanwhile the quantity of financial, social, educational and military aid being supplied by the USSR and some other countries close to it also grew in decisive size and value. By this time, unfortunately, the Chinese government had withdrawn all aid from the PAIGC, on the surprising grounds that the PAIGC was a hostile party — because, no doubt, it received aid from the Soviet bloc — and even went so far, as in the case of Angola and Mozambique, to lend propaganda support to the fake-nationalist 'parties' such as the Dakar-based FLING (which had no presence of any kind in Guinea-Bissau). This Chinese policy was eventually modified, but only after independence. Cuban aid, in contrast, proved especially valuable in the training of civilian cadres, and in the provision of medical volunteers and small teams for training in the use of artillery.

Yet the big breakthrough on a wide international front came only in the early months of 1972. In March of that year, responding to proposals by the Organization of African Unity and by the PAIGC, the UN Special Committee on Decolonization recommended the sending of a special mission to the liberated zones of Guinea-Bissau. This took place in April 1972, and was a notable success.

Spinola, naturally, did his level best to stop the UN three-man mission from entering the country, and then, failing in that, to destroy it while it was there. He tried to bar the frontier, vainly, and then put in intensive aerial bombardments. But Cabral and his comrades saw to it that the mission was taken safely into Guinea-Bissau, was able to walk for some 200 kms through liberated zones and meet many persons and representatives, and was then convoyed safely out again. Its extensive report[8] was an eye-witness vindication of the claims of the PAIGC. It was thus a major setback to the Lisbon dictatorship and personally to Spinola. It directly paved the way for the UN recognition of the independent state of Guinea-Bissau that was to follow a year later.

The last months of 1972, in short, saw the PAIGC winning on every front; and its name across the world, epitomized so clearly by Cabral's, became a household word among all those who wished for a world without imperialism. This David had struck down its Goliath. Victory now could not be far ahead.

Then disaster struck at the PAIGC itself.

* * *

Told afterwards, all this story of success may sound an easy one. In fact, it was never less than harshly difficult. On those in command, above all, it imposed a relentless effort not only against the enemy and the problems caused by the enemy, but against exhaustion, loneliness, every kind of physical discouragement.

The disaster that struck now came partly from exhaustion, but its instrument was betrayal.

Cabral had warned repeatedly of the enemy's attempts to penetrate PAIGC ranks with men and women ready to betray. As late as March 1972, as it happened, he gave an especially sharp warning. In that document, circulated internally to all PAIGC organizations and units, Cabral warned of the existence of a colonialist plot to eliminate the leadership of the PAIGC, to form an alternative 'leadership' based on racist and tribalist elements secretly in colonial service, and, by this means, to secure an 'internal solution' by which the Portuguese regime would give the country a measure of autonomy under direct Portuguese control. The warning was very detailed; in hindsight, it was also particularly grim. For the plot which it described was more or less precisely the plot that murdered him in January 1973.

How could this happen? For what it may be worth, my own view is that the fault lay in the sheer attrition of the struggle upon those who led it. Briefly they relaxed their vigilance; betrayal did the rest.

Arrived back at the frontier with the Republic of Guinea early in December of that year of 1972, I found Cabral who had come to meet me before going on to training camps in the Boe region of Guinea-Bissau, somewhat to the north-east. We went up there by motor transport and then returned to the external base in Conakry. He was extremely tired, even desperately so. Some days later we dined together at his two-roomed 'house' in that little base or open 'compound', on the outskirts of the old colonial city of Conakry, so as to say good-bye for the time being: he and Ana Maria, his wife, and Aristides Pereira, who shared his exhaustion as he shared everything else with Cabral and always had, ever since they had first begun together in the middle 1950s.

Cabral said little; and he was so tired, or so it seemed to me, that he had even gone beyond the chance of easy sleep, while Aristides was in little better shape. They were confident, as I always found them to be, but they were overwhelmed with work. They had carried all the chief responsibilities for so long, and now they were in sight of new responsibilities. Cabral was thinking, as usual, of the next steps and talked a little of them: of the Assembly that would emerge from the general election and of what it would have to do. He felt its emergence as a turning point. They had travelled a long road; now the road turned, and another distance opened out before them. I recall some of his words. 'You have to think hard, very hard, about what you are really doing, about what you're aiming for. . . .' There had never been anything improvised about Cabral's planning for the long-term future; and it was just the same now. There would have to be, for example, a clear separation of functions, and eventually of powers, between legislature and executive.[9] There would have to be efficient measures to prevent any ossification of command in the years of independence that must soon begin.

Outside his little house, as I left that night to go back to my hotel, the guards were in a ring around the otherwise open compound, barring intrusion from the surrounding bush and its scattered habitations. Tough, well-armed men. At least, I remember thinking, there's no danger here.

Yet these guards were among the men already gathered to betray him.

He was shot down outside his house at about ten o'clock on the evening of 22 January 1973 in the presence of his wife.

References

1. See B. Davidson et al., *Southern Africa,* Penguin, London, 1976, p.60. My essay in this volume tried to synthesize the experience gained by liberation struggles in the Portuguese colonies.
2. See, for instance, Spinola's 1971 interview with the South African journalist, Al Venter (note 4 below).
3. *Daily Telegraph,* London, 15 December 1970.
4. *The Times,* 12 January 1972. Compared with these remarkably mistaken judgements on the military situation, those of a pro-regime South African journalist, Al J. Venter, were the least ill-informed of any published by observers on the colonial side of the war. Venter kept his eyes open during a visit in April 1971, and his report (published in April 1973 as *Portugal's War in Guine-Bissau,* Munger Africana Library Notes, California Institute of Technology) remains a useful source not only for what he saw of the colonial forces but also for an interesting

interview with Spinola in which, for the first time so far as I know, that aspiring politician set forth some of the ideas which he was to try to apply in 1974.

5. A. Cabral, *Unity and Struggle,* Heinemann, London, Monthly Review Press, New York, 1980. (Collected writings translated by M. Wolfers).
6. Ibid: for a detailed report.
7. Reprinted in full in Cabral, ibid. Written by Cabral in French, it was translated into English by the present writer.
8. Reprinted in UN, *Objective Justice,* Vol. IV, No. 3, September 1972.
9. Given the position and prestige of the PAIGC as an embracing national movement to which all self-respecting persons gave their allegiance, any such separation of powers would have to be a task for the future. In 1980, people's power in Guinea-Bissau was still being exercised through party rather than non-party structures, so that, in a certain sense, this was still a 'party-state', even if the promotion of non-party forms of mass participation was also going ahead. In the somewhat different circumstances of Cape Verde, non-party forms of participation were taking shape in 1980 with the promotion of *comissoes de moradores,* 'local residents' committees' and their respective local and regional assemblies, consisting of men and women elected by their fellow-residents irrespective of party membership.

10. Meeting the Bitterest Loss: 1973

Nothing, no criminal action or conjuring trick by the
Portuguese colonialists, can prevent our African people,
masters of their own destiny and aware of their rights and
duties, from winning national independence and building,
in restored peace and dignity, their genuine progress under
the glorious banner of our Party.
AMILCAR CABRAL

The colonial dictators had tried it before with soldiers, as we have seen, and
had failed.

Picked units of Spinola's troops, after intensive training for the operation
on one of the Bijagos islands near Bissau, had landed on 22 November 1970,
shortly before dawn, on the long spit of land from which the capital of the
Republic of Guinea, Conakry, looks out upon the South Atlantic. With about
350 men backed by six naval vessels, the operation aimed at killing President
Sekou Toure, the Guinea leader who had done much for the PAIGC, together
with Amilcar Cabral and others of the PAIGC. No doubt because Spinola and
his henchmen were fascists, they had long shown themselves convinced that
the PAIGC would collapse if only its top leadership, and above all Cabral,
could be eliminated.

Divided into different parties according to assigned targets, the raiders of
November 1970 had come ashore on the beaches and made for their objectives. Those ordered to eliminate the PAIGC leadership climbed through
undergrowth from their beach, a few hundred metres' distant, to the compound where Cabral and Pereira lived with their families. The raiders thus
achieved surprise, but they failed to exploit it. Challenged by PAIGC guards,
they opened fire and the fire was returned. Within minutes they were in flight
back to their boats, though not before putting a bazooka shell through the
front wall of the Cabrals' bungalow; mercifully, Ana Maria and the two
children were in the back room and untouched, while Cabral himself was not
in Conakry at the time.

The other raiding parties met with much the same fate. A fiasco.

But now, two years later, they tried again, this time with traitors.

137

It was not unforeseen. Cabral's internal message to militants of March 1972, mentioned at the end of the last chapter, had described what was in the wind.[2] 'You know,' he told them, 'that the criminal Portuguese colonialists have made and are making plans to take or kill the Party's leaders, particularly the Secretary-General, because they are convinced that the imprisonment or death of the Party's principal leader would mean the end of the Party and of our struggle.' Now it had become known to him, he continued, that another such plan was in hand and could soon be set in motion. This plan envisaged three phases.

In the first phase there would be the recruitment by Spinola's secret services of 'several African agents' to whom 'Spinola has promised fame and fortune' if they could infiltrate into PAIGC ranks after 'training by the PIDE [the dictatorship's political police] in political sabotage, provocation, and the making of confusion' in PAIGC ranks. These agents were to act as 'good militants', and, under cover of that reputation, seek out problems and organizational weaknesses, and then recruit 'discontented' militants in any way they could. Above all, these agents were to work on 'tribalist' or regionalist sentiments 'so as to try to set the Guineans [of Guinea-Bissau] against the Cape Verdians' and vice versa 'and people of one tribe against people of another, people with education against people without, Muslims against non-Muslims'.

If these agents could succeed in this first phase, they were to pass to a second. In this they were to organize a network of conspirators topped by a 'parallel' leadership, to make what foreign contacts they could, and prepare the elimination of Cabral. At this point, moreover, Spinola and company would launch a big propaganda campaign on the African and international scene, elaborating on alleged divisions within the PAIGC. After that, a third phase would begin: the phase of direct action. This would aim at the elimination of Cabral and his closest comrades in the leadership; and, having achieved that, the new 'parallel' leadership would 'take over' the Party 'at the top' and enter into negotiations with Spinola. These would lead to 'autonomy' for Guinea-Bissau with 'the formation of a puppet government under the Portuguese flag'. The chief conspirators would be rewarded with prominent positions and privileges in this fake independence, and would lead Guinea-Bissau into the 'Portuguese Community' as a supposedly autonomous state.

Having thus set forth the plot in a detail which was to be confirmed almost to the letter — save that the plot failed in all except the killing of Cabral — this penetrating document concluded with an appeal for greater vigilance. And greater vigilance was in fact applied; tragically, it was not enough.

On the fatal evening of January 1973 Amilcar drove home with Ana Maria from a diplomatic reception in Conakry. He stopped the car outside his bungalow and, getting out, was at once surrounded by armed men. One of them, I am not sure which, said that he was their prisoner and must come with them. He refused, replying that he would never be anybody's prisoner. Playing for time, not knowing what had happened, he began to argue. Whereupon a man called Innocencio Kani shot him down. As he collapsed on the ground, they finished him off.

Perhaps this killing was the work of panic and shame, and they had really been told to seize and take him to Bissau. There he could be paraded in public and killed later: the records of the colonial dictatorship have yet to reveal their secrets. But at least we know what actually happened. Having killed Cabral, the group at once went to find Pereira in another small bungalow fifty metres distant. And the guards? They had been changed, as we shall see, a few days earlier; and men in the plot were now the guards. They found Pereira and bound him with cords and hustled him into a car. Several of the plotters drove this car to the harbour at the seaward end of Conakry. There they had prepared one of the PAIGC's naval launches, diesel-engined, and, with their prisoner, they put to sea for Bissau along the coast, a distance of some 380 kms.

The remaining plotters, now in command of the compound, meanwhile set about rounding up all the PAIGC personnel they could find in neighbouring houses. They found many, though not before Vasco Cabral, coming up with a sub-machine gun, had killed one of the plotters. These prisoners were thrust into the little PAIGC prison from which two or three of the chief conspirators had been released by their fellow-plotters a few hours earlier. And the prisoners, who included two of the movement's women cadres, Ana Maria Cabral and Henriette Vieira, were told that all of them would be shot when dawn came.

Then the leading conspirators who had not gone with the launch to Bissau did a strange thing for which I have yet to hear a convincing explanation. They went to find President Sekou Toure. They found him and presented themselves and told, apparently with great satisfaction and a curious self-confidence, of what they had done. They informed Toure that they had killed Cabral and sent Pereira to Bissau because the PAIGC had fallen into the hands of Cape Verdians, had lost its way, needed a new leadership. It seems that they expected approval and support.

Whatever reasons may have led them to such expectations, they got neither from Sekou Toure. Instead, he called for guards and had these men arrested. Learning from them what they had done with Pereira, he ordered his own naval craft to overtake the launch and bring it back. They came up with it shortly before it entered Portuguese colonial waters; for Pereira, in the nick of time.

Next day, instead of being shot, the PAIGC militants in prison were released. And some days later, though oddly not at once, the Guinean police put the imprisoned conspirators into a truck and sent them to the PAIGC. These conspirators, again very oddly, still appeared to think that they would be forgiven. They were not forgiven.

* * *

With that, the plot was over and done with: even so, how could it have gone so far? Not everything on the non-PAIGC side has yet been explained. But apart from the question of external collusions, the facts concerning the conspirators were established by PAIGC interrogation and by much collateral evidence, and are not in doubt.

They confirmed the plot that Cabral had described in the previous March, ten months earlier. The chief conspirators, three or four in number, were former PAIGC militants arrested in Bissau many years before but released in 1969. The fact of their release was known, and some of them had already made their way across the frontier and had joined the PAIGC external base in Conakry. They had been welcomed but treated with initial prudence, and given minor responsibilities to show what they were worth. Two of them were named Barbosa and Momu; and these two, as it was to turn out, were already the chief colonialist agents in the conspiracy now set afoot. Secretly, they began to form a 'group' in Conakry; and from time to time they were reinforced by new arrivals from Bissau, among them a man called Valentim Mangana, another who was to lead the plot.

Early in 1972 the always steady stream of arrivals from Bissau began to grow bigger. This was noticed, but was explained by the belief that Rafael Barbosa in Bissau – the former Party President arrested in 1962 and released in 1969[3] – had remained loyal in spite of his sufferings during seven years of harsh imprisonment, and was sending new recruits. In fact he was playing a double game, and, of course in secret, was already Spinola's nominee for president of a stooge 'movement of liberation' in Bissau. Known as FUL (*Frente de Libertacao da Guine*), this 'movement' was billed to makes its public appearance as soon as the plot against Cabral came off, and to call for negotiations with the Portuguese together – as it was imagined – with a decapitated and suborned PAIGC. But first of all the plot had to come off.

Thus reinforced in numbers, the plotters at the PAIGC external base in Conakry added up to some fifty men by the end of 1972. Only a handful of these were in the inner secrets of the conspiracy; most, as it transpired, were hangers-on suborned by 'tribalist' and regionalist arguments and, still more, by the offer of personal rewards. Several, as we shall see, were guilty of various forms of petty crime for which they had been punished.

The principal argument used by these traitors was that the PAIGC had been taken over by Cape Verdians at the expense of the people of the mainland. Now this argument could carry no weight in the fighting units inside the country or in the liberated zones (as the outcome would most dramatically prove), for there the notion that Cape Verdians were depriving the mainlanders of the fruits of the liberation struggle could only appear absurd. But the primitive political thinking of the Portuguese fascists was right in supposing that it might carry some weight – enough weight – among personnel in the external base where the temptations of corruption could not be absent. And the argument, as we have seen, did win over two or three dozen persons in that external base.

Subsequent investigation helped to explain why. Barbosa and Momu, the chief conspirators infiltrated from Bissau, were joined by others at the Conakry base who had met with serious criticism and even imprisonment for acts of personal misbehaviour. Yet Cabral's constant policy was to try to recuperate such persons. He seldom lost sight of the frailties that derive from the colonial condition, and he held that it was a part of the liberation struggle to make good such frailties whenever this was possible. He liked to shorten prisoners' sentences, and keep such persons close to him so that they could complete their own rehabilitation. It was a generosity of spirit; a characteristic one, but fatal now.

In this little gang of 'malcontents', four were important. One of them was Goda, whom I myself knew very well as Cabral's personal bodyguard in the months previous to the murder. An excellent fighter, he had come under sharp censure for personal misdemeanours; but it was believed that he had genuinely repented and become worthy of trust again. So they put him in charge of the PAIGC's little disciplinary prison in Conakry. Among his prisoners there were Momu and Barbosa, who, by this time, were already under accusations of major betrayal and were now under arrest in Conakry. On the day of the murder it was Goda who released these two; and these two then led the others. Arrested himself on the day after the murder, Goda seized a rifle from one of his guards and shot himself.

Another of the 'malcontents' was Mamadu Ndiaje, also a good fighting man, but whose morale had suffered from a long spell in the rear. He had refused to go back to the fighting front, and was not sent. After all, this was a volunteer army, and even staunch fighters could have enough of forest conditions and constant danger. But Mamadu remained a doubtful character, and worked poorly. I happened to be present at the Boe training centre on 9 December 1972 when Cabral censured him again. He replied that he was ill and needed treatment. Cabral agreed to that but, since the man seemed not very ill, ordered him to undergo treatment in Conakry and, meanwhile, to take charge of the small guard detachment assigned to the PAIGC compound there. So it came about that the plotters could count not only on Goda, the man in charge of the prison, but also on Mamadu, the man in charge of the guards. It was this Mamadu who changed the guards a few days before the murder, putting in men from among the conspirators.

A third person among the 'malcontents' was Joao Tomas, a PAIGC militant arrested and tried for receiving presents from the Portuguese, and sentenced to ten years' hard labour. But Cabral's humanity had intervened, and Tomas was granted amnesty in September 1972, afterwards remaining in Conakry. A fourth of the 'malcontents' — absurdly described in Portuguese-inspired reports as 'one of the founders of the PAIGC' — was the actual murderer, Innocencio Kani. I knew him too. He had similarly 'come over' from the Portuguese, and subsequently been given command of one of the PAIGC's naval launches. This Kani had also fallen foul of the law when he had sold one of the engines of his launch on the Conakry black market, claiming to his superiors that it was no longer fit for use. Yet he too had duly shown himself contrite, and had been forgiven, for there were many temptations in Conakry; even good militants could be unsettled by them.

And so the murder was committed: incredibly, and yet all too credibly when the wretched details became known.

* * *

Once they knew that Cabral was dead, even if they had failed to get Pereira, the Portuguese in command of Bissau and Lisbon were jubilant. If ever they proclaimed their guilt, they did so now, calling on all their scribes, paid or unpaid, to celebrate the collapse of the liberation struggle. This was a propaganda campaign which completely failed within the PAIGC and among the principal allies and supporters of the PAIGC. Yet in Conakry, oddly enough, strange oppositions were seen to develop. There, criticism was heard; more hostile still, it was heard in public.

President Sekou Toure of Guine (formerly French Guinee) had generally given good support to the PAIGC after about 1962, although always, as was noticed at the time, with an air of condescension. What this might conceal was glimpsed even as early as the middle 1960s when Toure calmly laid claim to a large segment of the territorial waters of Guinea-Bissau, still then, of course, formally a Portuguese colony or 'overseas province'. Later again, towards the end of the 1970s, when it became clear that there might be off-shore oil in those territorial waters, Toure raised the matter to the level of a major dispute by signing an agreement in 1980 with Union Oil of Texas for prospecting in waters clearly belonging to Guinea-Bissau — an agreement at once contested by the government of Guinea-Bissau. When Cabral was murdered, much of this still lay in the future; but Toure's behaviour on that occasion was certainly prophetic.

In the wake of the murder, and timed for the funeral, Toure called a 'symposium' on the work and life of Cabral. This he opened by one of his customarily verbose addresses. With the whole thing running to some 80 pages of subsequently printed text, the third part concerned itself with 'contradictions within the liberation movements, and how to resolve them'. And here in public, under the guise of a generally acceptable theoretical approach, he made himself the spokesman of those same 'criticisms' of the PAIGC which he had just heard from the lips of the assassins.

It was indeed a strange way of showing solidarity with the PAIGC in the desperate moment of their losing Cabral. Perhaps, one may ask, he did not know that the assassins were enemy agents? But he could not fail to have known, for it was he who had ordered his naval craft to prevent them from delivering Pereira into the hands of the Portuguese in Bissau. Perhaps he did not know that their 'criticisms' were the common coin of enemy propaganda? It is far from easy to believe that.

For it was everybody's knowledge that colonial rule had long sought to maximize the differences between the two populations. It had worked on real differences which Cabral and his comrades had confronted from the start, and which were constantly revived and discussed by the opponents and enemies of the PAIGC. Unity between the two countries, as planned by the PAIGC, was accepted as a necessarily long process of mutual understanding and cultural enlargement among the two populations. Within the PAIGC, however, the common aims and fraternal alliance of Cape Verdians and mainlanders were never in doubt; and those who knew the PAIGC, whether in its fighting units or civilian structures, well saw that this was so. Yet Toure's airing of an imaginary disunity within the PAIGC, however indirectly expressed, was to be only the first of later moments of hostility. Was he hoping, perhaps, to supplant the PAIGC and incorporate Guinea-Bissau within Guinea-Conakry? Had he once again lost grip on reality? As for the PAIGC, they said nothing in reply to Toure's lecture. But they acted.

Those who knew the PAIGC could see what would happen, even if the news of Cabral's murder still came with sickening impact. I was myself at home in London when a voice on the 'phone said to me: 'BBC here. This killing of Cabral — will you please comment?' I refused to believe it, but I had to. I said into the 'phone: 'They will close their ranks, they will fight on.' It wasn't bravado; it wasn't even clever. It was simply what I knew would happen.

A three weeks' silence, and then the same answer came from the PAIGC. It took the form of a hard offensive on every fighting front, by individual units and combinations of units, and repeatedly for weeks thereafter. The colonial forces never recovered from it. What had come to seem like something of a stalemate was shattered, and the war entered a new phase — the phase that heralded the end.

Preparations had already been in hand for a New Year's offensive, but anger and bitterness, and perhaps an obscure sense of shame that they could have lost their leader in this way, gave new point and fury to this widespread operation. Yet the preparations helped, for on 23 March the PAIGC brought another weapon into play, and with it they broke the last superiority of Spinola's forces. They committed their SAM-7 ground-to-air heat-seeking missiles, and the effect was overwhelming.

Up to now, in all the three wars in Portuguese Africa, the colonial forces had enjoyed a complete mastery of the air. They could bomb and strafe as they pleased; even their helicopters had little to fear. The PAIGC , like FRELIMO and MPLA, had some anti-aircraft weaponry, mostly multi-barrelled cannon with hand-moved aiming levers of a type produced in Czechoslovakia and provided as part of military aid; but these were useless against fast-moving jets (though not always against helicopters) except as a means of boosting civilian morale. The movements knew that weapons such as the SAM-7 existed but failed, for a long time, to get any. In 1972, however, Cabral managed to persuade the Soviet Union that the PAIGC could handle these weapons with a suitable training, and their provision was agreed.

Now the SAM-7 (like its Western equivalents) proved a decisive innovation. Fired by a two-man team, and entirely portable, it required relatively little training except in its aiming requirements, which, broadly, are to fire sufficiently ahead of the target: with that, the missile simply finds its own course and explodes on contact. After the first hits of late March, the Portuguese forces put out stories that their aircraft were being downed by missiles fired from 'launching pads' in neighbouring Guinea. But there were of course no launching pads; the missiles were fired out of the forest of the liberated zones by two-man teams.

Within a little while Spinola had lost the flower of his hitherto invulnerable airforce. From 23 March 1973 to the end of July – at a time when Lisbon, through its various scribes and propagandists, was still trying to celebrate the collapse of the struggle – the SAM-7 teams of the liberation army downed twelve Fiat jet-bombers, three Harvard fighter-bombers, and three Dornier DO-67s, one of these piloted by the airforce commander himself, Almeida e Brito. The loss of eighteen aircrews to missiles which could not even be located, let alone hit, sufficiently demoralized the rest. After July there was next to no airforce activity till the war ended.

With air operations against them more or less stilled, the all-out offensive which had begun in March could undertake new targets. Of these, the most difficult had been a number of highly fortified and armed strong-points which could be attacked effectively only if attacking units could develop persistent artillery action against them. But any such action had meant, until now, the certainty of heavy aerial bombing and the dropping of helicoptered commandos as a prelude to the concentration of Portuguese reinforcements on the ground. All this was a risk that could be run, but unwillingly, for it offended against the basic guerrilla principle of refusing pitched battles. Now, with the air risk at an end, things were different.

Just how different was revealed that July. Under the general command of Joao Bernardo Vieira (Nino), the artillery commander Julio de Carvalho (Julinho) opened a mortar and cannon offensive against a key strong-point, that of Guileje on the southern lines of communication west of the (ex-French) Guinea frontier. Guileje had long been a thorn in the side of the PAIGC, and, though shot into many times, had never been seriously disturbed. Built on a square pattern in a wide forest clearing, heavily wired and fortified (as I myself saw it afterwards) and garrisoned by two picked companies, Guileje would need to be mightily hammered before it would fall.

After long planning and reconnaissance for range and cover, the PAIGC brought up six 120 mm. mortars and two 95 mm. cannon and began dropping shells right into the camp, regularly every half hour, from a distance of three to four kms. I was told later that they had assembled enough ammunition to go on doing this for days, knowing now that they ran little or no risk from the air and having made sure that access roads were barred to reinforcements. But the garrison had enough of it after four days, and those of the original 400 defenders who were still alive got away down the forest trail to the tiny 'port' of Gadamael on the neighbouring Cacine river. Well satisfied by this operation, code named 'Amilcar Cabral', the PAIGC let them go; they would (and they did) carry their demoralization further. Behind them they left a rich booty, including cannon, mortars, bazookas, no fewer than forty-seven Bren machine-guns, three armoured cars, four Berliet trucks, and one Jeep: all in good working order, and with much ammunition. It was indeed the signal for the end.

With the rainy season's torrential downpours beginning in July, there had to be the usual annual pause. This continued until the end of October, or thereabouts, when the PAIGC resumed its general offensive of the previous March. A year earlier, in what proved to be Spinola's last desperate throw, the Portuguese had tried to occupy the central zones of the southern region (Cubucare and its environs), and had failed after hard fighting.[4] Now the tables were turned, and it was the PAIGC which encircled Spinola's units and their fortified camps, and kept them pinned down. There was more hard fighting till the end of 1973, but the PAIGC encirclements remained unbroken. Then this situation was progressively generalized in the rest of the country. Everywhere, even around Bissau itself, the colonial forces were bottled up in their fortified camps by besieging PAIGC forces. And with the opening of the New Year of 1974, just twelve months after Cabral's murder, it was clear that the enemy's will to fight was practically at an end.

Meanwhile, a few weeks earlier, the executive had presided over the realization of another of Cabral's planned moves. At Boe on 24 September in that same year of 1973, the People's National Assembly elected in 1972 held its inaugural session at which it proclaimed, through its chairman Joao Bernardo Vieira,[5] the independence of their country even though a part of the national territory was still occupied by the colonial enemy. Speaking on the day before, Secretary-General Aristides Pereira said:

> Today our people stands up and affirms, with all its strength, its identity as an African people and its capacity to assume the responsibilities needed to realize its own progress and happiness, participating actively in the forward march of all the people of the world.

The independent state of Guinea-Bissau thus proclaimed by its sovereign Assembly, he went on,

> will have as its principal objective the complete liberation of Guinea-Bissau and the Islands of Cape Verde. It assumes the far-reaching task of unifying these two entities of our national territory in one unified state, and of building a society capable of creating the political, economic and cultural conditions which can end the exploitation of man by man in all its forms of subjection of the human person to degrading interests, to the profit of individuals, groups or class.

Within three months of this proclamation no fewer than seventy-five countries had recognized the new Republic; and on 2 November 1973 the United Nations General Assembly passed a very significant resolution with the overwhelming support of member states. This demanded that the Portuguese Government should immediately cease its violation of the sovereignty and independence of the new Republic, and all acts of aggression committed not only against the people of Guinea-Bissau but also against those of Cape Verde, and, further, that the Portuguese Government should promptly withdraw its forces from those two territories. On 19 November the Organization of African Unity received Guinea-Bissau as its forty-second member state.

Characteristically for the PAIGC, the great military gains of 1973 were made to go together with a political gain which was, if anything, still more decisive.

And then came the collapse of the dictatorship in Lisbon.

References

1. New Year's Message, 1973.
2. A. Cabral, *Vamos reforcar a nossa vigilancia . . . . : aos dirigentes e responsaveis do Partido*, PAIGC, March 1972.
3. See pp.17, 24 above.
4. We saw, in the last chapter, its prelude in the colonial attempt to tar the road between the Cufar airstrip and Catio: see pp.122-3.
5. Afterwards Minister of Defence, and then in 1978, First Commissioner (Prime Minister) of Guinea-Bissau.

11. The End of Colonial Rule

We have fought our war for national independence without
hatred for the people of Portugal, and we are now ending it
without hatred.
LUIZ CABRAL, 15 August 1974

In Lisbon on 25 April 1974, the officers of the Portuguese Armed Forces
Movement (*Movimento das Forcas Armadas:* MFA) overthrew the dictatorship which had ruled their country for nearly half a century, and declared for
'democratization and decolonization'. It was an action both generous and
humane, reflecting not only the weariness induced by long and painful wars
in Africa and the still longer and courageous anti-colonial campaigning of
radical Portuguese, but, beyond all that, a determination to return this abused
and misgoverned people to the respect and interest of the world. A victory for
freedom and good sense, an upsurge of that peculiar genius for civility and
realism which has somehow survived among the Portuguese in spite of all their
history of dictatorship, this action of the MFA was also a victory won by
lessons of liberation learned in Africa. For, as Aristides Pereira laid it on the
record a little later, 'most of the principal leaders of the MFA were officers
who had served at the front in Guine, where little by little they had understood the futility of a criminal colonial war, the real interests of the Portuguese, and our own inalienable right to independence '[1] – a statement, as will
be seen, that was confirmed by Portuguese officers at the time.
  The Portuguese thus joined themselves to the community of the world
after a long absence; and it was much to their credit. Sorely hit though they
were, they could have continued for a while with their colonial wars; they
preferred to end them. Whatever might come afterwards, nothing would
lessen the value of this act of dignity and hope.
  All this should be said, and more; yet nothing can lessen another fact. The
Africans of the Portuguese empire were in no sense given their independence
by Portugal; they had to take this independence for themselves. During the
war: but also now, in 1974.
  The actual and dramatic story of their taking of independence in 1974 is a
complex one. In what follows I will set forth the decisive points so far as the

147

PAIGC was concerned. Although very different in circumstances, the same course of events governed the liberation of Mozambique, and even that of the still more complex case of Angola, in all basic essentials. FRELIMO in Mozambique and the MPLA in Angola faced the same intrinsic situation. They responded to it in the same intrinsic ways.

* * *

The PAIGC had ceaselessly studied the Portuguese, and knew them well. What its leadership particularly knew about them on 25 April was that the colonial army, at least many of its young officers and most of its rank-and-file, wished to end the war; but, secondly, that many of its senior commanders believed that the war could still be ended with a 'neo-colonial' compromise such as would ensure a continued if less direct Portuguese control. The PAIGC also knew that long years of fascist distortion and isolation had deprived most Portuguese of any useful grasp of political realities in Africa, and that this could play into the hands of fascist generals who were still upon the scene. These last included the odious Spinola, now in Lisbon after retirement from his Guine command the previous September 'for reasons of personal exhaustion'; the equally beaten and even more abrasive Kaulza de Arriaga; and others of their kidney.

True enough, there were senior officers of a different make, most notably General Vasco Goncalves, who were now seen to possess the patriotic clarity of mind and moral courage to recognize that any useful change in Portugal must be undermined without a genuine decolonization, and who were ready to act on this perception. But these others were a few at that level. Much was to be hoped from the parties of the Left, now fully legal once again; and yet even here there had to be doubts. The Portuguese socialists had yet to prove that they were ready to press for decolonization, or even to accept it as desirable; while the Portuguese communists, although evidently ready to do both, were now involved in support for a regime which, whatever its merits and prospects, was still presided over by Spinola, to whom the MFA had awarded leadership. This last fact alone was in any case enough to counsel prudence.

Those who led the PAIGC had respect for democratic Portuguese, and many had an affection for Portugal. They had campaigned for peace and good relations with a democratic Portugal, as document after document since 1956 is there to prove. But they knew now, very well, that even this partially renewed Portugal would not willingly concede a full independence to its colonies. No matter what revolutionary waves might surge in Lisbon, Spinola and his kind would twist and manoeuvre. A trap would be set. Pereira and his comrades waited for the trap.

While waiting, they took a step of their own. Eleven days after the Lisbon coup, on 6 May, their executive met at Boe in Eastern Guinea-Bissau, and issued their conditions for peace. The document in question is another that deserves to be remembered, for it largely foretold what the outcome was really going to be, no matter how many traps were set in the meantime.[2] They offered 'a concrete proposal' for ending the colonial war. This supposed that Lisbon would first accept the 'complete liberation of our people of Guine and Cape Verde', and would therewith recognize the Republic of Guinea-Bissau (declared the previous September), and the right of the Cape Verdian people to self-determination and independence. They also posed a second condition for peace, having no intention of forgetting their comrades in Mozambique and Angola. Lisbon must at the same time 'recognize the right to independence of the peoples of the other Portuguese colonies'. Given Lisbon's agreement to these conditions, immediate negotiations should follow 'with or without a ceasefire'. If Lisbon wanted a ceasefire, then two further conditions must be met. One was that all Portuguese garrisons and other units must be gathered at regional points of assembly for the purposes of ultimate evacuation; the other was that all acts of aggression must cease.

A reply came back through the good offices of the President of Senegal, Leopold Sedar Senghor. Would Secretary-General Pereira come to Dakar for a secret meeting with the new Portuguese foreign minister, the Socialist Party's Mario Soares? This meeting duly followed at the Ngor hotel, near Dakar, on May 16. Through Soares, Lisbon asked for a ceasefire before making any commitment. Pereira pointed to the PAIGC's conditions in its declaration of 6 May. Soares replied with Lisbon's 'difficulties': essentially, that Spinola had enough backing in the MFA to resist the PAIGC's conditions. Soares then repeated Lisbon's request for an unconditional ceasefire. Pereira refused this out of hand, since any such ceasefire might threaten a dismantling of the PAIGC's military positions before there was any promise, let alone guarantee, of colonial withdrawal. But Pereira was prepared to recommend his executive to accept a temporary truce on the understanding that this could in no way reduce the superiority of the PAIGC's tactical domination of the field of battle, and, thus, its capacity to begin the war again without incurring any disadvantage.[3]

So the Dakar meeting proved fruitful; it opened the process that was to lead to peace and independence. A conditional truce was agreed. This enabled the PAIGC to profit from the fact, well known to its executive, that the local MFA in Guinea-Bissau was determined to end the war: if progress could not be made with the Portuguese in Lisbon, in other words, then very possibly it could be made with the Portuguese in Bissau. From now onwards, in fact, the scenario became a dual one: in negotiations (in London and Algiers) with emissaries of Lisbon, and in parallel exchanges (in the bush) with the Portuguese in Bissau. These two 'sets of negotiations' formed a single one in PAIGC strategy, but for the sake of clarity they may best be followed separately.

After little delay, a first meeting with Lisbon's emissaries followed in London. Led by Pedro Pires, the PAIGC delegation restated its conditions as before: let the Portuguese agree to unconditional withdrawal from their colonies, and a ceasefire could follow in which the technicalities of their peaceful withdrawal would be settled, and friendly relations ensue. Soares, for Lisbon, again argued 'difficulties' and asked for 'understanding'. Any concessions made to Guinea-Bissau, he urged, would affect Mozambique and Angola, and Lisbon had received threats of counter-action by South Africa if it should go 'too far'; besides which, Soares let them understand, there were other pressures for 'moderation'. The PAIGC should not ask for too much; instead, it should help the democrats of Portugal.

But the trap was obvious now, and there for all to see: let the PAIGC only agree to end the war before Lisbon had promised anything substantial and concrete, and Spinola's neo-colonial game could be much advanced. Soares and his colleagues (who included two of Spinola's known henchmen) therefore met with blank refusal, coupled again with a restatement of PAIGC conditions for peace and full independence. At this point the meeting was suspended while Soares reported back to Lisbon. He returned to London with nothing new to offer. Pulling back even from their previous position, Lisbon's men would only talk now of a possible 'self-determination' for Guinea-Bissau; and, beyond that, they wanted to treat the country as a 'special case' setting no precedent for Mozambique and Angola. On this the London meeting ended. Pires said to Soares before they parted: 'Last time we met we gave you a tree in full flower to take to Lisbon, and here you've brought it back a withered twig.' It was no more than the manifest truth.

One may note in passing that here was another occasion on which Sekou Toure showed hostility to PAIGC leadership. Evidently unaware of or indifferent to the real strength of their position, whether military or political, he greeted the PAIGC decision to meet the Portuguese in London with a broadcast speech, which, among other things, said that 'it would be an aberration and a most grave danger if negotiations should take place in a country [that is, Britain] which has not only not recognized the independence of Guinea-Bissau, but openly supports the policies of Portuguese fascism and those of *apartheid* in Africa.' The case is all the odder in that it appears that the PAIGC had fully informed him of their position and intentions, and he had indicated no dissent. However that may be, Toure caused his speech to be rebroadcast repeatedly in Portuguese and in several African languages. In the circumstances, one could scarcely fail to see several of the passages in this speech as another direct attack on PAIGC leadership, and even as an appeal for revolt against it.

Yet Toure, in this, was once more wide of grasping the truth of what was really going on. Aside from what passed in London, the other 'internal' scenario had begun to move inside Guinea-Bissau. As we shall see in a moment, the MFA there was taking matters into its own hands, and moving towards separate talks with the PAIGC; informal contacts between Portuguese and PAIGC officers began to take place, in fact, soon after the initial Dakar meeting between Pereira and Soares. Such contacts occurred, for instance, between the PAIGC southern command and the garrison at Gadamael, where there had been much tough fighting in past months. These were without commitment by either side, but they gave a chance for later development. 'Our aim at that stage,' the PAIGC leader Julio de Carvalho (Julinho) told me later, 'was to show the Portuguese troops, especially their African troops, that it was unreasonable to go on with the war. Even troops from Portugal responded, in some cases sending out trucks with messages to say they were with us.'

Learning of all this, if obscurely, Lisbon had to move again, and this time faster than before. But Pereira and his comrades refused another London meeting. Although PAIGC representatives had been invited a few months earlier to the Labour Party congress of 1973, the newly elected British Labour Government still refused to join some eighty other governments in recognizing the independent state of Guinea-Bissau, while the British Foreign Office, if less surprisingly in view of its pro-Spinola preferences, had barely troubled to conceal its distaste for the PAIGC delegates during the London meeting. On 13 June the talks resumed. But on PAIGC suggestion they resumed in Algiers.

Again the Portuguese brought nothing fresh. They made it once more sufficiently clear, however, that Spinola and his backers[4] still hoped to induce the PAIGC to agree to his terms rather than having to give way to theirs. It was partly, the Lisbon men explained with some embarrassment, because Spinola wished to conserve the 'heroic image' he believed himself to possess. In any case, his terms were unacceptable. Very clearly, now as before, the key factor for Spinola was to secure an unconditional ceasefire; but on this, as before and after, the PAIGC would not budge from summary refusal.

Leading for the PAIGC, Pedro Pires thereupon told the Portuguese side that since it was evidently not ready for serious negotiations, his executive would now consider if the truce could still go on. The PAIGC had agreed to it in order to find out if the Portuguese would make peace by recognizing the national independence of Guinea-Bissau proclaimed in the previous September, and already recognized by some eighty states up and down the world. If the Portuguese would now accept and recognize this reality, well and good: the way would be clear for negotiation on the technical aspects of complete Portuguese withdrawal, and on subsequent relations between the two states. But if they would not, then the truce had no more value, and war would have to begin again.

This brought matters to a head. For the fact by now, thanks to the action of the MFA in Guinea-Bissau, and still more to the action of PAIGC militants in talking to the colonial troops, was that the 'falcons' in Lisbon no longer had an army to fight with. Soares put this on record at Algiers with an 'historic declaration'. The Portuguese, he said, would in any case no longer make war.

But by what further means could they be got to make peace?

The answer had to come from within Guinea-Bissau.

* * *

Things began to move in the capital of Bissau, with its large Portuguese garrisons behind their barbed wire and concrete pill-boxes, very soon after 25 April. The general in charge, Spinola's successor there, was Bethencourt Rodrigues, who had come from long service against the MPLA in Angola.[5] Strong for the dictatorship and for Spinola, Bethencourt had henchmen of the same mind. Yet the bulk of the army thought otherwise, including officers who had fought hard and long and were in no way demoralized; and, as well as these, there were young MFA officers, captains and lieutenants, who were firmly for decolonization. Composed variously in this way, the territorial MFA saw that it must seize the reins of power in Bissau, and did so.

One of its early actions was to put Bethencourt on a plane to Lisbon; after that, for a while, there was no Portuguese commander-in-chief (or governor). Then a replacement arrived in the person of Brigadier Carlos Fabiao, who had served against the PAIGC in earlier years. Sent out now by Spinola with orders to 'take things in hand', Fabiao arrived with a reputation as a fire-eater. But he soon showed himself to be another who had learned the lessons of a fruitless war. Arriving in the governor's palace at the upper end of Bissau's main avenue, Fabiao proved favourable to a realistic assessment of the position, and thus to contacts with the PAIGC.

Informal contacts, as I have said, were already occurring, but they were clearly not enough. Even though only a small number of Portuguese units continued to show fight, the situation between the two sides remained tense, for they faced each other in fighting positions. No hostilities occurred after May 25, when the temporary truce began, save for one or two very minor flurries in the last days of that month. Yet hostilities might all too easily begin again by accident, especially if Portuguese troops made unannounced moves across the territory and were opposed, as they would be, by PAIGC besieging units. Foreseeing the danger of such clashes and the possibility that these might lead to a renewal of PAIGC offensive operations, the Portuguese emissaries at the London meeting had insistently asked for a means to avoid the danger. Lt.-Col. Almeida Bruno, who well knew the desperate situation of the Portuguese army in Guinea-Bissau, proposed that the PAIGC should send a liaison officer to Bissau, so that, through this officer, any proposed Portuguese troop movements for withdrawal on Bissau might be made known to the PAIGC command. This was agreed.

Duly appointed by the PAIGC, an intrepid Juvencio Gomes walked out of the southern forest to the long-contested airstrip at Cufar on 10 June. But Fabiao was there to receive him, and they flew at once to Bissau. There, Juvencio's chief task was to inform the PAIGC command by radio signals of all Portuguese troop movements as advised to him by Brigadier Fabiao or his staff, so that PAIGC units besieging or confronting Portuguese units would not attack if the latter should move; the chief objective of such movements, later developed much further, was to assemble outlying garrisons at points convenient to a later evacuation. The liaison worked well, and all clashes were avoided. Meanwhile the PAIGC command, continuing to push for its own 'local solution' no matter what might fail to happen in talks with Lisbon's emissaries, took measures to strengthen its political campaign.

For weeks, now, PAIGC units in the field had been reporting the arrival of peasant 'spokesmen' from within beleaguered towns or villages held by Portuguese garrisons. These men came out and said that 'their' garrisons were ready to end the war, and sometimes they even brought Portuguese officers who said the same thing. A certain fraternization continued to develop on the basis of 'no more war'. To such local approaches the PAIGC unit commanders replied with their orders: they would undertake no operations while the truce lasted, but would reinforce patrols and begin again as soon as the truce ended. And to make sure that these orders were fully known in Bissau, both for the concession they contained and the threat, the PAIGC high command had them radio'd *en clair* in good Portuguese, not in cipher. The net effect, together with the influence of informal meetings, was to broaden a local Portuguese conviction that there could be no alternative to unconditional colonial withdrawal.

So it was expected, and so it came about. Yet prudence on the side of the PAIGC continued to be justified in view of the failure to reach agreement, whether at London or later at Algiers. Faced with this diplomatic *impasse*, the central committee of the PAIGC decided to oblige the Portuguese to meet their conditions of 6 May: that is, to match the truce with a withdrawal of their troops on Bissau, from where, later, they could be withdrawn by ship to Portugal. They accordingly proposed to Brigadier Fabiao that he should meet the PAIGC secretly, somewhere in the bush, so as to fix terms for this withdrawal; the alternative being that the PAIGC would end the truce and go over again to the offensive. Conveyed through Juvencio Gomes and his radio-link in Bissau, this proposal for a meeting was accepted by Fabiao.

A most secret encounter followed on 13 July at a cross-trails in the forest of Medjo, part of the old liberated zone of Cubucare in the southern part of the country. Led by Constantino Texeira, a strong PAIGC delegation included Jose Araujo in order to emphasize continuity with the Algiers talks. They waited with some curiosity for the Portuguese to arrive. They could not be at all sure, after all, of what was going to happen. Would the Portuguese send a lame-duck representative? Would they come at all?

The Portuguese had to come by helicopter, since all the roads were closed to them. More or less on time, they showed up in no less than three helicopters. These landed in the Medjo clearing and the Portuguese got out. As soon as the PAIGC men met them, they knew that they had planned rightly: they had finished off the war. For the Bissau delegation was led by Fabiao himself, and included half a dozen other senior Portuguese officers whose functions were quickly explained by Juvencio Gomes, who had come with them. A wise patriotism among the Portuguese had evidently prevailed; the war could end with an unconditional colonial withdrawal.

And so it proved. Two days of fruitful discussions ensued. Gradually, suspicions thawed. Each night the Portuguese officers returned by helicopter to Catio, while the PAIGC remained in the bush. After all, it was their bush, their country, and they insisted on the point, tactfully, by providing food and drink in that forest clearing through the organization of their senior militant on the civilian side, Carmen Pereira.

Part of the agreement reached at Medjo was that the Portuguese armed forces in Guinea-Bissau would regroup in an orderly way and retire on Bissau. Since there were about 130 Portuguese garrisons spread around the country (garrisons, that is, with Portuguese personnel apart from African troops in Portuguese service), this had to be a complex matter. It was disposed of in two chief stages of agreement. A timetable for the phased withdrawal of several dozen of these garrisons was agreed at Medjo; later, another timetable for the withdrawal of the rest was agreed at a meeting in the Portuguese barracks of the town of Gabu (in the north-east of the country).

Another aspect of the agreement concerned the several thousand African troops and militias in Portuguese service. The Medjo meeting agreed that the Portuguese command would now disarm all their African troops and send them home, and that the PAIGC would help them to do this; at the same time, the PAIGC confirmed that there would be no persecution of these former colonial troops, this being in line with PAIGC policies on national unity and peace, except for any individuals who were regarded as war criminals.

This was a huge advance for the PAIGC; yet doubts as to the future still remained so long as Spinola and others like him reigned in Lisbon. It was known, too, that Spinola still had his own hope of regaining some kind of indirect control. At about the time of the Medjo meeting he informed Fabiao, in Bissau, that he wished to come to the territory and there meet PAIGC Secretary-General Pereira. Would Fabiao get the PAIGC liaison officer in Bissau (Juvencio Gomes) to inform the PAIGC central committee of this project, and ask their agreement to it? The idea, as it transpired, was that Spinola and Pereira would together attend a session of the phony 'Congress of the People' — another fake like FUL[6] — which had been set up by Spinola in 1973. This 'congress' would 'demonstrate' for 'a sufficient self-determination', and Spinola would go home with the outlines of a neo-colonial control in his pocket and with bolstered prestige.

This was so patent a trap as to be absurd in itself. Apart from anything else, the obvious aim was to set aside the credentials and constitutional authority of the People's National Assembly which had declared independence the previous September; besides which, the last thing that the PAIGC intended was to have dealings with the man whom they regarded as responsible for the plot that killed Cabral. To Spinola's 'project' they replied short and sharp: if Spinola should arrive in Bissau, or anywhere else on the territory of Guinea-Bissau, they would at once resume the war on all fronts. And on that same day they sent orders to all senior commanders in the field that units should stand by to attack their targets as soon as an action signal was received, probably within the next few days: probably on 2 August, when Spinola was expected to arrive in Bissau.

Spinola never arrived, warned off by Fabiao. Instead, at this point, there came another of those 'turns of history' which make a difference.

* * *

It occurred thanks to Bobo Keita who, with permission, gave me the details some time later. One of those staunch young men who had reached maturity through Cabral's teachings and the experience of the liberation war, Bobo had

fought all through that war, had risen to positions of command, and now in
1974, as a senior commander of the eastern region, had been a member of the
PAIGC delegation to the London talks. These yielding nothing, he had
returned to his command, ready to begin the war again. Afterwards a member
of the general staff of the army for Guinea-Bissau, Bobo is a stalwart figure
who unites a shrewd judgment with a sense of humour. Both qualities came in
useful now.

Here in the east he had control of pretty well all its territory save for
several strongly held Portuguese camps and villages, notably Burumtuna and
Canquelifa. All these he had completely severed from ground contact with
each other or with Bissau and, since the fighting petered out after 25 May, he
had received messages from peasants and Portuguese officers, inside those
fortified camps, suggesting peace. Bobo had replied with his orders: truce
until agreement on unconditional withdrawal, or war to begin again.

Now came orders to stand by to begin again at the shortest notice. 'Of
course', Bobo recalled:

> I contacted my sector commanders that same night, and we analysed the
> orders so as to be able to carry them out when the action signal came.
> But at the same time I was bothered by two things. The peasants held
> by the Portuguese in those camps had told us that the troops there
> didn't want to begin again, and, besides, if we began again, those
> peasants would suffer no matter how we tried to save them. Then, too,
> we had our own militants inside those camps to contact the people and
> the Portuguese, so as to strengthen the will for peace. If ordered we
> should certainly begin again, but there were these problems.

In other words, Bobo was going to have to shoot at people who clearly wanted
peace, a very unwelcome prospect. So, taking thought, he 'decided on a
variation, a manoeuvre'. The PAIGC had always put value on personal initiative; Bobo used his now. He got his units into positions of assault, as usual
explaining to them why, but in two cases (those of the camps at Burumtuna
and Canquelifa) he took steps to make sure that their Portuguese commanders
knew that assault on them was imminent.

This provoked an immediately useful response. The Portuguese commander
in Burumtuna asked for a meeting with his opposite number among the
PAIGC besiegers. The latter, at Bobo's orders, said that assault could be
avoided only by immediate Portuguese evacuation, for which purpose the
PAIGC would open the road for withdrawal. This had to be today: at once.
The commander, a man who certainly had no lack of courage, objected that
he would need twenty-four hours to get out of Burumtuna, because he had
heavy equipment to load and move. Applied to, Bobo agreed to that delay.

So the Portuguese evacuation of Burumtuna began on 2 August, the day
that Spinola was expected but failed to arrive. It continued the next day with
PAIGC units helping the Portuguese to load their trucks. There was no
trouble; on the contrary, it seems that everything went with a friendly swing.

This was not the retreat of a physically shattered army, after all, but the with-drawal of an army which had decided, out of its own good sense, to fight no more. Nor was there on that strange scene, with PAIGC troops helping their old enemy to go, any spite or hostility recorded; again to the contrary, it seems there was the kind of respect that fighting soldiers feel for one another. In this atmosphere the last Portuguese withdrew from Burumtuna on 4 August, retiring to begin with, before going on to Bissau, to a chief point of concentration at Pitche.

And then, getting to hear of this, other PAIGC commanders began to apply other 'ultimatums', and other garrisons began speedily to follow the Burum-tuna precedent. By 10 August the colonial forces had cleared themselves out of the whole north-eastern region, except for Pitche and Gabu (evacuated later), with besieging PAIGC units standing aside to let them through. And now, rapidly, the timetable prepared at Medjo was brought into effect, so that a total withdrawal on Bissau could be made without confusion.

And this was how the end of colonial rule arrived without another shot being fired. Yet its actual ending in these ways was so unprecedented, so original in many of its aspects, that a more direct and personal account may help to convey its strange and peaceful drama.

* * *

Back in England, during all these obscure developments, there had been no means for a private person to understand what was going forward. All the negotiations were in secret; even to its friends, the PAIGC naturally respected the full confidentiality demanded by Lisbon. Yet it was desirable, even urgent, to have at least some notion of the truth. So on 12 July (the day, as it happened, before the crucial but very secret meeting at the Medjo cross-trail), I wrote to Secretary-General Pereira asking for information. On 24 July he replied by telegram that an immediate visit would be more useful. I couldn't get away at once; all the same, I reached Conakry on 13 August.

Life has radiant moments; and this was one of them.

Pedro Pires, whom I hadn't seen since 1972, met me at the Conakry airport. Yes, he said after mutual greetings, everyone was well. Yes, things looked quite promising . . . For Pires, that was saying a lot, and I knew it.

'But what's going forward, then?'

Pires smiled. 'You'll see.'

He took me to Secretary-General Pereira, and the extraordinary facts unfolded, then, and in surprising days that followed. Like Pires, Aristides prefers doing things to saying them; but on this occasion it was different. His vivid smile of welcome told me at once that all was well. Of the develop-ments I have related in the last section there were some still unknown and others still uncertain, but he offered a rapid sketch of what was clear and sure. He added that we would go tomorrow to Boke, the old PAIGC base on the Guinea-Conakry side of the frontier with Guinea-Bissau, where I had first been with Amilcar in 1967 at the beginning of this book; there we would find

Deputy Secretary-General Luiz Cabral and the latest news from across the border. That I had happily arrived at the right moment became further clear when Aristides Pereira explained that another meeting with Lisbon's emissaries, again in Algiers but this time with positive prospects of success, was nearing a successful end.

At Boke, Luiz Cabral was equally radiant and calm, and the latest available details were made clear, including some of the surprising facts about Bobo's 'ultimatum' and what had flowed from it. Luiz enlarged on Bobo's dilemma: that all his formation in the PAIGC had prepared him to spare innocent people and spill blood only when there was no other way, and here was Bobo facing the prospect of orders to shoot into people who were relying on him not to. Bobo had found his way out of that dilemma – and it was characteristic. 'We have fought our war for national independence without hatred for the people of Portugal', Luiz commented, 'and we are ending it now without hatred.' Over our meal together I thought to myself of the epic of these men who had 'begun with nothing' back in 1956 – and that was almost literally true – and yet come through to the end with such good sanity and confidence. Here, surely, was an example that the whole wide world could mark with profit and admire.

For the rest I listened, writing hard. 'Really a joyful time,' my notes record, 'everyone says so.' And no wonder. For now it became certain that the Algiers meeting had at last produced Lisbon's agreement to the conditions posed by the PAIGC from the start: and this agreement was in fact about to be signed. Peace and independence were conceded by the Portuguese. PAIGC units were to move into Bissau within days, and Brigadier Fabiao, for Lisbon, was to hand over formally on September 10, on what would have been Amilcar Cabral's fiftieth birthday, while evacuation of all remaining colonial forces would follow the established timetable. Commenting on this in our talk at Boke, the President of the Republic of Guinea-Bissau, as he would now become as well as remaining Deputy Secretary-General of the PAIGC, remarked that:

> We believe that we have a great responsibility to end this struggle in an orderly and humane way: not only for our own country's sake, but also as a useful precedent in helping the Portuguese to follow suit in Angola and Mozambique.

Luiz Cabral was by no means claiming too much.

With this the talk turned to problems of the future that were now to become problems of the present: to problems of the colonial heritage, unemployment, dislocation, material ruin, and lesser difficulties, for instance the certainty of countless landmines to be lifted . . . so that now, said Luiz Cabral, 'the most difficult part will begin: less hard, yes, but more difficult.' Even in the joy of those days, realism stayed the keynote.

Immediately, the need was for speed in ensuring that nothing went awry. I learned now that Juvencio Gomes and Julio de Carvalho were in Bissau, and

that Joaquim da Silva and Humberto Gomes had joined them in order to disarm the African commandos in Portuguese pay — something, as I was to see,
that they managed successfully — and that now, within a day or possibly two,
others would go from Boke to join them: Silvino da Luz and Osvaldo da Silva
heading for their native Cape Verdes, Dr. Manuel Boal who would extend his
medical responsibilities to Bissau, Carmen Pereira, Jose Buscardini, Lilica Boal
and other senior cadres.

This was astonishing news, since of course I still knew very little of the
events set forth in my previous pages here. I was trying to take it all in when
Aristides asked: 'Would you like to go with them? There's a truck to Cacine,
and then there'll be a Portuguese plane to take you with the others to Bissau?'

He went on: 'After all, you've seen something of this war through the years.
Why not see the end of it as well?' And he added with an affectionate smile:
'You won't even have to walk.'

* * *

Truly, a memorable journey. We crossed the frontier in a truck and headed for
Cacine through blinding rain storms and along roads like craters. These were
forest trails they had all walked many times, and even I on several occasions;
but now the trails seemed short and easy in spite of all the weather. We
bumped through the forest clearing at Guileje, and stopped for long enough for
me to look at that smashed-up stronghold, while Osvaldo da Silva explained
how PAIGC artillery had smashed it. We passed through Gadamael, evacuated
two days earlier, with its buildings bearing squalid witness to its garrison's
swift departure. Little else was left save rubble and rubbish and piles of empty
beercans and discarded bottles. No retreating army's track is ever pleasant to
the eye, and this was another echo of scenes that I had witnessed in 1944 and
1945, coming into evacuated towns and villages on the heels of other fascist
armies withdrawing in defeat.

A limping carburettor delayed us a little in reaching Cacine, evacuated by
the colonial forces a day or so before, but we got there without further mishap.
It proved another of the surprises of those days. Cacine had been the chief
base of the Portuguese marines during the war, and a hard one to attack, for it
fronted on the wide Cacine river; while along its landward side the colonial
commanders had installed a string of hutments for corralled peasants, these in
turn being screened by barbed wire and defensive posts. Entering Cacine, I
also expected some solid evidence of Portugal's 'five centuries of civilizing
presence'.

There was precious little such evidence: not much more, in fact, than a
plaque on the wall of a single-storeyed military clinic, announcing 1954 as the
'Fifth Centenary of the Discovery'. Otherwise all the pompous claims of the
dictatorship seemed empty. As was mentioned in the last chapter, even the
'port' on the Cacine river, reached by a narrow dirt road, consisted only of a
dismal jetty and a hand-cranked crane capable of lifting, I thought, no more
than half a ton. The school, another of Spinola's vaunted contributions to a

'better Guine', was a filthy single room with a dozen benches but no desks or blackboard. For years the dictatorship had basked in a self-proclaimed odour of Christian sanctity; yet this chief marine port on the Cacine river had one small chapel, Number 5 of Fatima, Portugal's latest miracle saint, and even this was stacked with iron bedsteads and miscellaneous junk.

Such were the pathetic truths of Portugal's imperial 'presence' through all these years. Otherwise it was all military barracks and stores. Alongside the seaward buildings was a bar called 'The Volcano' with various legends painted on its inside walls. One was in English: 'Peppers Lonely Hearts Band'; another had the word 'Ranger' in tall letters, and I wondered what echo of the US Ranger outfit had put it there.

We overnighted in a foully dirty officers' mess, and drank warm water from bottles labelled 'Old Parr Whisky, reserved for the Armed Forces', one more dispiriting experience left to us by the departed army. But happily the Portuguese ferry-plane showed up next morning. It could take three passengers as well as the pilot, and for the rest of the day would ferry our group of fifteen or so to Bissau. The first trio consisted of Silvino da Luz (afterwards Cape Verdian minister of defence), Jose Buscardini, another veteran on his way to take over the broadcasting system in Bissau, and myself.

We embarked in that Portuguese army plane and swapped greetings with a taciturn pilot. For my part, at least, I seemed to have got myself into a very strange scenario; and I wasn't alone in thinking this. Buscardini, who never lacked for the appropriate comment, said as we taxied off: 'The last time I was in one of these planes it was when the PIDE were taking me to prison in Bissau, back in 1963. I sat for six months then. . . .' This time we sat for little more than half an hour, swooping over the forests where the PAIGC had marched and fought for years. And we came to the major airport of Bissalanca on the outskirts of Bissau.

With evacuation to Portugal going ahead, Bissalanca was full of big transport aircraft and scurrying personnel. We sat around and felt lonely for half an hour, and then Joaquim da Silva came with a car and took us into town. Joaquim and Humberto Gomes had just succeeded in persuading the 700-strong African commando battalion, Spinola's worst invention, to accept disbandment and lay down their arms, a success for which the Portuguese command was also duly grateful, since they had failed to achieve it themselves. Individuals from this commando battalion were to give trouble in after years, attempting at least one coup d'etat, but in those crucial days they gave way almost happily to forceful arguments and unassailable self-confidence.

In a two-storeyed house next to the governor's palace, nowadays the central office of the PAIGC in Bissau, we found Juvencio Gomes; and here, with the rest of our group, we made our base for the next days. The rest of our group came in on time, Carmen Pereira and other leaders arriving to ensure, if possible, that nothing should now go wrong. And it can be said that nothing did.

Responding to the PAIGC's spirit of reconciliation, Portuguese officers and men called up unknown reserves of good sense and judgment. Having decided to end the war, they continued with their evacuation in a sensible and work-manlike way. The movement set going by the lucky 'ultimatums' had become an orderly withdrawal on Bissau; I travelled about a little with Joaquim da Silva, going up as far as Mansoa and Farim, and saw that it was so. By 20 August (the day on which we reached Bissau), no fewer than 41 fortified camps and defended garrisons had withdrawn without incident. By 10 September the number had grown to 109, and by 18 September all troops stationed outside the capital had assembled at Bissau (with a few at Bolama) for evacuation by sea. I watched some of their transports leaving the port; at least one of them, such were the excitements of those days, was decked with red flags and its railings manned by troops singing The Internationale. With that kind of thing going on, the sense of never-never-land inevitably lingered, and yet it was also the sense of a nightmare being ended in the good and plain light of a merciful day. For these Portuguese – and I got to know a few of them, and watched many more – gave the impression of a people who at last had won out over their own misery and released themselves from their own imprisonment. The Algiers agreement had provided that all colonial personnel whether military or civil, should be evacuated by 31 October; in fact, on PAIGC request and thanks to the prevailing spirit on both sides, all were gone by 15 October.

In all this huge withdrawal of some 30,000 troops there were no acts of hostility, no affrays, no shootings, no casualties (save three, I believe, from a road accident). Had the world ever seen a most bitter war end like this? For bitter it had certainly been, and long: eleven years long. It had ended in colonial defeat; yet the bulk of these Portuguese troops, from a military point of view, had nothing to be ashamed of save the folly and the crimes of their leaders. They had fought hard, held out, gone through various kinds of hell in these dense, damp, malarial and immensely discouraging forests. And the casualty figures for the Portuguese show that these wars, though fought hard in Angola and Mozambique, were fought hardest of all in Guinea-Bissau.

Portuguese casualty figures have remained open to serious doubt as to their accuracy in absolute totals, long concealed by the dictatorship, but have a realistic value in relative terms. Thus their official documents show that the proportions of all Portuguese effectives killed in action in Africa since 1961 were 33 per cent in Guinea-Bissau, 35 per cent in Angola, and 32 per cent in Mozambique; while comparable percentages for military deaths suffered 'for other reasons' were 26, 50 and 24. The admitted percentages of men wounded in action were 48 in Guinea-Bissau, 35 in Angola, and 17 in Mozambique. Yet the PAIGC, inflicting these casualties, could draw on a population of less than three-quarters of a million, compared with some five or six millions in Angola, and some nine millions in Mozambique. Taking these percentages into account, it will be seen that Portuguese casualty totals for Guinea-Bissau were proportionately very much higher than elsewhere. For what they may be worth, admitted Portuguese absolute totals confirm this. They have been given as 6,340 Portuguese killed in action or 'for other reasons', of whom 1,875 died in Guinea-Bissau, 2,671 in Angola, and 1,794 in Mozambique; and although these absolute figures certainly understate the truth, and apparently take no account of African troops killed in Portuguese service, they are still by no means small.[7] (See also note 5, p.120.)

Against these painful Portuguese casualties, one may add, PAIGC military losses were comparatively light, as tends to happen with guerrilla armies which are led with skill. The total of PAIGC combatants killed in action had still to be securely ascertained in 1980. But the relevant government department believed that the total of men who had survived serious wounds was 345, of whom 150 had suffered amputations; that there were about 600 war-widows (but some, of course, belonging to polygamous families); and that about 2,800 children had lost a parent or both parents (though not always parents who were combatants). Indicative rather than final assessments, these totals suggest a smaller total of military dead than might have been expected, and in any case much smaller than the total on the colonialist side.

Those who have known the party of Cabral may not be surprised that it could achieve the ending of war, even of such a war as this had been, without revenge or bitterness. History will award due credit to the MFA as well. Perhaps the most moving tribute to the party of Cabral and its teachings about human liberation, in some ways the most convincing tribute, came from that quarter. For on 29 July, before the first evacuations had begun, the territorial assembly of the MFA met in session at Bissau, and unanimously passed a resolution that speaks volumes for the liberating nature of this victory over fascism and colonialism. The declaration ran:

> The colonized peoples and the people of Portugal are allies. The struggle for national liberation has contributed powerfully to the overthrow of fascism and, in large degree, has lain at the base of the Armed Forces Movement (MFA) whose officers have learned in Africa the horrors of a war without prospect (*sem finalidade*), and have therefore understood the roots of the evils which afflict the society of Portugal.[8]

It was indeed a prospectus for regeneration. The national liberation ideas and struggles of Africa had helped to liberate Portugal as well.

And so the great evacuation came to its end, and the PAIGC was left in sovereign control. It was also left to pick up the pieces. On 15 October, troops of the PAIGC accompanied the last Portuguese troops to their waiting ship. 'And we were left', recalled Bobo Keita when we were talking it over two years later, 'to lift the landmines they had sown. Around Burumtuma alone we lifted more than 8,000. . . .'

But not only landmines.

* * *

Many terrible problems, and not only in Guinea-Bissau.

Yet the capacity to tackle and solve these problems was available, as events now showed, in Cape Verde as well as on the mainland.

During the liberation war it had long seemed that success on the mainland could not at once lead to success on the islands. Far out to sea, these appeared likely to require a more prolonged effort. But it fell out otherwise.

Several hundreds of Cape Verdian militants had rallied to the fight on the mainland and some of them, as we have seen, played decisive roles there. But others were told to stay put and organize a clandestine political campaign in the archipelago. They had a hard time. Seized by the political police, not a few leading militants passed long years in the dreaded prison at Tarrafal on the island of Santiago; at least a dozen were deported to the Angolan prison camp of Sao Nicolau, and others to still more remote regions of the far Angolan south.

Yet an underground organization managed somehow to survive all these arrests. Its cells were small, but generally they were staunch. After 25 April 1974, with the dictatorship swept away in Lisbon but its organization still intact in the islands, these men and women began to venture into the open and promote public meetings. At the first big one of these, on 1 May, they openly presented themselves as PAIGC and began to speak of independence.

These meetings won a mass response, and the work could now be rein-forced by the release from Tarrafal of a number of experienced militants, such as Luiz Fonseca, who had himself spent five years there. Their task, largely, was to explain to these isolated island populations what was going forward in their world, and to prepare them for a different future. They had also to un-mask the true nature of two little 'administrative parties' set going against them by the colonial government (*Uniao Democratica de Cabo Verde*, and, a little later when this had failed to 'take', another such effort called *Uniao das Popolacoes de Cabo Verde* which, in the outcome, did no better). These were essentially the same in kind as Spinola's 'Congress of the People' or FUL on the mainland, though they varied a little in drawing on some Cape Verdians established in Dakar (Senegal).

This semi-legal campaign for independence continued through the events I have described in Guinea-Bissau. It went well, but more experienced leaders were required. In early August, as we have seen, the executive decided it could send them some, including Silvino da Luz and Osvaldo da Silva. Arriving in Bissau, these asked at once for military air transport to the islands, but, because of delays in this being provided, decided to fly by TAP, the Portuguese airline, on 25 August. Eager to get back to London with all the news I now possessed, I went with them as far as the desert island airport of Sal.

It is more than an hour's flight from Bissau to Sal, and on the way we talked. I learned a little of the history of these extraordinary island populations on their bare volcanic crags and hills, of the long drought they had suffered since 1968, of the complexities of their politics and culture. Intensely patriotic as perhaps only islanders can be, these people were now determined to seize an independence that had seemed, only yesterday, little more than a dream. 'But so far, in the islands', said Osvaldo, 'it's been euphoria. Now it's got to be organization.'

The euphoria burst upon us, or rather upon them, as soon as we had landed on Sal, for the airport was packed with happy people who had come from the other islands to welcome their veterans. I lost my spectacles in the crush, but an appeal put out on the Tannoy soon restored them; it was altogether that kind of day. The last I saw of Silvino and his comrades on this occasion was a fine panorama of waving arms, and their heads bobbing above the shoulders on which, triumphantly, they were carried to the inter-island plane for the capital of Praia on the island of Santiago.

As for me, I continued on to Lisbon. Not, I confess, without one or two misgivings as to the reception I might find there. But Lisbon had its own euphoria, and even a traveller such as I was embraced by it. Seeing the name on my passport the transfer-booking clerk cried excitedly: 'Ah, it's you! We know you! You want to go to London? Here, we'll show you, we'll carry your bag for you, we'll make you comfortable. . . .' No other booking clerk had ever done that for me before (or has ever done it since); I went on to London in a happy daze.

* * *

The story of the Cape Verdians, of how they lived through the long colonial period, of how they took part in the fight for the independence of the mainland as a means to win their own independence, of how they won that independence, and of how they then began to confront the tragic problems of their heritage of poverty made deeper by years of unrelenting drought, will merit many books. It is a story that is very human, dramatic and instructive, an epic in the conquest of despair and isolation by an ingenious people who produced for themselves, after 1955, a leadership of enormous distinction. The list of those who rallied to the struggle, proclaimed from the first as a united struggle by the two peoples, those of the mainland and those of the islands, has combined many different characters and talents.

Here I will relate only the chief facts about the winning of the islands' independence. In August 1974, with Spinola and his kind still influential in Lisbon, a new governor arrived to assert Portuguese 'continuity'. Billed for the town hall of Praia, the capital of the archipelago, his 'programmatic' speech was drowned with calls for independence, while people hauled down the Portuguese flag above the building and raised the PAIGC flag in its place. On 15 September, making his last bid for a 'controlled decolonization', Spinola himself came to Sal, also for a meeting with President Mobutu of Zaire (largely, to ensure Mobutu's continued intervention against the MPLA in Angola). The governor, it seems, had promised Spinola an enthusiastic welcome in Praia. But by this time the governor knew better; and now he warned Spinola not to go on to the capital. Spinola turned back to Lisbon, but visited his wrath upon the governor by taking him as well.

On 21 September a new governor, Sergio Fonseca, arrived to apply the 'strong hand'. He duly applied it. On 24 September, for example, some of his troops shot into protesting crowds at Mindelo on Sao Vicente. But by this time the full and accepted independence of Guinea-Bissau was nearly two weeks old, and the Cape Verdians were not going to be left behind. They bound up their wounded and enlarged their demonstrations. And now it appeared that the bulk of Portugal's troops on Cape Verde were of the same mind. As early as 3 July, moreover, Cape Verdian recruits called to take an oath to the Portuguese flag had refused, declaring that 'our flag from now on is the flag of the PAIGC.' The MFA saw that things had singularly changed, and sought contacts with the Cape Verdian leaders. Negotiations followed in Lisbon during October. They were not easy, and Portuguese propaganda continued to assert 'continuity'. But on 9 December the PAIGC organized the occupation of the inter-island broadcasting system, and held it for three days and nights. With this and other unmistakable signs of mass support, the PAIGC once more won the day.

This was fully displayed in the following June of 1975. A general election under Portuguese supervision swept the polls for the PAIGC, turning out 85 per cent of the electorate, of whom 92 per cent endorsed the candidates of the PAIGC. Independence followed on 5 July with Secretary-General Aristides Pereira as President of the new republic. Here too, a new era now began.

References

1. A. Pereira, *Balanco de 20 Anos de Luta. . . .*, PAIGC, Bissau, 19 September 1976, p.12.
2. *Declaracao do Comite Executivo da Luta*, PAIGC, Boe, 6 May 1974.
3. Much the same scenario was unfolded by Lisbon *vis-a-vis* FRELIMO at a formal meeting in Lusaka (Zambia) during June, and with much the same outcome. This provided another demonstration of how little the Portuguese of the MFA had understood the realities of the position occupied so confidently by their adversaries. Here was another Portuguese handicap deriving from the years of fascism.
4. Chiefly, in Lisbon, the Champalimaud finance group; but of course Spinola remained Washington's and London's hope at this stage.
5. One of those who would afterwards claim (see *A Vitoria Traida*, Intervencao, Lisbon, 1977) that the fascist generals had won their wars in Africa only to be stabbed in the back by the 'home front', Bethencourt warrants a footnote as being the man who, with General Luz Cunha, organized and accepted the defection to the Portuguese side of Savimbi and UNITA in Eastern Angola. Though kept secret at the time, this was revealed in a series of letters of 1972 between Savimbi and Luz Cunha, as well as Col. Ramires de Oliveira (Portuguese chief of staff in Eastern Angola in 1972); these letters were handed by MFA sources to the Paris journal *Afrique-Asie*, which published them on 8 July 1974.
6. 'United Liberation Front', see p.140.
7. Generals J. da Luz Cunha, Kaulza de Arriaga, Bethencourt Rodrigues, Silvino Silverio Marques, *A Vitoria Traida*, Intervencao, Lisbon 1977, p.68.
8. Quoted from the then MFA-edited newspaper *Voz da Guine*, Bissau 10 August 1974.

12. Building and Rebuilding

The model which our party builds is one in which participation at the base is guaranteed in all decisions, and at every
level, by a democratic organization and method. ... This
organization and method presuppose the existence, alongside
every executive committee, of an assembly of delegates
elected from the level of that committee, an assembly which
elects and controls the committee in question.
ARISTIDES PEREIRA, August 1976

As in Mozambique and Angola, liberated in the same years, the immediate
problems were two-fold. They were material and technological poverty, backwardness, widespread physical ruin; and, on the other hand, a more or less
profound moral and political confusion in several areas still under colonial
control at the end of the war. This heritage of a long foreign domination was
a grim one, but was at least foreseen and measured by the leaders in the work
of liberation. They knew that they could not avoid any of the problems of
this heritage; but they were also sure that there were certain policies they
could follow in order to contain and progressively solve those problems.

The rapid ending of the war, in 1974, did not find these leaders unprepared.
They had already considered the various ways in which the war might end,
including the possibility of a rapid Portuguese collapse. So long as the war was
on, there had been little they could do to grapple with the actual daily problems of the colonial heritage outside their liberated zones; but they had looked
ahead to the time when they would control the entire country, and they had
laid down guidelines of basic method and objective. I will look at these in a
moment; they were derived partly from the socialist choices of the PAIGC,
but decisively, so far as organizational forms and methods were concerned,
from the experience of the liberated zones of which, by 1974, the more
advanced had nearly a decade of effective independence and local self-government behind them. This experience on the mainland could now be applied to
the Cape Verde archipelago as well. The two new republics did not have to
come into their sovereignty with ideas and methods untested or unknown.
They arrived there with the advantages of a rich practice and a consistent

theory. The colonial dictatorships were not brought to an end in a vacuum of political thought and action.

On all that, the outlook was understandably clear and optimistic. Immediately, however, the unavoidable problems were many and enormous. Four basic policies were brought to bear so as to rebuild first whatever could be serviceable, and then to build anew, and from the start, all those things that were lacking. 'We are going to build a new society,' proclaimed the earliest PAIGC banners in liberated Bissau, bravely flapping in the August rains of 1974 (as I saw them myself) even while the last Portuguese military patrols were still on duty; and it was not intended, not for a moment, as an idle boast.

The first of these basic policies was to end the war as quickly and cleanly as possible, avoiding revenge and reducing bitterness, so as to absorb into the community of the PAIGC all those groups and persons who had remained till the last under colonial influence. We have seen something of the persistent success with which this work was done in the months following the April coup d'etat in Lisbon.

Intimately linked with, and continuing this first policy, was a second objective. This was to extend to the zones freed from colonial control only in 1974 the structures, attitudes and culture of the wartime liberated zones, where the outlines of a new society had indeed begun to take shape and where the morality of its values had become part of everyday life. Target areas were the whole of the Cape Verde archipelago; and on the mainland, chiefly the capital, Bissau, where about one-eighth of the mainland population was living by the end of the war.

This 'Bissau problem' was especially difficult, for its 80,000-odd people contained by 1974, a not insignificant proportion of those who had lived for years off the Portuguese military economy, whether by petty trade or petty crime, jobs in the Portuguese service, prostitution or the peddling of drugs. It was the problem posed by all the large colonial cities liberated in these years, whether in Africa or Asia. How to 'reconvert' such a population, give it a decent livelihood, inspire it with a new morality? The defenders of the colonial order have seldom cared to consider this aspect of a departing colonialism.

The PAIGC began to tackle their 'Bissau problem' without delay : first, by an intensive effort of politicization, which largely, for that bemused and ignorant city population, meant simple explanation and discussion; and, secondly, by the installation of urban assemblies and elected citizens' committees through which a trend towards mass participation was launched, and then deepened. They met with remarkably little trouble, a fact explained by the ease and speed with which the mass of the city population could and did assimilate the good sense of PAIGC methods and objectives.

Bissau's 'colonial bourgeoisie', naturally, proved more difficult, and, as later developments were to show in 1979-80, was going to make a big and not always unsuccessful attempt to win control of the new state's bureaucratic apparatus. Its best individuals had long joined the struggle of the PAIGC. But the majority of its several hundred 'members' in Bissau (effectively, there were none elsewhere) included former officials and colonial hangers-on who had not the slightest intention of following Cabral's advice of 1964, and 'committing suicide as a class'. Although strictly speaking they did not form a class, they certainly formed a social grouping. They would find it hard to achieve a concept of life in line with the tasks of liberation; meanwhile they were simply 'there', waiting for the most part to see which way various cats were going to jump. Otherwise there were one or two minor plots of counter-revolutionary violence; these were chiefly the work of former African agents of the Portuguese dictatorship or of several of Spinola's former 'commando' mercenaries. They were easily put down.

A third policy, again characteristic of everything striven for since the 1950s, was to extend and strengthen links with all those foreign parties, groupings, governments and international organizations that might be ready to help without posing conditions. Here the PAIGC continued to gain from its determined policy of non-alignment in all matters that lay outside the scope of the Organization of African Unity. The scale of international response — now from the West as well as from the East — to this call for financial and technical aid testified not only to the seriousness of the PAIGC, but also to the prestige won in many countries by the party of Cabral. Guinea-Bissau and Cape Verde had been practically unknown in the world. Now these sister-republics of the PAIGC became a focus of worldwide attention. Problems relating to the scale of this aid — as to whether it might not bite into the sovereignty of these republics, and as to what would happen when it fell away and stopped — were also apparent; we will look at them a little further on.

From an early point, in any case, the PAIGC leadership began again to think ahead. They argued the need for a wide range of social, economic and political action, starting with basic things such as gaining command of currency and credit, moving on from there to constructing the foundations of national plans, and selecting immediate targets for rebuilding and building afresh. All this was generally put together under the label of 'reconstruction', a somewhat misleading word in that much which had now to be built had never existed before.

A fourth major policy, likewise promoted after liberation as an extension of what had gone before, was to begin the long-term cultural and structural work of creating an organic unity, a far-reaching but probably federal form of unity, between Guinea-Bissau and Cape Verde, now that the PAIGC had won an overwhelming success in both countries. This continued to be seen as being inseparable from other aspects of the struggle for liberation from the colonial heritage.

All these policies had their ramifying effect after 1974; and a full report would call for another book, or several books, at least as long as this one. Written in 1980, this outline can report only on initial progress, and indicate the problems as well as the solutions that remained on the scene. Fortunately, there is no lack of information on which to base judgments. The PAIGC has remained true to the thought and spirit of Cabral in this way, too: it has continued to explain itself in detail and in public, as well as opening its frontiers to all who have wished to probe the explanation on the spot.

I draw attention, therefore, to several documents of crucial importance for the years immediately after 1974, all of which were made public and most of which are available in English. First, there is the detailed report (*relatorio*) given in August 1976 by Secretary-General Pereira on behalf of the Conselho Superior da Luta, the supreme executive council of the PAIGC. Very factual, this sought 'to strike a balance sheet of our action and trace the lines of its prolongation' into the years ahead. A somewhat shorter version, entitled *Balanco de 20 Anos de Luta,* was published on 19 September of that year.

Thirdly, and concentrating now on the detail of new programmes for the long term as well as for the short, Pereira gave the Third Party Congress (held in Bissau, 15-20 November 1977) a 30,000-word review of every field of effort and intention, once again summing up the experience gained and drawing conclusions for the future.[1] Here the crucial issues of ideology and political intention are much discussed, and those readers who wish to find the key formulations that guide PAIGC thinking – on which I will say something later – are directed to this long review.

Fourthly, and more especially for Guinea-Bissau, President Luiz Cabral (and Deputy Secretary-General of the PAIGC) provided at various times a similar series of exhaustive reports, whether thematic or practical: to the opening session of the People's National Assembly, for example, in 1976, and at the first session of the legislature of 1978.[2] Fifthly, and to the same end, Luiz Cabral's opening speech to the same assembly a year later, in 1979, was devoted to questions of developmental strategy.[3]

Alongside these, there is for Cape Verde a corresponding series of basic documents on immediate problems, developmental strategy, and future aims. These include emergency plans drawn up in 1976, and after, for dealing with the long-term drought from which the islands continued to suffer.

Two other sources of information also came to hand. One consisted of the work of foreign observers, notably Rudebeck.[4] The second was a corpus of reports to the Economic and Social Council of the United Nations made by special missions sent by that organization to Guinea-Bissau and Cape Verde, especially in 1977-78-79. These are of consistent factual value, and may be thought to show the world organization at its most effective in the field of information. Here, too, it will be right to pay a tribute to the United Nations, and especially to its Special Committee (on decolonization) and its Department of Political Affairs, Trusteeship, and Decolonization, for the detailed work of reporting and analysis which its officials carried out continuously during the whole period of the armed struggles in the Portuguese colonies.[5] To all concerned with these struggles, this U.N. documentation in reports and summaries was often indispensable, and always useful. I do not really know what we should have done without it.

Other reports of varying interest and value were made by missions from a number of foreign governments after 1975, and a few of these became available. Drawing on all these sources, I have also had the advantage of visiting the two countries on four occasions since 1974.

* * *

What could be achieved in the years immediately after 1975 was necessarily
determined, in large part, by the condition these countries were in. If I am a
little repetitive here, the reason is simply that this condition may be hard to
grasp, in all its difficulties, by those who have not experienced it.

The sterility of the colonial heritage that the PAIGC found in 1974-75 is
indeed hard to overstate. In material terms, the situation of the 'marine port'
of Cacine with its single little hand-cranked crane could simply be generalized:
of installations geared to modern technology and processes of production
there were practically none. The solitary exception on the mainland was a
brewery and soft drinks factory finished in 1973, largely for the needs of the
Portuguese armed forces (who never had time to benefit from it). Admittedly
very up-to-date, with excellent beer-making equipment from several European
countries including Czechoslovakia, it depended on the import from abroad of
all the materials (except water). The position was little better on the Cape
Verde islands; and there, in another dimension, the colonial period had produced not a single hotel for the capital of Praia.

This dearth of any form of development was mental and cultural as well.
There were, for example, no statistics or statisticians, almost no resident or
indigenous doctors (outside the liberated areas on the mainland), almost no
teachers with anything beyond a basic education themselves and, behind all
this, a rate of illiteracy or pre-literacy of about 98 per cent on the mainland
and 70 per cent on the islands.

Summing up in 1977, Pereira recalled that colonial rule had left these
countries with a more or less complete absence of technicians and middle-
level personnel as well as this very high rate of illiteracy; with a feeble transport network, whether by land or sea, in no way corresponding even to elementary internal needs; with a virtually non-existent energy system; with an
almost complete failure to utilize natural resources in order to overcome
material backwardness; with a deficient and inadequate health and educational infrastructure, what little there was being concentrated in a few urban
centres; and, not least, with a lackadaisical and often anti-social conception
of life in certain strata of the urbanized population.

Of Guinea-Bissau a U.N. mission of 1978, in another summary, noted that
'The war had disrupted the economy, which was in any case weak and under-
developed, and had destroyed or damaged much of the very limited infrastructure. The country faced acute shortages in vital areas, especially in food
supplies, trained manpower, equipment and spare parts, budgetary finance
and foreign exchange. . . .' Of Cape Verde another U.N. mission enlarged
upon the tremendous problems which the still-continuing drought, which had
begun in the late 1960s, piled on top of colonial stagnation — to the point that
the rate of Cape Verdian unemployment at the end of 1976 was estimated at
about 60 per cent of the working population.

Among the few statistical data available, there were some for exports and
imports; they in themselves are enough to indicate the measure of the post-

liberation crisis. In the second half of 1974, for example, the exports of 'Portuguese Guine', then becoming the Republic of Guinea-Bissau, covered only 7 per cent of the cost of essential imports. For the whole of 1975, it very soon transpired, the exports of Guinea-Bissau could cover only 16 per cent of the cost of imports, and even less in 1976. Only in 1977 could the productive effort of the new regime and its people begin to reduce these appalling deficits, so that national exports between January and September 1977 were at least able to cover 41 per cent of import costs. The position in Cape Verde was still more adverse. There being no reserves of money in the colonial treasury — Lisbon was even to ask, though vainly, that Guinea-Bissau should meet the accumulated deficit run up by the country during the colonial period — only foreign aid could meet this emergency; and foreign aid, as we have noted, did in fact arrive from many sources.

So the going was tough. Much of the southern region of Guinea-Bissau is ideal for growing rice, with abundant supplies of fresh water in climatically normal times, as well as a relatively unexhausted soil; and rice had long become the staple diet of most of the population. These rice-growing areas were those in which the PAIGC had established its earliest and eventually largest liberated zones, and such was their success in growing rice, even under conditions of warfare, that the liberated zones were producing an export surplus by 1973. But this was too small, in 1974, to offer much to the zones still under Portuguese occupation. There, production of all commodities fell steeply through the late 1960s and early 1970s, and in 1974 there was almost no production at all. The shortfall which had to be bought abroad in that year was almost one-third of the total national need, or some 30,000 tons. If this continued, the country would remain bankrupt.

The PAIGC accordingly sponsored a major productive effort, and rice imports in 1975 were down to 20,000 tons; with the effort continuing, they were down to 11,000 tons in each of the two following years, 1976 and 1977. At the time it seemed likely that rice imports might be eliminated in 1978-79, and the country would then be self-supporting in its main item of food. Unhappily, the extension of the drought in the Sahel came in to kill that prospect; and in 1978 large rice imports were once again required. Aid monies earmarked for infrastructrual and social construction had to be diverted to meet the new emergency. By 1979 the productive situation had begun to improve, but was still unsatisfactory (and was then worsened by grave deficiencies in the distributive situation).

Progress was meanwhile made in other fields. The monopolist stranglehold on export-import trade exercised by the subsidiaries of the Lisbon-based CUP (Companha Uniao Fabril) were rapidly dismantled, and the PAIGC regime, while taking over control of these activities, likewise launched a country-wide system of wholesale and retail commerce, partly by enlarging the wartime system of 'people's shops', *armazens do povo,* and partly by the encouragement of price-controlled local traders. For the first few years, at least, these seem to have worked well. Post-colonial and anti-colonial administrative departments and state agencies continued to be installed with success. All banking, currency and credit were nationalized. A useful start was made in the collecting and collating of essential information, and statisticians were sent for training. Preliminary studies were undertaken to establish the nature of the country's natural resources, including oil; and some initial enter-prises were launched, partly as pilot schemes, partly as co-operatives, and partly as long-term investment. Other aspects of long-term planning provided for a gradual decentralization of urban effort and investment from Bissau, pinpointing such provincial centres as Bolama and Cacheu as points of future growth and development.

Comparable measures were taken by the PAIGC Government of the Cape Verdes, but there the ravages of cyclical drought were far more severe and called for much emergency action. In this respect the break with colonial methods and ideas was exceptionally sharp. The Portuguese had never done anything to alleviate the consequences of cyclical drought, from which the islands had often suffered in the past, except for a little charity now and then. To this latest drought they had reacted in their familiar way. Waking up to its seriousness in 1970, largely thanks to PAIGC agitation on the international scene, they had simply handed out 'relief money', or *apoio* as it was called; and while this could undoubtedly save some lives, it could do nothing to give the islanders any chance of defending themselves better in the future.

Taking power in July 1975, the new PAIGC government reacted very differently. It appealed for financial aid from any country that would give it without conditions, and much, happily, came to hand: not least, no doubt, because the Western Powers were now relieved to find that PAIGC non-alignment really meant what it said, and that the strategically well-placed Cape Verde archipelago would allow no foreign military bases on its soil.[6] This money the PAIGC used in its own way. Instead of handing it round as 'relief', the PAIGC turned the money into a wages fund. We shall see what they did with this fund.

With all this — and we will come back to some of the details — the colonial heritage began to be shaken and shifted. The future could be different.

* * *

Building that future could not be the brief affair of a few years. While tackling the immediate problems after liberation, PAIGC thinkers soon let you know that they were also looking at long perspectives. The armed struggle for national independence and unity had had to be protracted; so would this continued struggle for a new society. Meanwhile, what guidelines to that future did they follow? What was to be the structural and organizational nature of their new society?

People make their own history; and prophecies have never been much use, so far, in describing what they will make. The general aim here was that 'people should live better in ways they work for and recognize', in other words, the aim of everything the PAIGC had fought for since the 1950s. It expressed Cabral's well-known call for a stern realism: that people were not fighting for the ideas in anyone's head, but 'to win material benefits, to live better and in peace, to see their lives go forward, to guarantee the future of their children.'

First and foremost, this meant an end to all those forms of direct exploitation associated with colonial rule, and, beyond that, to all other types of exploitation the 'neo-colonial' countries had shown to be all too possible. So the PAIGC was pledged to end 'the exploitation of man by man in all its forms of subjection of the human person to degrading interests and the profit of individuals, groups, or classes'. This was the general formulation they had worked under during Cabral's leadership, re-stated in the above words by Pereira at the proclamation of the independent state in 1973, and on later occasions after that. Thus the PAIGC programme remained within a revolutionary and socialist perspective, defined in terms of a materialist analysis of productive forces and classes. Otherwise the PAIGC, disliking the use of terms that the masses had not yet learned to understand, and had therefore not yet learned to accept, continued to avoid them. A campaign could certainly have popularized the word 'socialism' as a slogan; but what precisely would this slogan have meant — could it have meant in this phase of development — to village farmers and rural herdsmen?

There is an interesting comparison to be made here, it seems to me, with the early years of preparation for the armed struggle. At that time the pioneering militants of the PAIGC, striving to win peasant participation, had never used 'big words' like 'colonialism' and 'imperialism'. Their leaders might well understand the meaning of those terms as real targets; but it would have been a merely intellectual paternalism to have flourished them, or relied upon them. What the leaders had to do, and what these leaders did do, was to become acutely aware of peasant targets — colonial taxes, administrative impositions, various coercions, and the rest — and then to fight against these targets in such a way as to link their meaning, gradually, to wider meanings concerned with system and ideology. So now the 'big words' like 'socialism' were left to emerge, in due course, from a mass understanding of actions to end this or that well-perceived inequality or injustice.

But meanwhile, to ensure and safeguard this future, the new states took care to abolish all major or external forms of capitalist exploitation. No nationalization of land (save of some urban land) was necessary or in any way desirable in Guinea-Bissau, where nearly all the land was collectively held and divided. But a handful of large landowners in the Cape Verdes were expropriated, and steps were prepared gradually to end *parceria*, a form of *mezzadria* (share-cropping is perhaps the nearest English word) that was widely practised there, often in complex forms which were also the fruit of a purely Cape Verdian history. The banks, as we have seen, were all nationalized, and foreign commercial companies disarmed or removed.

All this cleared the ground for action, as it were, on the 'home front'. Here the process of building a new society had to be many-sided and gradual. There remained contrasts of social system and local custom: just as the legal organs of the new regime, aiming now at an extension and regularization of a new system of justice, found itself, at first, having to accept the application of five or six local codes in relation to petty crime and even to homicide. Among the Balante, in certain circumstances, neither theft nor homicide was regarded as a punishable action; among the Fula, by contrast, both always were, at least in theory. There were differences, too, in regard to the usufruct of collectively held land, to the rights of women in the possession of the produce, of their work, or even of their children; and to the question of mutual aid and collective labour; and much else beside. There were fewer such contrasts in the more homogeneous society of the Cape Verdes, and yet here too there were considerable differences of land-holding and tenancy from island to island, as well as contrasts in means of livelihood between, for instance, Sao Vicente and its close neighbour, Sant'Antao.

PAIGC militants were quite at home in this maze of local usages, thanks to their intimate experiences with it during the long struggle before liberation. The immediate postwar years accordingly found them in the search for 'common denominators' of interest and understanding appropriate to the new period of liberation, just as they had sought and found such 'common denominators' in the fight against the colonial system. Much of the detailed story of these years is composed of this search and its various successes or setbacks: in terms of suitable types of producer co-operative, of vocational schooling, of organizations for the advancement of the equality of women, of methods of fitting army veterans back into civilian life, and a great deal else. It may probably go without saying that much of this was far from easy, and by no means all of it well done, or without a constant battle against egotism, provincialism, or individual folly. Nothing could worse describe these efforts at progress as merely triumphant; sometimes they failed altogether. A process of toil and constant reassessment would be nearer the truth.

There was also the problem, mentioned above, of the 'colonial bourgeoisie', or 'petty bourgeoisie', or however best one should describe this real but elusive grouping. Unavoidably, they had to be absorbed into the new regime, the new state; just as unavoidably, their presence would be a drag on innovating change. How to eliminate or even reduce their negative influence?

Various measures were taken after 1975. One of them, long-term, was to rewrite existing colonial programmes of education and textbooks, give these an anti-elitist content, broaden and extend their range to the working masses, and, meanwhile, 'hold the line' until a new generation could come forward, a generation that would no longer be the product of a colonial background. This, too, met with difficulties: the new educators were by no means always sure of what they should be doing – they themselves, after all, had also received a largely colonial schooling – and a satisfactory supply of progressive teachers could not be whistled out of thin air. Yet a start was made in those early years, and some of it was very promising.[7] Another measure was to select good militants for training abroad in urgently needed technical skills, including those of state administration.

The real problem posed by this 'petty bourgeoisie' – just as in Angola and Mozambique at the same time – belonged to the field of class conflict within these societies. Cabral, during the armed struggle, had gone to great lengths in analysing their 'class contradictions', and much of internal PAIGC debate had been devoted to the same end. No serious militant of urban upbringing any longer thought of the peasantry as an 'undifferentiated mass', even if the precise stratifications and opposing sets of interest were often hard to identify, and relatively 'uncrystallized'. Thrust into all these existing or potential conflicts of conception or ambition, just as evident in the towns, the PAIGC was no more neutral now than in the past. On the contrary, militants were called on to take sides with 'the most underprivileged strata, above all with those who work in the countryside': against exploitative groups or persons, against petty bourgeois elitism, and, of course, against such tendencies which could or did flow in from beyond the frontiers.

The latter danger, one may think, would remain one of some importance. Guinea-Bissau lives on a West African mainland largely subject to neo-colonial elitism and its petty bourgeois values, while Cape Verde must expect strong influences of the same kind from its migrants in America and Europe. In the nature of things, moreover, this class struggle against elitism or its simulacra in the state or society at large was no less a struggle against the same influences within the PAIGC itself, and more especially as the party widened its membership. Much of the everyday drama and dispute on the post-liberation scene — notably of a big internal upset in 1980 and its background — did indeed appear to derive, essentially, from this continuing and at times hotly contested form of class struggle. Let the 'bright lights' of Bissau remain the centre of attraction, let dispensable consumer goods flow in from outside, let 'free enterprise' flourish: all these, and others such, became issues of confrontation.

Given that all these issues, in a large sense, were a 'class question', a third group of initiatives was much discussed in 1976 and introduced in 1977. These aimed at restructuring and strengthening the PAIGC itself. Up to about that time, the leadership had securely relied upon one of its greatest achievements, perhaps the greatest of all outside the purely military sphere: beyond any doubt, it had acquired during the armed struggle a profound legitimacy in the eyes of the peasant masses. It had forged an ideology of liberation whose meaning was known, understood, and accepted. It had established a set of values, whether moral or material, for which men and women were willing to fight and if necessary to die. It had identified itself with the masses, and there is no rhetoric in saying that the same was true in reverse, or that every self-respecting person, though of course in varying degree, gave his or her loyalty to the party of Cabral.

But if 'everybody' had belonged to the PAIGC during the armed struggle, the same could not be allowed to remain the situation in the different circumstances of peace and reconstruction. If that should happen, then the necessary class struggle would sooner or later lose its edge, and all sorts of egoists and opportunists could use their talents for ends that were perfectly contrary to the party's declared aims. The danger of unselective membership was obvious.

New party statutes were presented to the Third Congress (November 1977) and were approved after discussion. These set out to embrace 'the best sons and daughters of our land' within a more structured party. Membership was to be broad, but limited to candidates, whether men or women, who were known to have demonstrated their social and moral value, their work for the party's programme, their capacity for political understanding, and their general worthiness to belong. As with the new parties being formed in Angola and Mozambique at the same time, such persons were not to be selected by any private or hidden process, but in the full light of local participation. From now onwards, but increasingly, this was to be a party of acknowledged militants. At the same time, Pereira defined the nature of the regime of the PAIGC as being that of 'a liberation movement in power', indicating thereby that its content and status were conceived as being in no way static, but so composed as to continue the tasks of liberation.

Given this content and status, the task of the PAIGC was neither to substitute itself for the state which it had brought into being, nor to monopolize the processes of democratization. Its task was to 'push and steer' towards an egalitarian and non-exploitative society. But this task of 'pushing and steering' wasn't conceived, it seems to me, as any simple relationship between 'developed militants' and 'population' On the contrary, and within the PAIGC itself as well, it was to wage those forms of class struggle — *for* the 'most underprivileged strata', *against* elitism and its abuses — which I have briefly touched on above.

* * *

What then was to be the relationship between this PAIGC — on the mainland and in the archipelago — and the two states which it had brought to life? It was another obvious question, given the general world experience of the past fifty years. It was both asked and answered; and the answer of these years since 1974-75 was that the leaders of the PAIGC, having destroyed a colonial dictatorship, had no intention of replacing it with a party dictatorship. In this respect the Third Congress discussions and resolutions were particularly interesting. They tackled a central problem that recurs in any revolutionary process: that is, the problem of making revolutionary leadership compatible with an increasing mass participation, of preventing the ossification of party and state into a bureaucratic authoritarianism, and thus of safeguarding the democratizing dynamism of a sane and liveable society.

The approach was indicated by Secretary-General Pereira at the same congress. In the course of his long analysis, he remarked that:

> In Guinea-Bissau, as in Cape Verde, the state is born for the realization of our programme. And it could not have been otherwise. The carrying out of this programme, in practice, calls for a whole series of practical, material, technical and administrative achievements; and these, by their very nature, a political party cannot effect. A political party acts by persuasion and influence from the basis of confidence won by its political and ideological activities and positions; and it aims, above all,

175

at raising, clarifying and orienting the consciousness of the masses. A political party, accordingly, is not equipped with the means of material, technical and administrative action that national reconstruction and economic independence demand.

So it is the state, led by the party, which has the task of carrying out our economic, social and cultural programmes, and of ensuring defence and security. This subordination of state to party is enshrined in the constitutional texts of our two Republics. Yet this cannot in any way mean a confusion between the two entities, or the substitution of the party for the state. Each has functions that are different. Confusion of the two, or their identification, is prejudicial to the one or the other: such confusion would lead to inefficiency in carrying out the tasks confided to the one or the other; and it would create or enlarge bureaucratism [*o burocratismo*].

Both party and state, in other words, had their functions and purposes as articulated parts of a process of democratization. A large measure of centra-lized control was unavoidable at a time when the colonial heritage still hung heavy, when habits of literacy were still rare, and when the sheer problems of launching new projects and keeping them underway imposed a constant strain on available experience. But the natural tendency for central control to degenerate into one or other form of bureaucratic dictatorship, into one or other form of state capitalism, was to be consciously and strenuously resisted. If the danger could not be avoided, it would have to be averted. First, by the conscious action of the PAIGC as a community of motivated militants acting under a leadership well aware of the problem. But secondly, and in the long run decisively, by continuing to promote structures of mass participation in which the 'most underprivileged strata' have their dominant place, precisely because they are the subject of PAIGC practice and theory.

How did this work out? We have seen that the regimes of the PAIGC were able to come to power with the fruitful experience of their liberated zones on the mainland, the zones which were the scene of all those years of 'mobiliz-ation' (to use the PAIGC's own term for the promoting of participation) that Cabral and his comrades had first set going early in the 1960s. All this experience, as Cabral used to say, was a large aspect of the 'compensation' obtained by these peoples in return for their sacrifices and suffering in the liberation war. This was the harvest of unity and understanding which they reaped through their wartime assemblies, committees, and social service.

Now it was a matter of building on that experience. The process of doing this, perhaps one should emphasise, could be neither easy nor automatic. It continued to exact a most conscious effort. And the effort was in some respects all the harder, on the mainland if not on the islands, because now the natural solidarities of wartime were no longer present, and must be replaced by the more complex solidarities of peacetime. In this crucial matter, representing another facet of the class struggle I have noted above, the sure results – the clear establishment, if you like, of a new social hegemony – would be measurable only in future years. Meanwhile, with mass backing, the leader-ship set out to reinforce participatory structures wherever they existed, and install them wherever they did not. These were to be the sinews of a new society, of a new model.

'The model which our Party builds,' Pereira laid it down[8], and it is worth repeating here from an earlier page because its implications are crucial:

> is one in which participation at the base is guaranteed in all decisions and at every level by a democratic organization and method. These pre-suppose the existence, alongside every executive committee, of an assembly of delegates elected from the level of that committee, an assembly which elects and controls the committee in question.

The effort became a constant one, if with varying results, and, on the main-land, with problems arising from the constant 'pull' of Bissau City on material resources and militant personnel. The evidence for this period is plentiful in success as well as setback; and I found it so myself during travels in 1976 and 1977. Writing from research completed in the latter year, the Swedish socio-logist Lars Rudeback noted that:

> The local committee (*comite de base*) is where the people of Guinea-Bissau are brought most directly into daily contact with the organized political structure of their country. This is a popularly elected five-member committee that the PAIGC attempts to establish in all villages and urban neighbourhoods. At least two of the five members have to be women, according to party rules.
>
> At the moment of total liberation, the local committees already existed almost everywhere in the liberated areas. They have since been gradually extended to cover the whole country, including the *bairros* [urban neighbourhoods] of Bissau, where close to 100,000 people live. No official figure on the number of base committees has been published, My own very rough estimate is that there are perhaps about, or a little over, 1,000 such committees spread all over the country. In the rural areas there may be at an average perhaps 500 inhabitants, including children, per committee, often even less, sometimes considerably more.[9]

In June 1979, the results of the country's first accurate census of population – of persons actually counted, that is, as distinct from 'natives' who were 'estimated' by colonial officials – gave Guinea-Bissau 777,214 inhabitants.[10] Accepting Rudeback's admittedly rough figure of 1,000 committees in 1977, this would give just under 800 persons per committee; but in 1979 there were more committees than in 1977, so that a rough estimate of 500-600 persons per committee might be fairly accurate for that year. Thus the effective democratization of political and social life was steadily advanced. And although the habits and traditions of male oppression of females remained powerful, women were beginning to count in public life as they had never done before.

All-country elections to regional councils meanwhile carried forward the democratization of national institutions. These were held in December 1976, after which, as during 1972 in the liberated zone elections, the regional councils elected their deputies to the People's National Assembly. Again as in 1972, all persons over eighteen were eligible to vote by secret ballot for candidates over twenty-one on PAIGC lists. There being no place for alternative political parties at this stage of development, or for a long time ahead, controls over the mediation of power were introduced by way of the selection of candidates, the selection being of course made after much local discussion; and, again as in 1972, lists with unpopular or distrusted candidates could and did attract 'no' votes. On this point the voting was instructive.

In the old liberated zones, where self-government through elected committees was no longer unfamiliar, the PAIGC lists carried the day by huge majorities: by 84.5 per cent in Oio, for example, and 93 per cent in Buba. But where the colonial system had retained control and influence till 1974, and above all wherever it had succeeded in winning the support of local chiefs (as, for example, among the Fula minority), the opposition was considerable: reaching 44 per cent in Gabu, and 49.6 per cent in Bafata. In these latter areas the running-in of democratic structures would evidently need more time.

Even so, it was sufficiently clear by 1977 that the extension to the whole country of the institutions of self-government was approaching a mature stage. This could not mean, of course, that the system of mass participation, as sketched above, was immune to error, occasional corruption, or misuse of authority. But it did mean that this country had now built, out of the institutional void left by the overthrow of the colonial dictatorship, the basis for democratic decision-making and for democratic checks on that process. The unity of struggle had acquired a national dimension.

In 1978-79 the same process continued to evolve. Non-party structures of local government and participation — *participacao popular* — were still seen as PAIGC assemblies and executives, as essentially party structures, by a people for whom all useful initiatives were identified with the PAIGC. But at the same time they acquired an increasingly democratic nature through the presence of village assemblies of control.

The position on the Cape Verdes was a little different, although the ideas and objectives were not. There the PAIGC had formed no liberated zones during the armed struggle, and therefore no structures of participation. What happened after liberation, accordingly, was that the colonial administrative void was filled not only by the new state organs of the independent regime, but also by newly formed party committees and groups of sympathizers. As early as the latter part of 1976, according to Pereira at the time, 'more than 1,800 militants and an even greater number of sympathizers are organized in party committees and groups'. In the following years, as one found in travelling around the islands, these party committees extended their scope and size; and by 1980 the PAIGC had already accepted some 4,000 men.

and women as party members (or rather more than 1 per cent of the population). Yet once again it was clearly desirable to extend *participacao popular* in regularly organized forms.

Beginning in 1979, the PAIGC moved on to the promotion of local assemblies which elected 'residents committees', *comissoes de moradores,* at the village or town-quarter level. These purely local assemblies and committees would elect upwards to district and island assemblies. A constitution for the Cape Verde Republic, together with new elections at the end of 1980, would confirm and complete these arrangements with the emergence of a People's National Assembly as the sovereign organ of state power. At this point the situation in Cape Verde, in respect of electoral organization, would become essentially the same as in Guinea-Bissau. The aims of all this would encompass what Pereira, speaking in October 1980, called 'a revolutionary democracy'.

The Cape Verde drought continued in 1978-79, although less severe than before. Economic problems remained many, and foreign aid indispensable. There were painful shortages, and many inefficiencies caused chiefly by a lack of properly trained cadres: technicians and other personnel required both by the structures of *participacao popular* and by the state administrations. Yet the central solution, that of ensuring the means of democratic participation in all public affairs, *active* participation, was being steadily achieved.

The mood by the end of 1980, it appeared to me, was one of quiet but self-critical confidence. They were into the 'long haul' now, and could measure its requirements. 'Those blocks of flats we've built,' commented a PAIGC militant as we looked at some new housing at Praia, the capital town, in 1980, 'are not bad. We had nothing at all like them before. But they're not enough, they're only a start. We need another twenty years to get things as they should be.'

* * *

Generally, the immediate needs in both countries had now acquired strong programmatic implications. They included new systems of education, public health, transport, commerce, and the rest; and in all these fields there was progress to report, even if much still remained to be done. The key, in any case, would lie in an all-round increase of productivity and in a steady extension of the means of production. Foreign aid had come from many countries; the task was to use it soundly, and, meanwhile, prevent this aid from diluting or diverting the policies and principles of the new regimes. Here was another danger that could not be avoided, but, with care, could be averted: the danger, among other things, that certain forms and pressures of foreign aid would push for neo-colonial degradation.

Pereira enlarged on all this in his long analysis of 1977. In this phase of transition to self-reliance and self-generating development they would need, he said, to 'proceed with an extreme prudence so as to ensure that whatever we build is built to advance our independent economic development.' They had 'to make very sure that we do not fall victims to a vicious circle that would direct production to the external market at a rate faster than the expansion of the internal market', and thus, by putting priority on exports, fall back into a quasi-colonial posture.

Self-reliance in these senses was quite impossible as yet, but must still be the constant aim. More exports were urgently needed; and the winning of these was going to call for more investment in the export-oriented sectors; 'But the evolution of our economy,' Pereira continued, 'must be activated, above all, by an internal dynamism', arising from the maximization of 'our own resources', whether human or material, and not from any reliance on a merely mechanical expansion won through spending foreign aid. This aid could not continue indefinitely, least of all on the scale of 1976-79, and here was another reason why it 'must remain complementary to a dynamic dictated by the needs of an independent internal development'.

If economic expansion should be launched on a different plan, and achieved for the benefit of the few at the expense of the many, he went on to emphasise, then 'our economy might grow, but it would not develop'. This rejection of policies of 'growth without development' — in their upshot, the essence of the neo-colonial situation, the familiar *vademecum* of hosts of foreign experts in Africa since 1960 — was among the principal defences raised against 'diversion and dilution' through the pressures of foreign aid. The policy of a radical non-alignment was another. The acceptance of aid from a very wide range of donors was a third. And, of course, the nature of new investments, of the actual use of the aid money, was a fourth.

It went without saying that there would have to be compromises. Here, again, was another reason for refraining from premature claims on the ideological front. It might be at least conceivable that a half-continent such as the USSR could 'build socialism in a single country', even though Lenin (or any other Bolshevik in Lenin's time) had never thought so; it would be merely absurd to think that Guinea-Bissau and Cape Verde could do it. What they could do was to continue on their line of practice and theory, as outlined in my pages here, while promoting and defending their independent development. To that end, but also with these thoughts in mind, they began to take their part in the world as it was. Guinea-Bissau joined the Economic Community of West African States (ECOWAS), and Cape Verde also did so. Guinea-Bissau became a member of the international oil producers' conference, even though its oil was not yet being produced. There were other such moves.

One compromise that could not be avoided was the Cape Verdian agreement to allow South African Airways to continue to enjoy its staging facility at the big airport on the desert island of Sal. Here was another aspect of the colonial heritage; but to have brought it to an end, in line with OAU sanctions against racist South Africa, would have imposed an acute financial hardship at a time when Cape Verde desperately needed every source of income it possessed. In this matter of Sal, in fact, the position was just the same as that of Mozambique in respect of continued South African use of the port of Maputo, or of the limits on sanctions against apartheid accepted by other states in the Southern African region. The OAU rapidly recognized this. Its Khartoum summit of 1978, with Resolution 623, asked for an inquiry into continued South African use of Sal. The commission of inquiry duly reported to the Monrovia summit of 1979 and, with Resolution 734, the OAU expressed 'its understanding for and sympathy with' the Cape Verdian position, while at the same time appealing (vainly as it turned out) for member states to produce financial aid on a scale that would make it possible for Cape Verde to ban South African Airways.

One may remark, in passing, that these intractable situations went together with work to discuss, prepare and start a range of economic enterprises aimed at self-generating development. What that meant in Guinea-Bissau was registered in detail in Luiz Cabral's long address on strategy for development, made in May 1979; and it would be out of place in this brief outline to embark on a long description. Cabral had plenty to say that was positive, and quite a bit to say that was not. Much was being well done: in better farming, in the building of storage silos, in the improvement of roads, in the provision of coastal shipping for the creeks and rivers of the country, in the erection of refrigerating plant and the protection of fisheries, and much else, as well as the social and cultural advances that I have touched on earlier. Other things were being badly done. Too much of the state's money was going in payment to state employees. Certain enterprises were a vast disappointment. Particularly bad was the case of a fishing boat enterprise financed by Algeria. Thanks to poor local work, 'this has got absolutely nowhere. On the contrary, at each meeting of this Assembly' — the People's National Assembly to which Luiz Cabral was speaking as the country's president — 'we have noted that it has taken a small step backwards.' There was a shortage of manufactured oxygen, even though a new factory set up to produce it (with acetylene) 'was ready about a year ago'. Yet the factory was not in operation 'because we have not yet managed to install a supply of water for it'. Bad inter-ministerial liaison was the guilty factor.[11]

In Cape Verde, too, there was no lack of self-critical exposure, but also, quietly, no lack of sound progress. I will mention here only the matter of the anti-drought campaign. The eternal problem in the archipelago has been that the Cape Verde islands are steep and rocky (save for the desert island of Sal), and much of the tumultuous tropical rains, whenever they fall, regularly rush down gullies and bounce away into the sea. Nothing serious was ever done about this during the long colonial period (making a vivid contrast, by the way, with the much better situation produced under Spanish rule in some of the Canary islands). But, establishing a 'wages' fund from aid money, the PAIGC set out to change the ecology of Cape Verde.

In 1977 it began to employ some 30,000 workers, a large proportion of the available but otherwise jobless labour force. By 1980 they had built 7,200 stone barrages, 199 kms of retaining walls in stone, and 2,300 kms of retaining walls in earth.[12] You see these water-retaining works in all the more densely populated islands, though especially on Santiago, Sant'Antao and Fogo. They have four purposes. They prevent a considerable proportion of

181

tropical rains from flowing down hillsides into the sea, and thus enable these rains to sink into the soil to enlarge areas of cultivation, feed springs, and form reservoirs. At the same time the PAIGC launched a major programme of afforestation. By the end of 1979, and thanks now to large-scale voluntary participation as the idea caught on, they had successfully planted some two million trees, mostly of drought-resistant varieties of acacia, and were due to plant another one and a half million before the end of 1980. With UN aid, new wells and boreholes were also being sunk. A long-term revolution in ecological improvement was on the way.

Referring back once again to the basic policies noted at the onset of this chapter, there was also the question of unity between the two countries. Given the prestige and popularity of the PAIGC in both of them, it would have been easy enough to introduce a federation, or its equivalent, by simple proclamation and imposition 'from the top'. Yet this would have violated PAIGC principles, and was never, I think, so much as considered. Instead, there came the introduction from 1976 onwards of a network of consultative and co-operative committees — technical, cultural, political — through which a process of promoting an eventual union between the two peoples could be realized. These committees worked for joint planning and complementary programmes of development; but unity would become possible, it was repeatedly emphasised, only when the political consciousness of both peoples was ready to want and make it.

There was never, I think, any organized opposition to eventual unity on a federal plan. Yet each of the two populations had its own identity; and much in either country showed that there was a need for prolonged campaigning work, after decades of colonial divisiveness, before unity could become popular. Stressing that PAIGC policy had not changed since the 1950s, Pereira said in March 1976 that:

> Our aim is to unite our two republics. But there's no question of allowing ourselves to be rushed. We are embarked upon a unique experience: two sovereign countries but the same party in each of them. Yet each has its own character, and we shall choose our road carefully.
>
> We secured the unity that was required to win independence both in Guinea-Bissau and in Cape Verde. Now it is a matter of method and timing to secure what has always been our declared aim, the union of our two countries.[13]

To which the Cape Verdean Prime Minister Pedro Pires, questioned on the same subject, added:

> What is quite sure is that we shall in any case adopt the most democratic method we can find. There is no question of any attempt to impose union. It must come when the people see the value of it. That has always been our line: not necessarily to choose the easiest or quickest route that people are ready to follow, or want to follow even if you

persuade them to.

Such attitudes were reflected in statements by Luiz Cabral and other mainland leaders. Meanwhile both countries continued to be governed by elected
militants who knew each other well, and whose experience had long convinced
them that unity must be their watchword: provided, always, that this was a
unity nourished from the base, and not imposed from the top.

Defending and advancing their principles and programmes, the two
countries were now in the forefront of Africa's effort to escape from under-
development and all it means. They could be seen as part of a trend now
sharply in contrast to the neo-colonial confusions, or even worse, continuing
to haunt various countries in every major region. Again without claiming any
exemplary role, the PAIGC continued to recognize such facts. They looked
for friends; they put such influence as they had behind an enlargement of
this innovating trend.

Among the disappointments, in this respect, was the emergence of a clear
hostility on the part of the Republic of Guinea-Conakry led by President
Sekou Toure. The roots of this hostility were not exactly new, as we have
seen in Toure's response to the events of 1973. But now it took a new form,
and offshore oil was the reason. Back in 1964 the government of Sekou
Toure had quietly laid claim to a large segment of the territorial waters of
'Portuguese Guine'. The Portuguese ignored this claim, and the PAIGC, then
fighting the battle for Como island, were in no position to say anything on
the subject. There the matter rested, and was largely forgotten. But in 1980
the government of Guinea just as quietly signed an agreement with Texas
Oil which conceded to that corporation offshore-oil prospecting rights in the
aforesaid territorial waters of what was now the Republic of Guinea-Bissau:
territorial waters extended, in 1965, to the 200-mile limit. To this the government of Guinea-Bissau reacted sharply, rejecting both the claim and the
Texas Oil licence. At the end of 1980 the outcome had still to be seen.

In another direction there were useful developments, especially in relations
with the like-minded regimes and parties of Angola and Mozambique. Luiz
Cabral in 1979 could 'stress the wealth of trust that exists between the
political leaderships of all the Portuguese-speaking African countries: a trust
which was born in the common struggle for independence and progress, and
in the identical choices made from the first moments of that struggle.' The
question was: how best to use this trust on the wider scene? A meeting of the
five foreign ministers, held on Sao Tome in 1976, decided not to launch a
post-liberation CONCP – the wartime committee which had acted, to some
extent, as a useful organ of liaison and common action – because conditions
were now different, and, at that time, the immediate problems of liberation
were especially acute. By the middle of 1980, however, one had an impression
that the wind was beginning to blow in the direction of forms of organic
co-operation. It seemed likely, for example, that air and sea transport in the
south Atlantic might become the subject of combined organization.

* * *

As the 1970s came to an end, a retrospective look at the long years of struggle, first to end colonial rule and then to begin the building of a new and self-regenerative society, showed an impressive continuity of thought and action. If the PAIGC had suffered painful losses along that route, above all the loss of Amilcar Cabral, a solid core of the veteran leadership had come through intact, and had repeatedly enlarged itself with new militants from the grass-roots of these peoples. No one who knew West Africa, or indeed any part of the continent, could doubt that a new force was here on the scene, capable of confronting the menace of regression or dependence with a will and wisdom rare to find elsewhere.

There would be upsets and reverses in that difficult confrontation, just as earlier against colonial rule. The PAIGC had all but died of self-inflicted wounds in 1963, and yet was continually strengthened in the outcome. Its militants had lost their unforgettable teacher in 1973, and yet had gone on rapidly to win the war and consolidate their victory. And by the middle months of 1980, it was again clear that another crisis might be on the threshold in Guinea-Bissau where, as signs began to indicate, the necessary struggle against 'petty-bourgeois' ambitions, against new forms of elitism, against an ossification of party and administrative power with all its negative consequences, might be falling short or being thrust aside. Ever watchful for a 'break in the front', outside enemies could also take advantage of that.

When the crisis did in fact explode, on 14 November 1980, this book was already going through the press, and the further outcome remained to be seen. Nino Vieira was at that time First Commissioner (Prime Minister) and Chairman of the National Council of Guinea-Bissau (the country's supreme party organ; there was a similar one in Cape Verde). He led a swift military *coup* which ousted President Luiz Cabral, abolished existing structures of government in favour of a newly formed 'revolutionary council', and then proclaimed a *movimento readjustador* (translatable, more or less, as 'revision movement').

Welcomed within hours by Sekou Toure's government in neighbouring Guinea, this action appeared at first to be counter-revolutionary. It was indeed so welcomed by various opposition circles outside the country. Large accusations against the ousted regime were made, and especially against Luiz Cabral who was placed under arrest. Among other things, he was accused of installing a personal dictatorship and of preventing democratic discussion, notably of a new constitution. Yet it was difficult to see how so powerful and popular a figure as Vieira could not have acted through the National Council, if required, in order to prevent such developments by democratic means. Commenting on these accusations in a telex to Vieira of 19 November, five days after the *coup*, Pereira remarked to him that:

> What in fact happened is that in place of your using the National
> Council and its Permanent Committee in order to oppose what you

describe as the anti-democratic attitude and positions of Comrade Luiz Cabral, you simply obstructed the functioning of these structures which the party had placed under your responsibility. The Permanent Committee practically ceased to function, and the National Council met only when there was no other way of settling immediate issues. The truth is that these two party structures died in your hands through not being used.

Why then should Vieira have allowed this to happen, and then taken power by military means? Pointing to various 'reservations and more or less explicit fears' aroused by Vieira's action, the Mozambican weekly *Tempo* answered this question with another: Did this *coup* 'mean not only the overthrow of Luiz Cabral, but also the overthrow of Amilcar Cabral, and hence the overthrow of PAIGC'?[14]

Vieira and his fellow *coup*-makers proceeded to deny this. Whether in telex messages to Secretary-General Pereira in Praia, or in speeches duly printed in the Bissau newspaper *No Pintcha*, they affirmed that they would remain loyal to the teachings and policies of Amilcar Cabral and the PAIGC, including eventual unity with Cape Verde; and that they would not harm Luiz Cabral.[15] As the early weeks passed, the outlines of an internal political struggle within the PAIGC of Guinea-Bissau became increasingly evident.

Anxieties naturally continued, and it was increasingly seen that this manner of 'revision' was as damaging to the reputation of the liberation movements as it was certainly unconstitutional. No matter what grievances there were — and some were undoubtedly real — it was also seen at the same time that the PAIGC in Guinea-Bissau remained what it had always been, a broad and deeply implanted movement of participation, and was not to be shoved aside. Some of the initial actions and statements of the *coup*-makers were rapidly denied by them. Several of the harshest accusations were seen to be baseless. But hot and sometimes wild words of self-justification continued to flow from the new rulers in Bissau. In this situation the PAIGC in Cape Verde met in extraordinary congress late in January 1981, and, drawing an obvious conclusion for the immediate future, if not longer, reluctantly formed itself into a new successor party, the PAICV.

And here at this point, while the decade of the 1980s opened on new challenges and opportunities, I have to end this account of the liberation of Guinea-Bissau and Cape Verde. The overriding successes scored in both countries were beyond all serious question. Yet this is a story, as one sees, that really has no ending. *A luta continua!*

References

1. *Report* of November 1977: the full text is available in English from the Mozambique/Angola/Guine Information Centre, (MAGIC), 34 Percy Street, London WC1P 9FG.
2. Abridged text available in English in *People's Power*, No.4, September-October 1976, MAGIC, London. Various issues of this quarterly journal also devoted useful reports to a number of subjects: e.g. on literacy campaigning, No. 7/8, June 1977.
3. Also available in English from MAGIC.
4. See, for instance, L. Rudebeck, 'Guinea-Bissau: Difficulties and Possibilities of Socialist Orientation', Uppsala University, January 1978; S. Urdang, *Fighting Two Colonialisms: Women in Guinea-Bissau*, Monthly Review Press, New York and London, 1979; C. Foy, 'Unidade e Luta: the Struggle for Unity between Guinea-Bissau and Cape Verde', *People's Power*, MAGIC, No.14, Winter 1979; J. Jones, 'Agricultural Development in Guinea-Bissau', *People's Power*, No. 14, Summer 1979 and No. 16, Spring 1980.
5. These U.N. reports and summaries are far too numerous to list; they form a central part of the factual dossier on which future historians will work.
6. This of course was also the case in Guinea-Bissau.
7. See especially Paulo Freire, *Pedagogy in Process: The Letters to Guinea-Bissau*, trans. C. St. J. Hunter, Writers and Readers Publishing Co-operative, London, 1978.
8. In his *Report* of November 1977 (see note 1).
9. Rudebeck, op. cit., p.18.
10. Carried out with UN aid, this accurate census produced a figure which may be compared with the colonial guess of 1950, which had given a total of 517,290.
11. Luiz Cabral, *Strategy in Guinea-Bissau*, May 1979, available in English from MAGIC, 34 Percy Street, London W1.
12. Facts, with many others bearing on new development, in A. Pereira's retrospective survey on 5th anniversary of Cape Verdian Independence, 5 July 1980, Praia. Also, my own impressions gained during a visit of that month: see *People's Power*, No. 17, MAGIC.
13. Interviewed by B.D. in *West Africa*, 'The PAIGC Republics: Unity and Non-Alignment', London, 26 April 1976.
14. Article by Mendes de Oliveira, *Tempo*, Maputo, 30 November 1980.
15. In telexed messages to Pereira dated 16 and 17 November, and publicly in *No Pintcha*, Bissau, No. 753 of 24 November 1980, No. 754 of 29 November, and No. 758 of 23 December.

Notes on Further Reading in English

On the early stages of the liberation struggle: G. Chaliand, *Armed Struggle in Africa,* Monthly Review Press, New York and London, 1969.

On later stages: B. Cornwall, *The Bush Rebels,* Deutsch, London, 1973; S. Urdang, *Fighting Two Colonialisms: Women in Guinea-Bissau,* Monthly Review Press, New York and London, 1979; L. Rudebeck, *Guinea-Bissau: A Study of Political Mobilization,* Scandinavian Institute of African Studies, Uppsala, 1974.

On various aspects of history and the liberation struggle, see papers in a special issue of *Tarikh,* 24, 'Portugal in Africa', Longman, London and Lagos, October 1980.

As noted in my text, a large collection of the most important writings of Amilcar Cabral, with a biography by Mario de Andrade and translated by Michael Wolfers, is in *Unity and Struggle,* Heinemann, London and Monthly Review Press, New York, 1980. For a more detailed biography: M. de Andrade, *Amilcar Cabral,* Maspero, Paris, 1980.